China's New Era

中国新时代

EDITED BY
Annie Luman Ren AND Ben Hillman

CHINA STORY YEARBOOK:
CHINA'S NEW ERA

中 全球研究中心
AUSTRALIAN CENTRE ON
CHINA IN THE WORLD

Australian
National
University

ANU PRESS

Australian
National
University
ANU PRESS

The China Story
中（國）的故事

Published by ANU Press
The Australian National University
Canberra ACT 2600, Australia
Email: anupress@anu.edu.au

Available to download for free at press.anu.edu.au

ISBN (print): 9781760466336
ISBN (online): 9781760466343

WorldCat (print): 1424479972
WorldCat (online): 1424480566

DOI: 10.22459/CSY.2024

Design concept by Markus Wernli; 'China's New Era' cover design by ANU Press, and chapter and foci openers by Chin-Jie Melodie Liu

Typesetting by Amelia Menzies

The Australian Centre on China in the World is an initiative of the Commonwealth Government of Australia and The Australian National University

本书概要

2023

根據官方論述，中國的『新時代』始于習近平被任命為中共中央總書記的2012年。十年後的2023年，當習近平開始他的第三個五年任期時，這個新時代的整體形態已變得非常清晰。在習近平的領導下，個人獨裁統治不但在繼毛澤東之後再次被鞏固強化，同時，共產黨也擴大了對政府、經濟和社會的監管與掌控。

2023年，中國也迎來了許多其它的『新時代』。儘管2022年底的疫情解封引發了人們對國家以及生活能夠回歸正軌的期待，然而2023年中國經濟卻依然面對著房地產行業的持續困境、創紀錄的失業率以及地方政府債務危機的衝擊。在全球範圍內，中國政府推出了一系列全新的、雄心勃勃的外交舉措來吸引全球南方的支持以便擴大其在世界舞臺上的發言權。《中國故事年鑒2023：中國新時代》對以上以及其它重要事件提供了深入的剖析。想必在未來幾年中這些事件會持續發酵並彰顯，引發更多關注。

Translation by Annie Luman Ren

Contents

中国新时代

CHINA'S NEW ERA

引言

INTRODUCTION

CHINA'S NEW ERA

Annie Luman Ren and Ben Hillman

The General Secretary of the Communist Party of China (CPC), Xi Jinping, has declared his rule to be a 'New Era' 新时代. The Party's Third Historical Resolution of 2021, which cemented Xi's place in history, declared his leadership 'the key to the great rejuvenation of the Chinese nation'. The Party distinguishes the New Era from the two previous eras in the history of the People's Republic of China (PRC). In the first—the Mao Zedong era (1940–78)—China stood up and threw off the yoke of Western and Japanese imperialism. The second era—the Deng Xiaoping era (1979–2012), which includes the administrations of Jiang Zemin and Hu Jintao, Xi Jinping's immediate predecessors—is recognised for its successful economic reforms and rapid industrial development. The third era (2013–), the era of Xi Jinping, promises to be the one in which China is restored to its place as one of the world's great and powerful nations. This goal is encapsulated in the 'China Dream' and the two centennial goals that Xi Jinping set for his administration; namely, that China would become moderately prosperous by 2021, the 100th anniversary of the founding of the CPC, and an advanced, high-income economy and global power by 2049.[1]

A new era of new eras

According to the official narrative China's 'New Era' began when Xi Jinping was anointed party boss in 2012. But arguably, the new era was cemented in place in 2023 when Xi Jinping, already declared to be the Party's 'Core', commenced his third five-era term as General Secretary of the CPC.[2] Abandoning the collective leadership that characterised the Reform period and the two-term rule it established, from 2023 the CPC concentrated power in the hands of one man, who continued to strengthen the Party's control over the state to carry out his vision for the 'great restoration of the Chinese nation' 中华民族伟大复兴.

If the year 2023 consolidated Xi's New Era, it saw new eras of other kinds begin for China too. Following widespread anti-lockdown protests across China's cities in November 2022, China's leaders abruptly ended the zero-COVID policy that was characterised by harsh lockdowns and other draconian controls on movement. Despite initial optimism that the end of restrictions would renew China's lost economic dynamism in the new year, business continued to languish on several fronts and unemployment skyrocketed, particularly among youth. The official youth unemployment rate hit 21.3 percent in June 2023 before the government stopped publishing statistics.[3] Some estimates, taking rural youth unemployment (typically excluded from official measures) into account, placed the youth unemployment rate as high as 46.5 percent.[4]

As they have done in the past, Chinese youth expressed their frustrations on social media with slang and memes, progressing from the 'lying flat' 躺平 of years past to 'let it rot' 摆烂. Xi chided disgruntled youth and told them to 'abandon arrogance and pampering' and embrace the Maoist spirit of self-sacrifice. On Youth Day in May 2023, a front-page article in the Party mouthpiece *People's Daily* repeatedly told Chinese youths to learn to 'eat bitterness' 吃苦—basically, to stop complaining and suck it up.[5] Chinese youth reacted to such official exhortations by mockingly describing themselves as 'garlic chives' 韭菜 (i.e. exploitable resources that grow again after being cut down); towards the end of 2022 they revived an even darker self-definition first mooted in the 1980s: 'human minerals' 人矿.[6] China's university graduates—unable to find suitable employment—likened themselves to Kong Yiji 孔乙己, the miserable scholar-turned-beggar depicted by the revolutionary writer Lu Xun 鲁迅 (1881–1936) more than a century ago. This is the subject of Annie Luman Ren's investigation in 'Why are China's Unemployed Graduates Comparing Themselves to Lu Xun's Character?'.

China's middle-class population, which has grown from roughly 15 million at the beginning of the century to between 350 and 700 million people, for decades had ridden the economic boom that transformed China from a poor, largely rural country into the world's second-largest economy.[7] Many built wealth through property ownership, helped by steady increases in property values in recent decades. But in 2023, the property sector, once a key driver of the Chinese economy and household wealth, experienced a sharp deterioration as major developers teetered on the edge of default and property values declined.

In November 2023, the story of a Chinese couple named Li Jun 丽君 and Liang Liang 亮亮 went viral on social media. The couple were small-town migrant workers who moved to the capital city of Henan province, Zhengzhou, in 2021, where they purchased an apartment off plan that would be due for completion by 2024. Exhausting their savings for the deposit, the couple also took out a mortgage of more than RMB 1 million, with monthly repayments of RMB 6,293 for 30 years. After signing the contract in November 2021, the couple enthusiastically shared the news on Douyin (the sister app of TikTok), saying, 'Soon, among tens and thousands of lights in the city, finally there's going to be a light that only shines for me.'[8] At the time, their words inspired millions of others struggling to lay down roots in a large city.

But things did not go as planned for the couple. During waves of COVID-19 lockdowns that forced business to shut for months in 2022, Li Jun's monthly salary was reduced by half. The couple's combined income fell under RMB 10,000 per month. Then news came that their real estate developer, Sunac—China's third-largest property developer—missed the deadline for coupon payments on a US$742 million offshore bond in May 2022.[9] Construction on Li Jun and Liang Liang's future home halted. Yet the couple had to continue to repay their mortgage (in China borrowers begin paying mortgages for new properties as soon as the contract is signed) plus rent (RMB 1,500) for their current dwelling. Money became even tighter when the couple's daughter was born in October 2022. A year later, in November 2023, the couple's plight gained wide attention as they shared dramatic details of their struggles with Sunac: Liang Liang claims to have been assaulted by staff members of the sales centre when demanding a promised refund and ended up in hospital with minor injuries, and Li Jun, who was recording the incident, had her phone snatched and her livestream was cut off.[10]

In a widely shared commentary that was later censored, an influencer on Bilibili concluded: 'The story of Li Jun and Liang Liang taught young people that even the most hard-working, most law-abiding and most optimistic Chinese citizens don't deserve to live the Chinese dream. There's no hope left for others. Thank you, Li Jun and Liang Liang, for showing us the cruel reality that is China today.'[11]

Headquarters of Sunac China Group, Beijing
Source: N509FZ, Wikimedia

Despite the sombre verdict, there may still be hope that Li Jun and Liang Liang will one day move into their apartment—in September 2023 Sunac announced that it had won approval from creditors to restructure about US$9 billion of debt.[12] However, experiences such as the couple's and the decline of the property sector more broadly have dampened consumer confidence, which is essential for the growth strategy known as 'dual circulation', announced in 2020, that seeks to balance state investment and export-led growth with domestic demand. As Jiao Wang notes in 'China's Macroeconomy in 2023: An Overview', China has been grappling with the challenge of slow and uneven household consumption recovery in the post-pandemic period. After reaching an all-time high of 127.00 points in February 2021, China's Consumer Confidence Index dropped to a record low of 85.50 points in November 2022 after the Twentieth Congress that cemented Xi's third term. Despite a brief upturn to 94.9 in March 2023, it subsequently dropped to below 90 and remained there to the end of the year.

Another cloud over the Chinese economy that darkened in 2023, and is closely linked to property sector woes, was the scale of local government debt. Local government debt had been building for years before spiralling under zero-COVID policies as the burden of testing and monitoring the population fell to local governments.[13] The value of outstanding local government bonds hit, by some estimates, RMB 50 trillion in 2023, representing a twenty-fold increase over the past decade, and, notably, this figure does not include other sources of government debt generated through local government finance vehicles (LGFVs) and shadow banking.[14] At the start of the year, debt servicing commitments exceeded income for 12 out of 31 province-level administrations, and the burden continued to grow throughout 2023.[15]

The local government debt crisis has driven cash-strapped governments to cut pensions, reduce contract work, and delaying payment of salaries for civil servants, teachers and postal workers.[16] In February, retirees in Wuhan and Dalian took to the streets to protest cuts in government-provided medical insurance for seniors.[17] In 'China's Local Government Debt', Jean C. Oi traces the local government debt crisis to China's state policies during the COVID-19 pandemic, which enforced fiscal discipline and deleveraged the real estate sector. In the summer of 2020, Beijing had implemented the 'Three Red Lines' policy 三条红线, which prohibited real estate firms from borrowing beyond set limits. This undermined the previously successful business model of property developers who had become accustomed to easy money, and squeezed revenues from land sales, which had become a vital source of income for local governments.

Although China's GDP was expected to grow at 5 percent in 2023, much stronger than many other countries, business and consumer confidence was hard hit and headwinds for the economy remained strong. The Xi Jinping administration has laid out an ambitious economic policy agenda as it seeks to move China up the value chain and towards high-income status, but it will struggle to achieve its goals unless businesses are investing and consumers are spending.

China also needs to grow the wealth of its rural population. The Xi administration claims to have lifted 99 million people above the official poverty line of 4000 yuan (US$620) per annum ($1.69 per day). Yet as Ben Hillman notes in 'From Poverty Elimination to Rural Revitalisation: The Party Takes Charge', this figure is less than the World Bank's threshold of

$2.15 a day, and far below the World's Bank recommended national poverty threshold for upper middle-income countries such as China, which currently stands at $6.85.[18]

An important way to grow incomes and the middle class is to incorporate rural migrant workers who have flocked to the cities to work in factories and on construction sites. Yet, as Dorien Emmers and Scott Rozelle argue in 'Inequality in China: The Challenge of Common Prosperity', China has failed to invest enough in the education and health of the rural population for decades. Having a large population of uneducated workers was not a problem while China was moving from low- to middle-income status. But such shortcomings in education and health will likely threaten China's future growth.

An overall sense of malaise and uncertainty about the future crystalised in spontaneous public grief over the death on 27 October of former state premier Li Keqiang 李克强, which some quarters interpreted as a collective mourning over the collapse of the Chinese Dream. Li, who was sidelined by Xi in favour of loyalists, was seen by many as an adherent of Deng's 'Reform and Opening Up' policies, in contrast to Xi, whom they see as pulling back on reform and closing China to the world.[19] Several sudden leadership changes compounded the uncertainty, as Willy Lam argues in 'The Mystery of Xi's Disappearing Officials'. The high-profile disappearances of former state councillor and foreign minister Qin Gang 秦刚 and former defence minister General Li Shangfu 李尚福 in August prompted questions about Xi Jinping's ability to run the party–military apparatus. Lam warns that the instability at the highest levels could undermine efforts to address economic headwinds.

Xi Jinping's response to the policy challenges that crystalised in 2023 has been to double-down on centralising governance of the state by the CPC. The Party has increasingly taken control of social and economic policy, expanding its presence in private companies, schools, and civic associations as well as local urban and rural communities. Even multinational corporations have been subjected to increasing political pressure and economic coercion, as Debby Chen writes in 'How Multinational Corporations are Coopted into Becoming China's Agents of Repression'.

The most notable interventions have been in the tech sector, which suffered a wipe-out of US$2 trillion in market capitalisation, leading to widespread speculation about the Xi administration's commitment to market reforms and the future of innovation in China. Yet, as Rogier Creemers explains in 'The Dreary and the Dramatic: What Happened to China's Platform Economy?', this regulatory wave was not a sudden whim of Xi's, nor was it triggered by Alibaba founder Jack Ma's public criticism of the financial regulator. Creemers points out that since 2018, the Chinese state has sought to impose regulatory measures on the fintech sector such as exist in the European Union and elsewhere. What happened, he argues, should be understood as a 'rectification': the introduction of a new governance paradigm for a sector that Chinese authorities view as highly strategic and therefore in need of effective regulation and state supervision.

At the start of 2023, the Party released its Document No. 1 on rural affairs, which highlighted a more dominant role for the Party in rural governance as part of its ambitious 'rural revitalisation' 乡村振兴 agenda for the countryside. In 'From Poverty Elimination to Rural Revitalisation: The Party Takes Charge' in this volume, Ben Hillman explains the important changes underway in China's 700,000 villages. After four decades in which self-governing village committees and directly elected village leaders played a leading role in decision-making, village-level party branches and village party secretaries are now taking charge of all key decisions on village affairs, including economic affairs. The centralisation of rural governance under the leadership of the Party has been buttressed by the expansion of 'rural enforcement teams', which gained wide attention this year with viral videos featuring rural enforcement teams (known colloquially as the *nongguan* 农管) confiscating farmers' livestock or forcefully removing crops. Tan Zhao discusses the expanded responsibilities and powers of the rural enforcement teams in 'Are the Nongguan Coming? The Evolution of the Rural Comprehensive Administrative Enforcement Team in China's Rural Governance'. Tan Zhao links the expanded role of the rural enforcement teams in 2023 and rising complaints about their heavy-handed tactics to leadership concerns about food security. He also notes that the management of its local agents continues to be a challenge for the Party as it intervenes more in local social and economic affairs.

A new era of global ambitions

The year 2023 also marked a new era in China's global ambitions. On 18 May 2023, as leaders from the world's seven advanced economies gathered in Hiroshima for the Group of Seven (G7) summit, Xi Jinping welcomed the heads of state of five former Soviet republics—Kazakhstan, Kyrgyzstan, Tajikistan, Turkmenistan and Uzbekistan—in the historic city of Xi'an, Shaanxi province, for the inaugural China–Central Asia Summit. As evening fell, Xi and his wife Peng Liyuan hosted a welcome ceremony and banquet inspired by the traditions of the Tang dynasty inside a sumptuous garden complex built on the site of an imperial garden dating back to the Tang (618–907). Standing in front of the brightly lit towers and pavilions, Xi outlined his 'vision of a China–Central Asia community with a shared future' and proclaimed 'a new era' of ties between China and Central Asia.[20]

Chinese state media quickly hailed this meeting as a triumph of China's regional diplomacy. For Beijing, Central Asia is key to its trillion-dollar Belt and Road Initiative (BRI), launched a decade ago. The region is critical for China in terms of trade (which reached a record US$70 billion in 2022), natural resources (Kazakhstan has some of the world's largest oil fields outside the Middle East) and, not least, maintaining control and security in far-western Xinjiang, which borders Central Asia.[21]

The pomp and circumstance of the China–Central Asia Summit is one marked example of how China envisages itself on the global stage. The city of Xi'an had been chosen for its historical and political significance. Once the capital city of the Tang dynasty, a period characterised by cultural openness and economic prosperity, Xi'an (then known as Chang'an) was the eastern starting point of the ancient Silk Road, a cosmopolitan centre welcoming Persians, Arabs, Indians, Koreans, Japanese and others to China for trade, education and cultural exchange.

Nearly two decades ago, heartened by their country's newfound strength, scholars in mainland China turned to the past for inspirations for a uniquely Chinese approach to the theory and practice of international relations. Most notably, Professor Zhao Tingyang 赵汀阳 at the Chinese Academy of Social Sciences remoulded the ancient Chinese ideal of *Tianxia* 天下, or 'All-Under-Heaven', into a new vision for the international system that is 'explicitly inclusive and implicitly puts China at its centre'.[22] Reverberations of the *Tianxia* belief can be observed in the catch-all slogan of 'Community of Shared Destiny' 命运共同体 first proposed by Xi Jinping in 2013 during his first official visit to Russia as the new leader of China's party-state.[23]

| Tang Paradise, a Tang dynasty themed park in Xi'an where the China-Central Asia Summit took place
Source: rawpixel.com

While China has already pivoted away from the bellicose wolf warrior diplomacy that characterised Xi's second term in office, under Xi's third five-year term, it is likely that China will continue to promote its own vision of a global order on an even grander scale. Kevin Magee observes in 'From Riyadh and Tehran to Beijing: China's Diplomatic Role in a Changing World' that in 2023, China took on a series of new initiatives in areas where it hitherto played little or no diplomatic role, including brokering a peace deal between Saudi Arabia and Iran, as part of its new approach to diplomacy.

In 'The Belt and Road's Midlife Crisis: Perspectives from Latin America and the Caribbean', Ruben Gonzalez-Vicente reflects on how ten years of the BRI has reshaped the politics of development in the region. He characterises the BRI as being in a state of midlife crisis and questions whether it will be supplanted by the Global Development Initiative (GDI) announced by Xi in 2021. The GDI, along with two follow-up initiatives—the Global Security Initiative (2022) and the Global Civilisation Initiative (2023)—has been described by the *Financial Times* as 'China's boldest move yet to enlist the support of the "global south" to amplify Beijing's voice on the world stage'.[24]

For Graeme Smith, China has been using Australia's colonial history in the Pacific to 'tell the China Story well' 讲好中国故事 and to strength ties with Pacific Islands nations. In 'The Frontiers of History: China Discovers the Pacific's Dark Colonial Legacy', Smith calls on the Australian government to deal with its Pacific history with honesty and make reparations where appropriate, which would help to blunt China's criticisms.

Australia–China relations: Fifty years on

In November 2023, Prime Minister Anthony Albanese became the first Australian leader to visit China since 2016. Beijing hailed the visit as 'a new starting point' of China–Australia relations, coming after a period of turbulence that marked much of the Coalition's time in Canberra.[25] Among the more symbolic actions of the visit was Albanese's trip to the Temple of Heaven's circular Echo Wall, where he took a photo that paid homage to Gough Whitlam's ground-breaking visit to Beijing 50 years ago, which marked Australia's recognition of the PRC.

Beijing's decision to remove the tariffs on Australian barley it had imposed in 2020 in August and to review dumping tariffs of 218 percent on Australian wine helped to pave the way for Albanese's visit. In 'Ending Economic Sanctions: The Role of Chinese Industry Associations in the Removal of Barriers on Australian Barley and Wine', Scott Waldron, Darren Lim and Victor Ferguson examine China's decision to remove the barley tariff.

The authors also present fresh analysis that includes consideration of the influential role of domestic interest groups and lessons for future trade negotiations.

While trade relations have improved, the trilateral security pact between Australia, the United Kingdom and the United States known as AUKUS continues to a point of contention between Australia and China. This is the subject of Edward Sing Yue Chan's 'How Fearful is China's Military Rise?' In 'Caution and Compromise in Australia's China Strategy', Benjamin Herscovitch discusses the mix of tactical caution and policy compromise in the Labor government's China policy.

Voices from the 'other' China

The year 2023 also marked the ten-year anniversary of the '*Southern Weekly* Incident' 南方周末事件, when China's most influential and outspoken liberal newspaper found itself at odds with the Guangzhou Ministry of Propaganda. The annual New Year editorial 新年献词 published by this Guangzhou-based weekly had been a popular and influential tradition. Entitled 'The Chinese dream, the dream of constitutional rule' 中国梦，宪政梦, the original 2013 New Year editorial called on the party-state to fulfil promises made in the 1982 constitution to allow independent courts and the rule of law.[26] Instead, the paper was forced to run a commentary prepared by the provincial propaganda department praising the Communist Party. This sparked a three-day anti-censorship protest outside the paper's headquarters and a nation-wide dialogue about press freedom.[27] A 2023 commemorative piece published in Taiwan concluded: 'The *Southern Weekly* Incident was a watershed, it foreshowed the arrival of a new age ... looking back now, it signified the shrinking boundaries and scope of Chinese journalism.'[28]

The same diminishing space for candid discussion has been felt by millions of Internet users in China. Although censorship has always been prevalent, the advent of the Xi Jinping era marked a turning point for the Chinese Internet, with the Party instructing social media platforms to play a more active role in serving the Party's interests. As early as August 2013, Xi recognised that 'The Internet has become the main battlefield for the public opinion struggle'.[29] Since then, virulent nationalists fed on diets of 'positive energy' and 'the declining West' have come to dominate public discussion. Alarmingly, in 'Chinese 'Incels'? Misogynist Men on Chinese Social Media', Qian Huang shows that an increasingly gender-conservative media and educational system under Xi, combined with increasing gender imbalance and decreasing social mobility, have helped to foster widespread misogynist discourse on the Chinese Internet. This has damaging implications for China's gender equality.

Yet no matter how simultaneously clamorous and suffocating China's media landscape can appear, voices of humanity and decency, of wit and good humour, can still be heard. This includes Chinese-language podcasts, which, relatively free from official attention, have attracted more than 85 million subscribers tuning in to listen to authentic real-life accounts and nuanced, civilised discussions.[30] In this volume, we feature two translations from a popular Chinese language podcast, *Gushi FM* 故事FM. In one story, 'Loneliness, Death and Desolation: Why I Return to Antarctica Time and Again', the narrator Cao Jianxi 曹建西 describes his experiences working as a member of China's Antarctic Scientific Expedition, offering a personal account of China's pursuit of becoming a 'polar great power'.[31]

In another story, 'How AI Changed the Way We Work', employees from different industries share changes to their work routine brought on by AI. While some feel as if they are being washed away by the changing technological tide, others are surfing the wave with great excitement. By offering these two translations, we hope to present what Geremie Barmé, the founder of the China Story, describes as voices from the 'Other China': a China of 'quiet dignity and unflappable perseverance', where 'myriad expressions and ideas continue to exist', despite 'a political party that would bend all to its will'.[32]

Acknowledgements

Co-editors Ben Hillman and Annie Luman Ren are enormously grateful to all our contributors and to the China Story editors Graeme Smith and Linda Jaivin for their contributions throughout the year. We would like to thank Jan Borrie and Cathryn Game for copyediting the book, Amelia Menzies for typesetting the book, Melodie Chin-Jie Liu for the artwork on the internal pages, ANU Press for the cover design, and the anonymous referees for their helpful feedback.

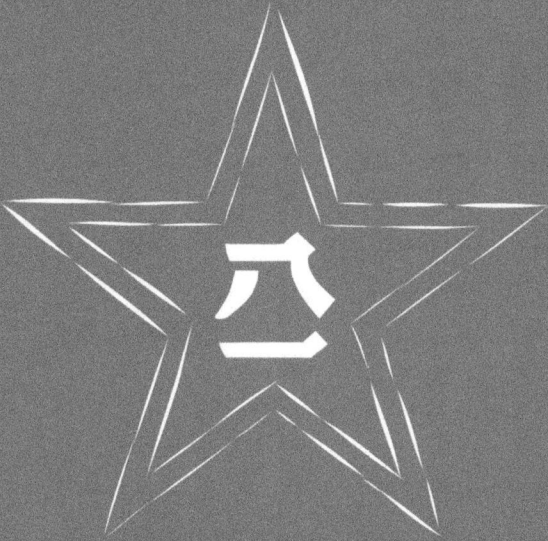

CHAPTER 1: POLITICAL LEADERSHIP AND ECONOMIC HEADWINDS

THE MYSTERY OF XI'S

DISAPPEARING OFFICIALS

Willy Lam

The disappearances of former state councilor and foreign minister Qin Gang秦刚 in June 2023 and the former defense minister General Li Shangfu 李尚福 in August raise questions about the supreme leader Xi Jinping's personnel management. A score of senior officers from the Rocket Force and departments in charge of weapons procurement also got the sack, prompting widespread speculation that they were being investigated for graft. Cadres in both the Rocket Force and the logistics departments are considered more prone to corruption because large sums of money changed hands when they were procuring equipment.

Given his apparent lack of expertise in economic and financial affairs, it has long been assumed that Xi's forte rests in pulling together a personally loyal clique of capable cadres. A master of Machiavellian-style palace intrigue, within ten years of assuming power, he had ensured that his clique dominated all major offices in the party-state apparatus.[1]

However, both former foreign minister Qin and General Li—as well as the disgraced commander and political commissar of the Rocket Force, Generals Li Yuchao 李玉超 and Xu Zhongbo 徐忠波—had been considered Xi protégés. The failure to disclose fully to the public the reasons behind their demise testifies to problems Xi is facing in running the party-military apparatus.[2] The lack of due process in senior-level appointments and sackings under Xi has opened him to criticism by other 'princelings' (the offspring of the PRC's founding fathers). In the run-up to the celebration of the 125th anniversary of former state president Liu Shaoqi's 刘少奇 birthday, Liu's son, General Liu Yuan 刘源, published an article entitled 'Affirm and insist upon the system of democratic centralism; strengthen the construction of organization and institutions' in the official journal *Research on Mao Zedong Thought*. General Liu—who reportedly does not see eye to eye with Xi—seems to be critiquing Xi's dictatorial ruling style.[3] Given that his father was persecuted to death by Mao at the start of the Cultural Revolution, General Liu's statement might have been more pointed than it seemed.

In general, the party-state apparatus since the 20th Party Congress has been dominated by apparatchiks (political officials responsible for issues including ideology, national security, personnel and propaganda) and not technocrats (often English-speaking cadres who might have been trained abroad in science or technological fields or economics, and who understand economic principles, modern financial tools and international trade). While quite a few of the current Xi-appointed Politburo have at least bachelor's degrees in technology-related subjects, they have built their careers in party affairs, especially ideology or organisation. The best example is the vice premier in charge of finance and economics, He Lifeng 何立峰, who worked with Xi for more than ten years when the latter was based in Fujian.[4] He has Xi's full trust, but he is not a technocrat and is a newcomer to policy-making in the areas of finance and international economics. He is therefore a far cry from his predecessor, former vice premier Liu He 刘鹤 (in office 19 March 2018–12 March 2023), an economist with a masters degree in public administration from Harvard. Liu He was in charge of negotiations with the United States over tariffs and other financial issues during a particularly tense time in bilateral relations. Liu He was also a close adviser to Xi before retiring.[5] Meanwhile, the older generation of technocrats employed by then premier Zhu Rongji and his successor Wen Jiabao in the late 1990s and early 2000s—including former People's Bank of China governor Zhou Xiaochuan 周小川 and minister of finance Lou Jiwei 楼继伟—have all stepped down due to age requirements.

Qin Gang, former minister for foreign affairs of China, addresses the Human Rights Council
Source: UN Geneva, Flickr

The rise of the 'national security faction'

The only Politburo Standing Committee (PBSC) member accompanying Xi during his recent summit with US President Joe Biden on 15 November in San Francisco was Cai Qi 蔡奇. Although ranked fifth in the PBSC pecking order, he controls the police-state apparatus in his capacity as a vice-chairman of the Central National Security Commission 中央国家安全委员会 as well as being the head of its General Office. His formal title is head of the CPC Central Committee Secretariat 中共中央书记处; other members of the Secretariat include Minister of Public Security Wang Xiaohong 王小洪 and Minister of State Security Chen Yixin 陈一新. It is the first time in CPC history that heads of the ministries of public security and state security have had slots on the Secretariat, signifying the centrality of security to Xi's administration. Moreover, Cai is director of the CPC Central Committee General Office 中央委员会办公厅主任, which controls all party-related decision-making and implementation. The General Office is the nerve centre of the entire party apparatus. It is the first time that a PBSC member has held this critical position. Cai is also responsible for the well-being and safety of Xi in his capacity as head of the Party General Secretary's Office 国家主席办公厅.[6]

There is speculation that a subtle power struggle has erupted between Cai Qi's faction of national security apparatchiks and Premier Li Qiang's 李强 State Council bureaucrats. Li Qiang is ranked No. 2 in the PBSC pecking order, just behind Xi. Yet his performance as premier—in theory the person responsible for the whole economy—since assuming the post this year has been low-profile and lacklustre, especially compared to his predecessor Li Keqiang 李克强, who was deemed a committed market-oriented reformer. Li Qiang has said publicly that the role of the State Council is to implement decisions made by top party committees—for example, the Central Commission on Finance and Economics—headed by Xi. Under Xi's instruction that party organs should take the lead in policy formulation, the status and power of the State Council has been truncated.

Li Qiang (a former governor of Zhejiang province, where Xi worked from 2002 to 2007) represents the Zhejiang subfaction of Xi Jinping's faction. Cai Qi and He Lifeng represent the Fujian subfaction (where Xi worked from 1985 to 2002). Appointments since the 20th Party Congress have demonstrated that the senior cadres of the Fujian subfaction have outnumbered those of the Zhejiang subfaction.[7]

Policy-making mismanagement

Xi's failures in managing high-level personnel and his apparent lack of success in putting together a team that can reverse the economic slowdown has been responsible for a series of ill-conceived policies, discussed below.

Putting national security concerns above attracting foreign direct investment

The weeks after the Biden–Xi summit in San Francisco witnessed more multinational corporations pulling out of the PRC. The purported 'smile diplomacy' pursued by the Xi delegation in the United States produced very little in terms of reviving the domestic economy. Foreign investers and businesses are aware that the Ministry of State Security has stepped up its harassment of foreign firms, particularly those handling due diligence, accounting and consultancy. It has launched a propaganda campaign urging Chinese citizens to report foreign spies, liberally defined, and even issued an instruction warning businesspeople (domestic and foreign) 'not to short' the stock market.[8] Several senior staff (including Americans) working for the China-based offices of multinationals have not been allowed to leave the country. Despite repeated requests from the CPC administration, Washington has yet to relax efforts to cut China off from US investment (including wealth funds) and from the global supply chain in high-tech areas such as IT, AI and pharmaceuticals. According to JPMorgan, in the second quarter of 2023, foreign direct investment fell to its lowest level in twenty-six years.[9] It is likely that the pace of foreign direct investment leaving China will further accelerate.[10] Yet even when Beijing talks about luring back multinationals, it has announced no favourable policies such as allowing them a bigger share of the market or giving them more flexibility in moving foreign exchange in and out of China. The Free Trade Zones advertised by the Chinese government in the past few years have failed to attract significant investment from multinationals, meaning that they are not attractive to potential investors in China. Initial public offerings (IPOs) of Chinese firms in both China and Hong Kong have also shrunk in both numbers and size of capital.[11]

President of China Xi Jinping and U.S. President Joe Biden
Source: 李季霖, Flickr

Too little, too late in saving the real estate sector

It was only in mid-November 2023 that the State Council announced one trillion yuan of low-cost financing to help a select list of struggling real estate firms to restructure their loans and ensure that they complete unfinished apartments already sold to customers. This is a case of too little, too late.[12] After Evergrande, the biggest developer in the PRC, announced its insolvency in late 2021, other property firms, including HK-based Country Garden and China Vanke, followed. Yet the party-state apparatus has done nothing to stop these overleveraged firms from continuing to draw huge loans from friendly state bankers and to raise bonds (for which they cannot even make the minimum interest payments). It is understood that these firms pay hefty bribes to bankers and bond issuers for their services.[13] Anti-graft operations have yet to start.

In September 2023, in response to massive complaints from home buyers—including millions who faced difficulty paying mortgages for unfinished apartments—Beijing dangled the possibility of the state rolling out 'subsidised housing' 保障房. Under the so-called Singapore model, by which the government provides good-quality subsidised flats to residents, state-backed housing would play a big role in China's housing market. This would put to an end the monopolisation of the housing market by developers of expensive 'commodity flats' 商品房. At this stage, details are lacking. State Council Document 14 on the this subject simply states that there will be a return to 'subsidised' housing. At time of writing there have been no detailed announcements as to who will be entitled to subsidised housing.[14]

Widening social economic unrest

After the official statistics showed that youth unemployment had risen to 21 percent in the first quarter of 2023, the State Statistical Bureau stopped releasing new figures on this sensitive issue.[15] Findings by a Peking University professor claim that as many as 46.5 percent of young people are jobless.[16]

A related point is the shrinking population. Government subsidies amounting to RMB 3,000 or more for urban couples to have a child are not working because raising a child in a city has become prohibitively expensive even for middle-class families—not to mention labourers who are struggling to make ends meet. As with the sudden ban on tutoring schools and restrictions on the hours students can spend on online gaming, it is a case of poor planning and untimely execution of policies.[17] These decisions have not been popular and have hurt business confidence.

As a result of unhappiness with such policies and the economic downturn, protests have increased in dozens of cities and towns. Protestors include laid-off workers, labourers who fail to receive their pay cheque in time, distressed mortgage payers, and depositors who can not withdraw money from accounts with local government banks.[18]

Meanwhile, local administrations have piled up debt amounting to 92 trillion yuan (see 'China's Local Government Debt', page 35).[19] Local-level government bankruptcies mean that not only civil servants and teachers but also police and people's armed police (PAP) members cannot get their salaries. A big chink in the armour of China's surveillance and police apparatus has appeared. In response, various levels of party cells have asked state-owned enterprises (SOEs) to revive their own security teams, which were active during the Mao years.[20] Called *renwubu* 人武部 (people's militia departments), these security teams are paid for by SOEs but also keep an eye on law and order in their areas.

The increasing police-state atmosphere has particularly alarmed some of the 400 million members of China's middle classes. The increasingly stringent control over the movement of foreign currency in and out of the country has made it difficult for Chinese who want to emigrate to Western countries.[21] But this has not stopped frustrated Chinese from taking dangerous and often illegal paths to leave China. The number of 'refugees' or 'escapees' from China trying to reach the United States by traversing dangerous terrain in South and Central America testifies to the loss of faith among many Chinese in the communist system.[22]

As of this writing, the Xi leadership has still not convened the much-anticipated Third Plenum of the 20th Central Committee. Usually, third plenums, which discuss economic and sociopolitical policies and reforms, are called in October or November. Xi's failure to assemble and keep a capable leadership team, or to introduce timely measures to address the nation's multifaceted problems, have cast on doubt Xi's ability to remain a 'leader for life'—and even, perhaps, the Party's own 'mandate of heaven'.

CHINA'S MACROECONOMY

IN 2023: AN OVERVIEW

Jiao Wang

China's economy experienced a bumpy journey in 2023, with fluctuations in each quarter. In the first quarter, GDP growth reached 4.5 percent, exceeding market expectations and marking a strong start to an economic recovery following the three-year COVID-19 prevention and control policy regime. In the second quarter, it grew by 6.3 percent, which, considering the low base of the previous year, was not particularly impressive. The quarter-on-quarter growth stood only at 0.8 percent, much lower than market expectations. Despite pessimistic speculation about the second half of 2023, GDP growth for the third quarter reached 4.9 percent, beating expectations once again. Although investment in the property market has continued declining since 2022, services, consumption and private business investment, particularly in the high-tech industry, contributed to robust growth in the third quarter. In the fourth quarter, China achieved 5.2 percent GDP growth, which was also the annual GDP growth rate for 2023. This figure is close to, but about 1 percent lower than, the pre-pandemic level, indicating an overall solid but incomplete recovery. Overall, the performance of China's economic growth in 2023 has made China the largest driving force of the global economy, likely contributing to more than 30 percent of global economic growth.[1]

Trade, high-tech industry and the services sectors showed resilience in 2023's post-pandemic recovery. In 2023, China's goods export volume grew by 0.6 percent compared to the previous year, while goods import volume experienced a 0.3 percent decline, likely reflecting a weaker domestic demand. High-tech manufacturing in areas such as solar cells, service robots and integrated circuits continued to grow steadily. In November alone, their output surged by about 45 percent, 33 percent and 28 percent respectively. Large high-tech manufacturing enterprises saw a 6.2 percent increase in added value relative to the previous November. The strong growth in the high-tech industry can be attributed in part to continuous support from the Chinese government. Beijing has recognised the potential of high-tech firms in driving economic growth and innovation, and this support is expected to continue in the near future.

In 2023, growth in the services sector gained significant momentum, driven by increased consumer and business demand as China removed COVID-related restrictions and reopened provincial and national borders.

The services sector grew by 5.8 percent, outperforming the other two pillars of the economy, agricultural (1.3 percent) and industrial production (4.6 percent).

China still faces significant challenges in several areas, including declining property investment (which has a flow-on effect on other industries, such as construction, architecture, real estate services, infrastructure and the financial sector), weak consumption growth and the risk of accumulating debt, all of which pose short-term risks to the Chinese economy.

Freight by a harbour
Source: Kurt Cotoaga, Unsplash

In 2023, real estate investment declined by 9.6 percent, slightly less precipitous than the decline the previous year (10 percent) but still considered a deep contraction. Property sales declined by 8.5 percent, which was significantly less severe than the contraction in 2022 (24.3 percent). Throughout the year, the real estate climate index, a monthly economic indicator measuring the overall prosperity of the real estate sector, was stuck in the below-95 region, indicating very low prosperity for the sector.

The contraction in the property market stems from a series of policy crackdowns that started in late 2020, notably the 'Three Red Lines' policy designed to mitigate the danger to the economy from developers' mounting debt. Beijing has since repeatedly emphasised that housing is for living in, not for speculation, reaffirming its determination to control the housing market. Despite a continuing decline in residential investment, the real estate sector showed signs of recovery in 2023, thanks to more positive government policies. For example, in January, the government announced a 21-point action plan aimed to improve the balance sheets of high-quality property developers. It has a strong focus on easing financial pressures of what they considered 'high-quality' developers. An important part of the plan is to ensure the completion and deliveries of houses from developers to buyers within the contracted timeframe 保交楼. The plan sets up special bonds and loans to support the said completion and deliveries. Another part of the plan is to relax the borrowing constraints set out by the 'Three Red Lines' policy and provide debt extensions to good-quality developers. Thirty pilot real estate developers will be the first to implement those new policies.

Beijing also eased mortgage rules and relaxed requirements for first-home buyers to boost buyer confidence.[2] The government even stepped in to tackle imminent collapses of property developer firms of systemic importance. The most prominent example was that the government dealt with the near bankruptcy of Evergrande, one of China's largest real estate developers. Beijing's heavy intervention in terms of debt restructuring and negotiation with global stakeholders ensured that Evergrande did not experience a full collapse, which might have caused a chain reaction that dragged down the real estate sector or even the banking sector more broadly.

The golden days of rapid property market expansion might be over. The era of high-leverage, high-debt and rapid market expansion created risks too huge to be ignored. The recent contraction caused pain and losses to many real estate firms, but was part of the process of establishing a sustainable, albeit much smaller, market with better-quality property developers and closer government oversight.

Local government debt poses another potential catalyst for a debt crisis in China. Beijing's deep concern over the scale and sustainability of local government debt led to a reform of the local financial regulatory framework announced in March 2023. The Chinese government has also initiated a gradual restructuring of local government debt, including rolling over existing debts, extending loan terms at lower interest rates, and issuing special-purpose bonds to fund large infrastructure projects. Local government debt restructuring is a complex issue. It must strike a balance between preventing large-scale crises and establishing sustainable paths for local government budgets ('China's Local Government Debt', page 35).

China has been grappling with the challenge of slow and uneven household consumption recovery in the post-pandemic period. Despite increases in total retail sales and services, the consumption of durable goods and big-ticket items remained sluggish in 2023. Chinese households appeared hesitant to spend. The National Bureau of Statistics Consumer Confidence Index (CCI) has remained below 100 since April 2022, suggesting a pessimistic sentiment among consumers. While the CCI inched up to 94.9 in March 2023, it subsequently slid down to below 90 and remained there to the end of the year.

The share of household consumption in China's GDP has been historically lower than in other countries of similar economic development levels, standing at 56 percent, compared to 66 percent in India and 67 percent in Thailand. The average consumption-to-GDP ratio in most advanced economies is around 80 percent. The COVID-19 pandemic exacerbated the situation because of its impact on household balance sheets. The Chinese government has implemented a series of fiscal and monetary policies, but these primarily affected businesses rather than households. Partly that was due to China's inadequate social security network, which prevented the government from directly extending support and relief to households. The sluggish recovery of household consumption is therefore primarily a structural issue rather than a cyclical one. Long-term structural reforms in social security, income redistribution and the household registration system are needed to address this issue.

In 2023, China's China Consumer Price Index (CPI) grew only by 0.2 percent, and the Chinese Producer Price Index (PPI) declined 15 months in a row. The prospect of very low inflation with an elevated debt poses more challenges to Beijing in stimulating the economy to restore it to its pre-pandemic growth level (the consensus on China's growth potential is 5–6 percent). Beijing has highlighted the critical role of internal circulation in promoting economic growth in the post-pandemic era as part of the Dual Circulation strategy first introduced in May 2020 by President Xi Jinping.[3] The goal of the Dual Circulation strategy is to foster a complementary and synergistic relationship between the domestic market (internal circulation) while maintaining openness to the global economy (external circulation) and integration with it.[4]

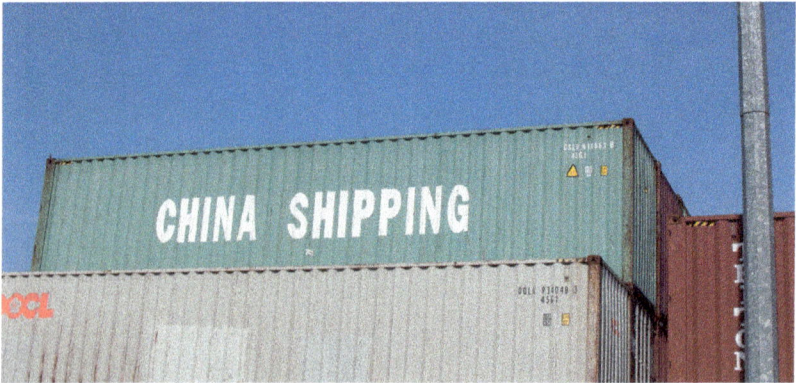

China Shipping cargo
Source: Anja Bauermann, Unsplash

On 11–12 December 2023, at the annual Central Economic Work Conference in Beijing, China's leaders outlined the country's economic priorities for 2024.[5] Echoing the former leader Deng Xiaoping's famous slogan, 'Development is the hard truth' 发展是硬道理, this year's conference prioritised 'Maintaining High-quality Development as the New era's "Hard Truth"' 必须把坚持高质量发展作为新时代的硬道理, reiterating the party's belief in the absolute importance of growth and development—but also high-quality growth that is sustainable, innovation-driven and consumption-led.

Since 2021, the central government has repeatedly emphasised the triple pressures of demand contraction, supply shock and weakened expectations for the Chinese economy. These pressures stemmed from various sources including the disruptions caused by its draconian lockdown policies around COVID-19, an unfavourable external economic environment, and rising geopolitical tensions. The 2023 Central Economic Work Conference reiterated those challenges and identified real estate, local government debt, and small and medium financial institutions (such as small and medium-sized banks, rural and community banks, and urban cooperative banks that serve regional or underserved segments of the population and are therefore more prone to economic shocks) as key areas of risk and advocated a coordinated national-level approach to resolving these problems.

Regarding the real estate sector, the conference proposed to establish a new development model for property developers, likely by 2024. As for local government debts, Beijing called upon major provinces to make their contributions to the overall debt restructuring effort. In addition, the conference reaffirmed the priorities of anchoring expectations and promoting growth and employment through active, likely stimulative, fiscal policy and prudent monetary policy. Notably, it placed anchoring expectations ahead of promoting growth and employment in the official statement, which has been interpreted as showing that Beijing's growing concern over weakened household and business confidence had surpassed its concern over slowing growth and promoting employment. Accordingly, one could expect to see more policies that are targeted to support household consumption and income, and reforms aimed at addressing inadequacies in the social security networks and household registration system, although the reforms will likely be gradual and incremental.

Looking ahead, the Chinese economy is experiencing increasingly difficult challenges. Faced with the challenge of a volatile external environment, the central government has identified the domestic market as the key driver of growth. The million-dollar question is how to build the demand and supply network to ensure a circular flow in the domestic economy. China's structural challenges, including broadening the reach of its social security system, making its household registration system flexible enough to allow a rational flow of labour between localities, the ageing population and rising labour costs, cannot be swiftly resolved. The three-year COVID-19 lockdowns and controls protected the world's most populous nation from an unimaginable public health disaster and its economic consequences but disrupted China's long-term growth trajectory. Technology and innovation, including in the digital economy, delivery services and the tech-intensive green trio of solar batteries, lithium-ion batteries and electric vehicles, hold the potential to drive growth. Navigating the challenges to achieve the party's stated goal of becoming a moderately developed economy within a decade will require political resolve.

CHINA'S LOCAL

GOVERNMENT DEBT

Jean C. Oi

The hidden debt of China's local governments, which is held by entities called local government financing vehicles (LGFVs), has rattled financial markets. Now some worry that it could threaten the entire economy. While there is no official data, one estimate of LGFVs debt puts it at 59 trillion yuan (US$8.25 trillion) at the end of 2022.[1] The International Monetary Fund estimates that the total might be even higher, more than 70 trillion yuan (US$9.79 trillion).[2] To put these numbers in perspective, another estimate puts local government debt held by LGFVs at nearly half of China's total GDP in 2021, or about twice the size of Germany's economy.[3] A more recent estimate has upped the number closer to US$10 trillion, which would be roughly double the GDP of Japan.[4] These off-the-books LGFV borrowings are almost the same size as official (on-the-books) central and local government debt combined.[5] While we do not know the precise figure, we do know that the prospects for local government finances are going to remain dire unless the real estate sector—the major source of local government financing—rebounds. The severe decline in the cash flow from the real estate sector to local government means that an increasing number of LGFVs will face liquidity risks, unable to pay their debts as they become due.

For most readers, the most puzzling thing about China's local government debt might be why it is considered 'hidden' and why local government financing vehicles (LGFVs) are holding the bag for local governments. To understand this, it is necessary to understand what LGFVs are and why the collapse of the real estate sector has created such problems for them. The bigger question is why China's powerful central government let this problem grow to this degree. Why didn't Beijing do something about it earlier? LGFV debt skyrocketed during the zero-COVID policies, so is the pandemic to blame? Finally, what is Beijing doing about this crisis, and is it enough to solve the problem?

LGFVs and 'hidden' debt

While local government debt is common in all countries, China's story is unique in several respects. First, if one looks at the on-the-books debt of local governments, the situation is manageable and relatively stable—one would not know there was a debt problem. What makes the China case so curious but also worrisome for Beijing is that the local government debt that has skyrocketed is 'hidden'. In this context, the adjective 'hidden' does not imply that the debt is illegal, but rather that it is off-the-books or unrecorded. Local governments do this off the books because Chinese law forbids them from bank borrowing. To circumvent this restriction, local governments were allowed by Beijing to create institutional middlemen to borrow on their behalf—these are the special purpose vehicles, called local government financing vehicles (LGFVs), which incur and hold this 'hidden' debt. It is these LGFVs that now are teetering on default. Hence, while this debt is technically 'hidden', it is an expected and condoned outcome of a deal made between Beijing and the localities.

To understand why and how LGFVs are left holding the bag of local government debt, one needs to go back to the early 1990s when Beijing reformed the fiscal system, which had been in place since 1980. The 1994 fiscal reform stemmed from the 1980 fiscal system, which was called a revenue sharing-system. The reason why that system proved to be such a potent incentive for local state-led development was that there was a category of taxes and fees, called extrabudgetary revenues, that localities did not have to share but could keep in their entirety. The most important and the fastest growing of these revenues was the collective and individual enterprise tax, which took off with the development of the township and village enterprises, the TVEs. It was these TVEs that allowed China's economy to take off. The problem was that all the new revenue from this sector was staying in the localities. By the early 1990s, Beijing was only receiving less than a quarter of total revenues.

To grab a bigger share of total revenues, in 1994, Beijing restructured the fiscal system by dividing taxes into those that would go exclusively to the centre, those that would go to the localities, and those that would be shared; this is known as the 'tax-sharing system' 分税制. The hitch was that this 1994 fiscal reform would leave localities with insufficient tax revenues to meet their basic expenditures. Localities would face an annual fiscal gap—a shortfall between the amount of tax revenues left to them and their fiscal expenditures. The then vice premier of China, Zhu Rongji 朱镕基, and others, including the then minister of finance Xiang Huaicheng 项怀诚, recognised the problem and knew that localities needed new incentives to pursue local state-led development to make up for the revenues that were taken away.

Zhu Rongji came up with a grand bargain that would allow Beijing to have its cake and eat it too. Beijing could recentralise tax revenues, and the localities would be given the rights and tools to raise new non-tax revenues that they could keep to replace the extra budgetary funds that were taken away. To make the bargain operable, localities were given the right to run local state banks and then establish LGFVs to circumvent the legal prohibition on government borrowing.[6]

The dependence of LGFVs and local governments on the real estate sector

Local governments established LGFVs as middlemen to borrow on their behalf. LGFVs were also tasked with selling land to real estate developers, who then paid land transaction fees to local governments. Using land to generate revenue is known as 'land finance' 土地财政. This strategy allowed localities to fill the fiscal gap left by the 1994 fiscal reforms, which recentralised taxes to Beijing. Yes, localities had to borrow and incur debt, but the steady stream of revenues from land transactions allowed them to repay debt and have funds to drive growth.

Problems began with the Global Financial Crisis, when China implemented its stimulus package to keep the economy going. Nominally, the stimulus package provided RMB 4 trillion. In reality, however, the central government provided only 30 percent of that amount, and local governments were expected to find the rest.[7] All of that borrowing created a huge debt burden for local governments around 2013 when many of those loans started to come due. To help repay these debts, local governments started to issue bonds. Although debt was becoming more burdensome, it was manageable because land finance was still viable as the housing market continued to boom.

Construction sites have been left empty or half built since Beijing implemented the 'Three Red Lines' policy
Source: Markus Winkler, Unsplash

The current crisis stems from the collapse of the real estate sector, when the demand for land vaporised, rendering the land finance strategy inoperable. Because of their dependence on the real estate sector for revenues, its collapse left local government budgets with no incoming revenue stream. LGFVs must now borrow more on behalf of their local government to ensure the continued operation of public services and to service existing loans. Some localities have already had to cut back on social services or laid off government employees because of fiscal shortcomings. But the other options are also limited because there are now also restrictions on the ability of LGFVs to issue bonds if they are already holding too much debt.

COVID-19 and the current crisis

One might think that the current local government debt problem can be blamed on COVID-19. The costs of testing, isolating and treating COVID-19 was borne almost entirely by local governments. Yet COVID-19 does not sufficiently explain the problem. While COVID-19 certainly raised expenditures for local governments, it was pandemic-era state policies, which enforced fiscal discipline and deleveraged the real estate sector, that triggered the crisis of local government debt. The mountains of debt facing local governments across China are largely an unintended byproduct of these policies. A few factors came together, including COVID-19, to create a perfect storm that then magnified and made intractable an institutional problem that had its origins in the mid-1990s.

Before COVID-19, starting in 2016, Beijing had already begun to tamp down the real estate sector with a deleveraging campaign that tried to limit the sector's borrowing and ensure that borrowers would have cash on hand to repay debt. The arrival of COVID-19 led Beijing to pause its efforts to enforce fiscal discipline. From about January to June of 2020, the central authorities provided substantial aid to localities to offset some of the costs to local governments during the initial phase of the pandemic, such as special low-interest COVID-19 bonds 抗疫特别国债.

Ironically, it was China's success in tackling COVID-19 during the first six months that set it on the road that led to the local government debt problems. After a rocky start in Wuhan, Beijing was highly rated by the Nikkei COVID-19 Recovery Index for its handling of COVID-19, as measured by case numbers, vaccination rates, mobility and functioning economic life.[8] Beijing became so confident that in the summer of 2020, the central government returned to its pre-COVID-19 economic agenda to try to enforce fiscal discipline on the real estate sector and curbing debt more generally, especially that of local governments.

Beijing implemented the 'Three Red Lines' policy 三条红线, which prohibited real estate firms from borrowing beyond set limits. Overnight, the developers' heretofore successful business model of borrowing to grow became inoperable. This left them with few or no new sources of funding to keep operating or repay debt, leaving many scrambling to sell assets for quick cash. Some stopped building, leaving construction sites empty or half built. Suppliers went unpaid. Some developers defaulted, but few were buying land from local governments. But the consequences did not stop with the developers not being able to get loans. Because homebuyers in China had start making mortgage payments before construction was complete, once they realised what was happening to the real estate developers, they went on mortgage strikes, refusing to make further payments out of fear that they would never get a finished apartment.

Ultimately, the failures of the real estate companies meant that revenues from land sales and preparation sank to almost nothing, leaving local governments cut off from the source of non-tax revenue that made up the gaps in funding of their local budgets each year. The impact of the loss of land sales revenues was made worse by the decrease in tax revenues after central authorities cracked down on the tech and the afterschool tutoring sectors during this same period.

The final factor that contributed to the perfect storm was the arrival of a new COVID-19 variant, Omicron, in January 2022. The resulting lockdowns further cost local governments as COVID-related expenses for testing, quarantining, and treatment soared, while revenues plummeted due to the near halt of most economic activity. It became increasingly difficult, if not impossible, for local governments to repay their debts and cover rising expenditures. The real estate sector and housing market have yet to recover despite the end of zero-COVID restrictions at the end of 2022, as the economy—after a brief bump in activity—has remained in a slump.

To make matters worse for local governments, Beijing pushed aside concerns about curbing local debt. In an about-face, it instructed LGFVs to take up the slack from the demise of the real estate sector and make land purchases, even if it mean going into more debt, to provide revenues for local government coffers. It remains unclear what LGFVs are doing with this land. Reports suggest that few have actually used that land for new development. Recent reports reveal that although some LGFVs did buy land, others faked these transactions to comply with upper-level directives.[9] These must have decided that they simply did not have the funds to do so, nor did they want to assume more debt. We await details of how local governments dealt with these directives, which are simply trying to make the on-the-books local government budgets look stronger even if the off-the-books borrowing skyrockets even further.

Why did Beijing not stop this hidden debt problem earlier?

CHINA STORY YEARBOOK | China's Local Government Debt
CHINA'S NEW ERA | Jean C. Oi

Since 2014, when the costs of the stimulus package loans became evident, Beijing has been trying to rein in local government debt. This included Beijing swapping out the LGFV bonds, which were most costly in terms of interest with shorter maturity dates, to longer maturing, lower-cost, centrally approved and guaranteed local government municipal bonds that could be more easily repaid. Importantly, these municipal bonds were strictly limited in the amounts issued and required approval by the upper levels. The assumption was that if they cleaned up these existing bonds and required approval for the municipal bonds, the centre could control local government debt. After the bond swaps, in 2018 another campaign was started to get rid of hidden debt, including having local governments sell assets or stakes in state-owned enterprises (SOEs). But none of the many attempts were successful because none addressed the root of the problem: the flawed fiscal system instituted in 1994 that left localities with a fiscal gap. The approved municipal bonds were insufficient to cover local fiscal needs.

Banks such as ICBC are now offering 25-year loans
Source: Adrian-Grycuk, Wikimedia Commons

The point that must be understood is that LGFVs and their borrowing on behalf of local government was an expected outcome of the grand bargain to mobilise support from the localities for its 1994 fiscal reforms. Beijing even assured localities that they should not fear upper-level intervention in revenue-generating activities, as long as they sent up the requisite tax revenues. This also explains why Beijing had no official accounting of local government debt until 2011. Beijing had agreed that it would not seek to know the details.

What Beijing is doing to resolve the crisis

Allowing the establishment of LGFVs was an effective short-term workaround for local government borrowing. As indicated in the introduction, the terms 'legal' or 'illegal' are useless in understanding their actions because they were condoned and created to get around official prohibitions against local governments borrowing from banks. But the grand bargain between the centre and the localities that allowed their creation also has created ambiguity around who is responsible for repaying LGFV debt and allows Beijing to pretend that local government finances are not in jeopardy.

As financial analysts around the world have become more rattled by the sheer size of this hidden debt and the possible consequences for the larger economy, Beijing has tried to calm markets by describing it as enterprise debt (LGFVs are state-owned enterprises) and denying that it counts as local government debt. As China's Ministry of Finance has said, the liability for LGFV debt 'lies with the entity that issued it'.[10] It added, 'local governments do not bear the responsibility to repay the debt of LGFVs and other state-owned enterprises', citing the amended Budget Law in 2014. That means, however, that there is no explicit guarantee of payment; that is, local governments never promised to pay this debt. This ignores the fact that local governments also have what is called implicit debt, which is debt that they may pay if the original borrowing cannot pay. To thwart any hope of a central government rescue, the ministry has explicitly said: 'If it's your baby, you own it. There will be no bailout from the central government.'[11] Such statements seem at least implicitly to recognise that the problem will be the local governments'.

At the same time, Beijing has taken steps to buy more time for LGFVs and local governments to repay their debt. Banks have been asked to give LGFVs new loans with 'ultra-long maturities and temporary interest relief to prevent a credit crunch'. Instead of the ten-year loans previously given to LGFVs, banks, including some of the big four such as ICBC and China Construction Bank, are now offering 25-year loans.[12] But this strategy has moved huge risks onto the banks. As a result, Goldman Sachs downgraded its rating of China's big banks,[13] which led to a rout in bank stocks on foreign exchanges.[14]

None of the above strategies solves the institutional problem of local government debt in China. The state can formally separate local governments from their LGFVs, but at the end of the day, somebody must take responsibility for their debts. But even if someone takes over existing LGFV debt, more local debt will reappear each year because of how the fiscal system is structured. Beijing must reconfigure the system or find an alternative source of revenue to plug the fiscal gap.

China realises that a property tax like that in the United States where the revenue would belong to the localities is a solution. A few cities have limited pilot programs, but Beijing keeps delaying its implementation. Such a tax would alienate a rising middle class, and in the current context it would further hurt a depressed housing market.

Ultimately, to end hidden debt, Beijing must address the fundamental flaws in the system established by the 1994 fiscal reforms. Without thorough fiscal reform, the problem of local government debt, hidden or not, will persist. It might be time for Chinese leadership to stop kicking the can down the road. There is no other sustainable solution.

CHAPTER 2: PARTY-STATE CAPITALISM

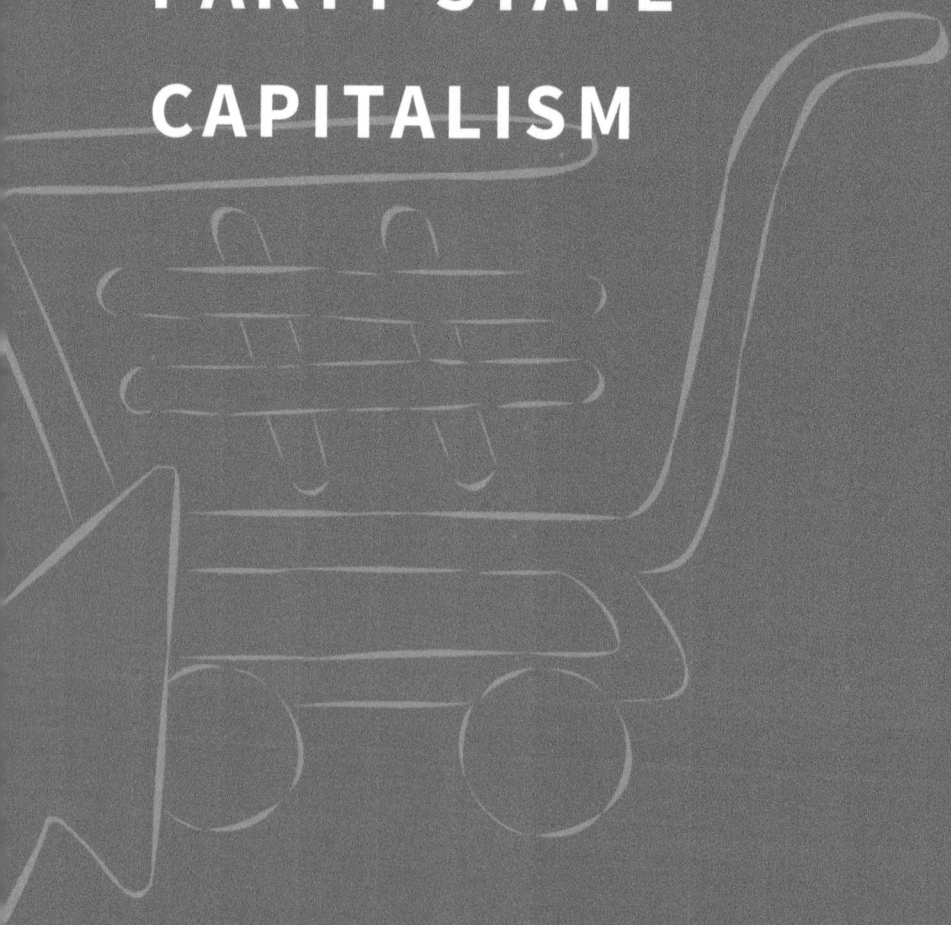

THE DREARY AND THE DRAMATIC: WHAT HAPPENED TO CHINA'S PLATFORM ECONOMY?

Rogier Creemers

It is no coincidence that Desmond Shum's *Red Roulette* has been one of the most popular books among China watchers to come out in recent years. For many of us, his lurid descriptions of the drama and debauchery taking place among the great and gilded in Beijing are as thrilling as *The Godfather*, a real-life version of *Downton Abbey* (or perhaps, more appropriately, *Crazy Rich Asians*)—a professionally justifiable guilty pleasure. Yet such depictions also often come with an almost conspiratorial tone, in which the *real* drivers of Chinese government decision-making are the personal interests of senior Party leaders and their cliques of hangers-on, and the backstabbery going on between them.

One of the most fertile grounds for such personalised speculation in recent years has been the regulatory offensive against the platform economy. Why, for instance, did Jack Ma 马云 disappear from public view for three months after the Ant Financial IPO—slated to be the largest in history—was cancelled?[1] Did Xi Jinping personally axe the deal because Jiang Zemin's grandson, Jiang Zhicheng 江志成, was a major investor through Boyu Capital, a private equity firm he co-founded, as one shot in a larger, internecine battle?[2] Did Tencent get into trouble, as an academic colleague attempted to convince me at a conference, because it had been prominently posting information favourable to Li Keqiang in the run-up to the 20th Party Congress? What happened to Bao Fan 包凡, the rainmaker for big tech investment deals, who resurfaced in early March 2023 after being reported as missing by his firm in late February? It was subsequently revealed that he is assisting authorities with an inquiry into Cong Lin, the former president of Renaissance Holdings, an investment company he founded.[3]

The standard story presented by foreign news media of what became known in the West as the 'tech crackdown' is as follows.[4] Xi Jinping got angry with Jack Ma after the latter gave a speech in October 2020 to the good and the great in China's financial sector at the Bund Summit of China Finance 40, a leading economic think tank. Ma belittled regulators and government banks as being behind the times, directly opposing the message of greater regulatory prudence delivered by Wang Qishan at the same meeting, that same morning. Seeing an opportunity not just to take an uppity Ma down a peg but also to take a swing at the interests of the Jiang family, Xi killed off the Ant Financial IPO and, for good measure, fired off a barrage of rules to constrain other platform companies and ensure absolute Party control over the digital sector. Predictably, this crackdown has gone too far. Faced with catastrophic consequences in the platform economy,[5] and economic malaise across the board, the leadership is now seeking ways to roll it back and return to growth.[6]

Jack Ma disappeared from public view after the Ant Financial IPO
Source: Paul Kagame, Flickr

This common narrative attempts to provide an explanation for something Western observers have found difficult to fathom: why would China inflict so much damage on the most innovative sector of its economy? Moreover, it is an explanation that confirms our prior assumptions: authoritarian states are going to do authoritarian things, Xi Jinping is the puppet master of the entire Party apparat, Chinese policy decisions are primarily taken in view of top leaders' personal political interests, and as long as those decisions diverge from the dictates of neoliberal market economics, they are predictably misguided and incompetent.

The problem with that story, however, is that it is highly selective in many instances and plain incorrect in others. This regulatory wave was not a sudden whim of Xi Jinping's but had been in preparation for quite some time. The drafting of the Personal Information Protection Law 个人信息保护法, for instance, started in 2018.[7] In 2019, the State Council published a document outlining the problems and abuses it saw existing within the platform economy, and listing the regulatory tasks intended to be undertaken as well as the ministries to which those would be assigned.[8] In other words, anyone claiming that the regulatory offensive came from nowhere simply was not paying attention.

The problems identified in this 2019 document and elsewhere are real. For example, the success of platform companies depends on legions of immiserated delivery drivers and gig workers, as well as overworked programmers and software engineers.[9] Third-party merchants, reliant on platform firms for their businesses, suffer from onerous contract obligations and monopolistic practices.[10] Telecommunications fraud, enabled by platform firms' lax data protection practices, is rife.[11] Poor risk management practices in fintech (i.e. financial technology) had already caused the meltdown of the P2P (i.e. peer to peer) lending industry, evaporating the savings of millions of retail investors.[12] Stricter regulations on the fintech industry were already being drafted, and it is scarcely believable that Jack Ma and Ant's legal department did not have a fairly solid understanding of what the new requirements were, or how they would affect Ant's business operations. If that is the case, Jack Ma's speech was not the trigger for central authorities to embark on regulatory measures they otherwise would not have. Rather, it might have been an unsuccessful last-ditch effort to use his personal influence to stave off regulatory interventions that would damage Ant's profitability and Ma's wealth, and one that only slightly accelerated moves that would have happened in any case.

Those elements are, however, far less dramatic and eye-catching than the disappearance or detention of high-profile CEOs or gossip about palace intrigue. Moreover, to assess them requires consistent engagement with the drudgery of analysing Chinese policy and regulatory documents—a Calvary the great Belgian Sinologist Simon Leys (Pierre Ryckmans) memorably described as 'akin to munching rhinoceros sausage, or to swallowing sawdust by the bucketful'.[13] Doing so reveals a stack of dozens of texts, issued by multiple Party and government organs, which paint a somewhat more complex picture, where there is no single discernible cause or motivation, nor even clear evidence of much interagency coordination. Regulations in fintech, for instance, have evolved nearly in parallel with interventions in the realm of competition, or protection for consumers and workers more generally.[14] Some of the fintech rules resemble market regulation initiatives undertaken elsewhere, most notably in the European Union. The Personal Information Protection Law, for instance, reproduces many of the General Data Protection Regulation's (GDPR) terms, concepts and mechanisms, defining largely similar legal grounds for personal information processing, introducing similar procedures for data transfer abroad, and imposing similar levels of punishment for violations.[15] New Chinese regulations on competition in the platform sector contain similar definitions for large-scale 'gatekeepers' to Europe's Digital Markets Act.[16]

Traversing the turgid prose of such documents is time-consuming. Journalists, think tank experts and even academics are rarely able to concentrate on tracing single policy areas across time, beholden as they are to the demands of their editors, to news cycles and to the demands of immediate hot takes. The Chinese written language, too, forms a layer of encryption: many non-native readers (myself included) simply process Chinese documents far more slowly than texts in English. In those circumstances, it is easier to reach for a standard narrative, spice it up with details of the latest scandal, and serve while it is piping hot. Deep engagement with the matter at hand does not necessarily carry a reward: 'Chinese regulators attempt incremental improvement of working conditions for gig workers' is a far less attractive headline than 'Xi Jinping assaults Jack Ma's empire'.

Doing the work requires taking Chinese policy thinking around certain questions seriously, and recognising that it might diverge from Western instincts for reasons other than the wielding of blunt authoritarian power. Consumer-oriented online services might be seen as the pinnacle of innovation in the United States, but policy-makers in Beijing disagree somewhat. Beijing recognises that big tech has contributed in no small way to enhancing the convenience of Chinese citizens' daily lives but, at the same time, does not believe that it makes a durable contribution to the fundamental qualities of the Chinese economy. Instead, China's techno-industrial policy under the Fourteenth Five-Year Plan (2021–25) focuses on upgrading the efficiency and productivity of the manufacturing industry.[17] Platform firms are expected to support that effort, for instance, by providing innovative services in logistics and supply chain management. Cryptocurrencies, in the eyes of Chinese regulators, moreover, are mere vehicles for non-productive speculation and law-breaking, and consume vast amounts of electricity to boot.[18] No wonder they have now been banned completely.

Chinese authorities view the fintech sector as highly important and therefore in need of effective and strict regulation
Source: Dong Fang, Wikimedia

Beijing's willingness to damage the fintech sector, which has lost more than US$2 trillion in market capitalisation, for instance, becomes a lot more explicable when it is recognised that nearly all publicly traded Chinese fintech companies are listed on stock exchanges outside mainland China. The shareholders receiving a haircut are therefore far less Chinese than one might initially think. However, to admit that Chinese authorities might have good reasons for acting in the way they do implies that the Western political and economic model is not universally applicable, and undermines an easy dismissal of Chinese policy solutions. The fact is that China acts in many ways similar to, say, the European Union, and the bureaucracy in Beijing is beset by the same pathologies that trouble Washington, Brussels, Canberra or any other capital.

A similar problem lies in discussions of the 'end of the crackdown'. This phrase seems to imply that the regulatory campaign was temporary and that the normal order of business will resume. This is incorrect: it is better to understand what happened as a 'rectification': the introduction of a new governance paradigm for a sector that Chinese authorities view as highly important and therefore in need of effective and strict regulation. Safety requirements in cars are not an effort to stop people driving but to ensure they are not killed or maimed so often while doing so. Not only are the new rules here to stay but so also are the structures designed to enforce them. The State Administration of Market Regulation, China's relatively new competition regulator, has established a new Anti-Monopoly Bureau and hired scores of new enforcement personnel.[19]

The definitive end of this rectification came in the northern summer of 2023. Regulators imposed fines of RMB 7 and 3 billion respectively on Ant Financial and Tencent for a series of regulatory infractions.[20] Ant was also ordered to shut down its mutual-aid insurance arm Xuxiangbao. In an accompanying statement, the People's Bank of China stated that 'most of the prominent problems in the financial business of platform enterprises have been corrected' and that it would now focus on everyday supervision rather than major regulatory overhauls. In the subsequent weeks, a series of events demonstrated that the platform economy was back in Beijing's good graces. Premier Li Qiang 李强 hosted a seminar on the sector's 'healthy and sustained development' attended by the CEOs of Meituan, Xiaohongshu, Huolala, Alibaba Cloud, Douyin, Pinduoduo and JD.com, among others. This was the first time the premier had directly met platform companies since 2019. The policy measure was, however, clear: in his speech, Li highlighted the sector's potential but also called on platform companies to invest more in research and development, particularly of 'core' technologies, to integrate with manufacturing businesses and develop the industrial internet.[21] In return, government would increase investment, streamline bureaucratic procedures, and maintain regulatory predictability. This proposed *quid pro quo* was formalised in a Central Committee and State Council policy document on the development of the private economy published a week after this conference.[22] The Beijing municipal government subsequently published draft policies to support the platform economy, which included faster licensing procedures, relaxed codes of conduct for live-streamers, and the establishment of demonstration zones for best business practices.[23] Interestingly, the measures also announced a higher level of 'error tolerance', under which companies would be warned earlier and given more time to redress identified compliance issues. The State Administration of Market Regulation, too, has signalled that it will regularise oversight to avoid sudden actions that disrupt normal operations.[24]

However, none of these measures should be taken as evidence that Chinese authorities intend to roll back any of the measures that were introduced. If that results in the sector's profitability being permanently depressed, so be it: those profits would have come from unsustainable or undesirable practices anyway. Instead, the platform economy is encouraged to move towards practices that policy-makers are in greater favour of, particularly the industrial policies included in the Fourteenth Five-Year Plan, which focus on using digital capabilities to upgrade the manufacturing sector, and on supporting strategic and emerging technologies. One can reasonably disagree with that logic, but we need to recognise why it exists in the first place.

The inability or unwillingness of much Western commentary and analysis to engage with the drudgery of deep policy analysis relates both to our human fondness for a good yarn and to a predisposition for making sense of China in ways that are psychologically comfortable to those of us who closely identify with the Western liberal order. However, that comes at a cost: we are less able to make sense of the Communist Party of China's motivations and actions. This influences not only our direct engagement with China but also the broader world with which it is inextricably intertwined.

HOW MULTINATIONAL

CORPORATIONS ARE

COOPTED INTO BECOMING

CHINA'S AGENTS OF

REPRESSION

Debby Chan

Informal economic sanctions reinforced by state-sponsored consumer boycotts have made the Chinese market volatile for multinational corporations (MNCs) over the past decade. MNCs must be careful not to offend Beijing and nationalists in the People's Republic of China (PRC). Nonetheless, a definition of what it means to 'offend China' 辱华 is rather elusive. Examples range from refusing to procure cotton from Xinjiang,[1] and defending employees' freedom of speech in support of anti-government protesters in Hong Kong,[2] to failing to conceal the freckles of an East Asian–looking model in a fashion advertisement.[3] Chinese consumers even accused a Chinese condiment producer of offending China by including in its domestic products food additives not used in its exported products due to different food safety standards in the two markets.[4]

A recent example of 'offending China' involved alleged discrimination against mainlanders by the cabin crew of Hong Kong's flagship airline, Cathay Pacific. On a Cathay Pacific flight from Chengdu to Hong Kong on 21 May 2023, three flight attendants were accused of mocking a passenger who confused the English words 'carpet' and 'blanket'. 'If you can't say "blanket", you can't have it,' one flight attendant said. Another added, 'Carpet is on the floor.' The conversation was overheard and recorded by another Chinese passenger, who was sitting near the cabin crew's rest area. The clip was posted on Xiaohongshu 小红书 (an Instagram-like social media platform) the next day and went viral.

Making fun of the passenger's English was misconduct; however, it is not known whether the crew member treated the passenger less favourably when they requested a blanket. Within a day, Cathay Pacific issued three public apologies in simplified Chinese and Mandarin to the passengers involved and to mainland consumers. Chief Executive Officer (CEO) Ronald Lam 林绍波 declared that the airline 'had a zero-tolerance approach to any serious breach of the company's policies and code of conduct' and announced the three flight attendants had been dismissed.[5] He also stressed that passengers with diverse cultural backgrounds must be respected. To prevent similar incidents in the future, the airline would review its flight attendants' training.[6] As part of this reform, in July, the airline began to recruit flight attendants from mainland China.[7]

Despite prompt action by the airline, the scandal was elevated to a political controversy, unleashing a flood of mainland Chinese grievances against Hongkongers. Political actors and state media took turns condemning the airline. Hong Kong Chief Executive John Lee 李家超 reprimanded Cathay Pacific for the cabin crew's disrespectful words, claiming they had hurt the feelings of the people of both Hong Kong and mainland China[8] and tarnished Hong Kong's reputation as a courteous and hospitable place.[9] Other Hong Kong government officials and lawmakers lined up to express anger and disappointment at the airline to ensure that their stance on the incident was communicated to Beijing.

Cathay Pacific's alleged discrimation against mainlanders was elevated to a political controversy
Source: Issac Struna, Unsplash

Chinese state media characterised the incident as an exemplar of Hongkongers' weak national identity and Cathay Pacific's arrogance. Xinhua warned that consumers would vote with their feet. From a business perspective, the incident cost Cathay not only its reputation, but also one of its markets.[10] China Central Television (CCTV) claimed it was not an isolated incident and criticised Cathay Pacific for neglecting the root of the problem in their governance.[11] An online commentary published by the *People's Daily* condemned the airline for worshipping foreigners and looking down on mainland Chinese twenty-five years after the city had returned to the 'motherland' and the more recent imposition of the territory's National

Security Law. The commentary also attributed Hong Kong's prosperity to the Chinese state's support and Chinese tourists' spending. It demanded Cathay Pacific 'take heavy-handed measures to rectify the situation, establish rules and regulations, and fundamentally put an end to this iniquitous corporate culture'.[12] A *Global Times* commentary accused Hongkongers of having 'a colonial mentality in their hearts'. It urged the Hong Kong government to develop a strategic plan through education and public communication to achieve decolonialisation of its society.[13]

Cathay Pacific is a subsidiary of British conglomerate Swire Group, but 30 percent of its shares are held by Air China. The airline was one of the MNCs that faced tremendous pressure amid Hong Kong's political turmoil in 2019, which was sparked by a proposed extradition bill that would have destroyed the legal firewall between Hong Kong and mainland China.[14] A labour and market strike was called for 12 June 2019—the day the Bill was expected to pass. Working from home was rare before the COVID-19 pandemic, but HSBC, Standard Chartered, the 'Big Four' accounting firms, and other corporations permitted employees to have special work arrangements on the day of the strike, signalling their acquiescence to employees' participation in the protests.

Cosmetic company Lancôme faced pressure following the 2014 Umbrella Movement
Source: Wpcpey, Wikimedia

Political tensions escalated over the next few months and another strike was called for 5 August. Some 2,300 staff in the aviation sector, including 1,200 Cathay Pacific employees, joined the strike. At least 200 flights were cancelled.[15] Two days later, the Hong Kong and Macau Affairs Office of the State Council and the Liaison Office of the Central People's Government Office in Hong Kong jointly organised a closed-door meeting with 500 pro-Beijing members, including business elites, in Shenzhen.[16] In this united-front meeting, Chinese officials asserted the protests had developed 'colour revolution characteristics', which sent an unequivocal signal from Beijing that it would intervene in the political chaos in Hong Kong.[17] After attending the meeting, several leading conglomerates that had previously been silent about the protests swiftly displayed their loyalty to Beijing. Hong Kong's General Chamber of Commerce and the Real Estate Developers Association made statements denouncing the escalating violence in the movement.[18] In the same week, the Civil Aviation Administration of China demanded Cathay Pacific bar any cabin crew who participated in or supported the illegal protests from working on flights to the mainland. The aviation authorities also ordered the airline to submit crew members' identification information for their approval before the crew was rostered onto any flights entering China's airspace.[19] As well as the censure from state media, netizens called for a consumer boycott.[20]

John Slosar, then chairman of Cathay Pacific, initially defended the right to freedom of expression of his staff.[21] Faced with political pressure and financial jeopardy, both Slosar and Cathay Pacific's CEO Rupert Hogg handed in their resignations. More than thirty employees of Cathay Pacific and its subsidiary Dragon Airline were dismissed due to their political stance on the protests. Among them was union chairwoman Rebecca Sy, who had worked as a flight attendant for seventeen years and was immediately dismissed for lamenting the resignation of the CEO on her private Facebook account. Sy believed the private posts must have been passed on to management by her colleagues.[22] Similarly, several Cathay Pacific employees publicly stated they had been summoned by management and questioned about their private social media posts on the protests before being dismissed.[23] Employees who breach company regulations can expect to be disciplined, but the extent of Cathay Pacific's intrusion into employees' private lives was alarming.

Cathay Pacific's travails in both 2019 and 2023 present one of many examples of Beijing pressuring companies that operate in China to act as its agents in sanctioning individuals' political views. The following cases—one of which dates back almost twenty years—indicate how economic coercion, fortified by consumer nationalism, has led MNCs to suppress freedom of expression on behalf of the Chinese state:

- Yahoo! (2004): Human rights organisations, including Amnesty International and Human Rights Watch, accused Yahoo! of providing the Chinese government with Hunan-based journalist Shi Tao's 师涛 email communications with Democracy Forum, a New York–based website. He had sent them censorship directives related to the Tiananmen Incident's fifteenth anniversary from an anonymous email account. Shi was sentenced to ten years in prison for leaking state secrets.[24]

- Lancôme (2016): The cosmetic company abruptly cancelled a promotional concert featuring Denise Ho 何韻詩, a Hong Kong singer who supported the 2014 Umbrella Movement, after pressure from the *Global Times* and threats by Chinese consumers on social media of a boycott.[25]

- Cambridge University Press (2017): The press temporarily blocked readers in mainland China from accessing more than 300 *China Quarterly* articles at the request of China's General Administration of Press and Publication. The publisher restored the articles after widespread criticism from academia worldwide.[26]

- US National Basketball Association (NBA) (2019): A tweet on 4 October in support of the Hong Kong protests by Houston Rockets executive Daryl Morey led to a broadcast blackout of matches in China. The Chinese Consulate in Houston issued an online statement to condemn Morey's tweet and demanded the Rockets clarify the team's stance.[27] Chinese netizens also called for the dismissal of Morey.[28] Morey apologised for his tweet. In NBA's initial statement on 6 October, it regretted that

Morey's views 'deeply offended many of our friends and fans in China'. Two days later, NBA Commissioner Adam Silver defended Morey's freedom of expression in the wake of pushback from US politicians.[29] CCTV stopped airing NBA games from October 2019 to March 2022, except for one match in October 2020.[30]

- BNP Paribas (2019): The *Global Times* denounced Hong Kong–based BNP Paribas lawyer Jason Ng for his Facebook posts supporting the protests in the city and denouncing the police's management of them. Chinese netizens accused Ng of being a 'secessionist' and demanded the bank sack him. The bank apologised for Ng's comments and emphasised that they 'did not reflect the view of BNP Paribas'. Ng subsequently resigned.[31]

- HSBC (2023): HSBC terminated the bank accounts of the League of Social Democrats (LSD) without explanation along with the personal accounts of several LSD members. The LSD is the only opposition party that has maintained small-scale street activities in Hong Kong since the introduction of the National Security Law. LSD leaders were approached by national security police about their protest plans for 'sensitive dates', such as the anniversaries of the Tiananmen Incident and Hong Kong's handover to China, and China's national day. The homes of some members were raided ahead of those sensitive dates.[32]

Companies must comply with domestic laws where they operate. Doing business in or with China, however, comes with an additional requirement: be careful not to offend the authoritarian state. The above cases show the Chinese state and its consumers not only effectively compel MNCs to play by authoritarian rules and norms while operating in the PRC itself, but also insist that MNCs operating abroad censor the political views of their employees. MNCs may believe that profit justifies their political compliance; however, the effects of such a compromise on the erosion of democratic values and freedom of expression are borne by the liberal world at large. The more dependent a company is on the Chinese market, the more susceptible it is to coercion. Not many MNCs are willing to do anything that will endanger their access to the Chinese market. Google is one of the few exceptions. The tech giant ultimately refused to be complicit in China's censorship requirements and quit the lucrative market in 2010.[33] Despite an attempt to re-enter the Chinese market with a censored search engine, Dragonfly, the controversial project was dropped in 2019.[34]

China's spectacular economic growth and rising power have given it more resources to reshape norms and standards in the global order. Many studies have investigated the influence of China's foreign direct investment and foreign aid on target states.[35] Emerging research pinpoints how the Chinese government weaponises its domestic market to achieve political goals.[36] More work needs to be done to show how the Chinese government coopts and coerces MNCs to enforce its authoritarian values and policies— and the implications of this on the liberal world order. As consumer and shareholder activism for environmental and social justice expands to include human rights—by, for example, boycotting products produced by Myanmar junta-linked businesses—it will be interesting to see how companies negotiate the demands of their home markets and those of the world's largest one.

五

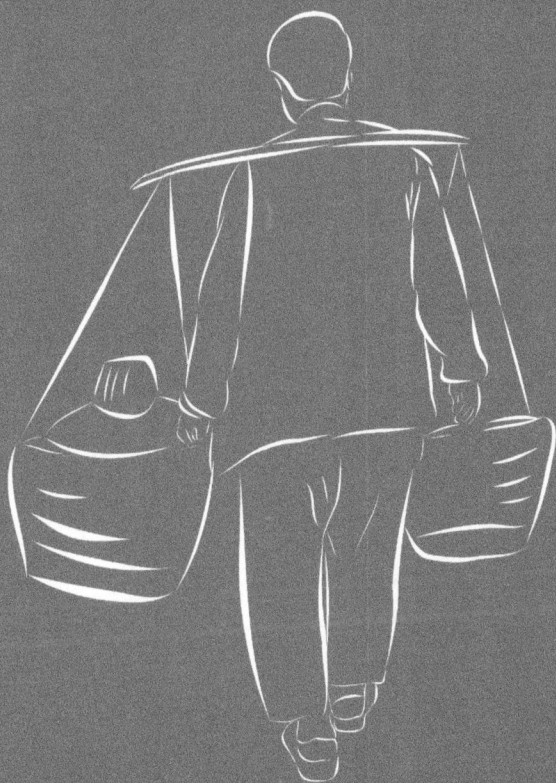

CHAPTER 3:
THE CHALLENGES
OF COMMON
PROSPERITY

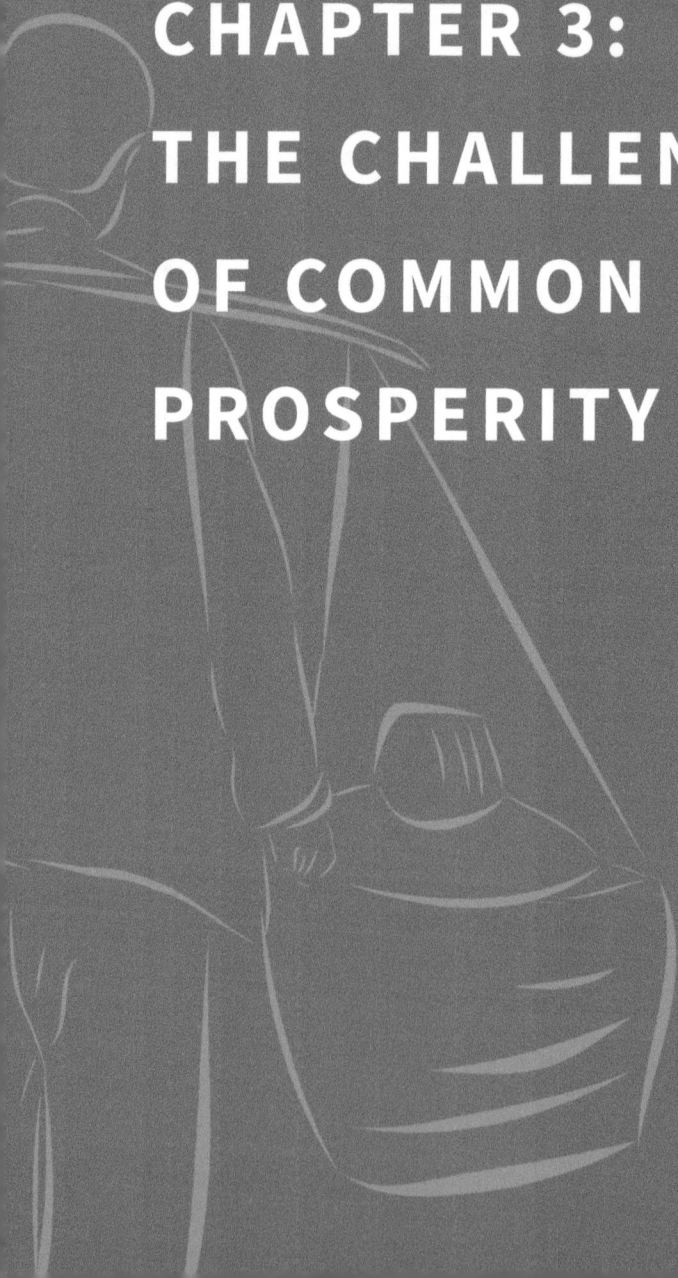

INEQUALITY IN CHINA:

THE CHALLENGE OF

COMMON PROSPERITY

Dorien Emmers and Scott Rozelle

According to World Bank data, only a handful of economies have risen from middle- to high-income status since 1960, when economic catch-up growth in many developing economies took off.[1] Examples include South Korea, Singapore, Israel and Ireland. Some countries that were high income in 1960 remain so today, such as Canada and France. Some that were poor, like Cambodia and Tanzania, have stayed poor. Many countries have stayed at middle-income status for decades, seemingly unable to reach high-income status.[2] They are in what is called the Middle-Income Trap, and this may include China too.

How does China compare to these other countries trapped at the middle-income level? Since the beginning of reforms under Deng Xiaoping in 1978, China has undergone remarkable development. After four decades of strong economic growth, China has become the second-largest economy (in terms of nominal GDP), the largest exporter and the second-largest importer in the world.[3] However, China's growth, even with double-digit growth rates, has relied heavily on unskilled labour. Most of the workers who have fuelled the country's rise come from rural villages and have never gone to high school. For all of its investment in physical infrastructure, for decades China failed to invest enough in the education and health of a large share of its people.[4]

One key factor that may account for disparate development paths among nations is education. According to the Organization for Economic Cooperation and Development (OECD), in 2015 in countries that graduated to high-income status (i.e. they escaped from middle income), 72 percent of the working age population (18–65 years) had completed secondary education when the country was still at middle-income status.[5] In countries stuck in the Middle-Income Trap, the share of the working-age population with a secondary education is much lower—only 36 percent on average.

Having a large supply of educated workers ensures that enough talent exists to meet and drive demand for high-value goods and services that drive an economy when it becomes a high-income one, thereby sustaining growth. When too many unskilled workers are squeezed out of upgraded industries, their wages tend to stagnate or fall, curtailing demand and hampering growth. This eventually leads to serious social problems, such as higher rates of unemployment and increased crime and social unrest. Nations with socially polarised work forces also suffer from political instability.

Young children in rural areas may be unprepared to learn complex skills as they age
Source: Samuel Vigier, Flickr

Shortcomings in education and health threaten China's growth

Education attainment metrics help reveal China's potential future development and growth trajectory. The share of uneducated workers in China's labour force is larger than that of virtually all upper middle-income countries. According to China's own 2015 micro-census data, there are between 450 to 500 million people in China between the ages of 18 and 65 who have never attended one day of high school, which is 70 percent of the labour force. This makes China one of the least educated middle-income countries in the world.[6]

A large population of uneducated workers was not a problem while China was moving from low- to middle-income status. Unskilled labour was in high demand. Unskilled wages were low, and low-cost manufacturing and construction were growing. But China's growth model has been changing over the past decade or more. Unskilled wages are much higher, so foreign investors have begun to shift their attention towards other countries with cheaper labour. China's own massive push to automate (also to avoid having to pay for labour that became increasingly expensive since the mid-2000s) also is rendering low-skilled workers redundant. Construction jobs have tapered off as investment in infrastructure cools as well. China's unskilled workers may become increasingly unemployable (and have actually begun to see wages falling) as the economy upgrades.

The only destination for China's unskilled workforce—new entrants to the labour force and laid-off workers alike—is the informal (or blue-collar) service sector. Data from the 2018 *China Statistical Yearbook* shows that informal employment is currently the fastest growing sector in China, increasing from 33 percent in 2004 to 56 percent in 2017.[7] A rising supply of unskilled workers (along with only moderately growing demand for services) means stagnating wages. With strong demand for skilled work in the white-collar sector, higher wages are going to those with higher levels of education. This result appears to have a large number of similarities to what happened in Mexico in the 1990s (although there are differences): Mexico had solid macroeconomic performance, export success and an accumulation of physical capital. However, despite these strengths, the nation's poorly educated labour force and the emergence of a dominating informal economy swamped and dragged down the development of the formal economy. Despite rapid growth in the 1970s and 1980s (which ended with Mexico being admitted to the OECD as a rapidly developing upper middle-income economy), Mexico has almost experienced no growth since the mid-1990s and today is a clearly a stagnant middle-income nation.

Recognising the critical need for secondary education, China's government expanded access to high school throughout the country in the mid-2000s.[8] High school attainment among the youngest cohorts in the labour force is close to 80 percent. But hundreds of millions of less educated people will remain in the labour force for the next thirty years.[9] The government will face huge challenges trying either to retrain workers or to provide a social safety net.

The quality of China's expanded secondary school education is also uncertain. Almost all low-skilled labour comes from rural areas, where school and health systems are under-resourced due to the legacy of national policies.[10] The household registration (*hukou* 戶口) system played an important role in the widening of China's rural/urban disparities. The system was introduced in the 1950s as a way of managing labour and population flows in an economy that was being run by central planners (as opposed to markets). Although *hukou*-related restrictions on labour mobility were relaxed gradually after the early 1990s, the system continued to limit educational, health and employment opportunities for rural *hukou* holders. Moreover, historically higher shares of public investments in infrastructure and services have been channelled towards urban areas in China. As a result, many of China's new secondary school graduates attended poor-quality vocational high schools and are not learning the maths, science, computer and language skills that China will need in the future in its labour force if the nation graduates to high-income status.

Systemic shortfalls in education and the health of young children in rural areas may also render many young people unprepared to learn complex skills as they age. Large-scale field studies showed that more than a quarter of Chinese school children were anemic; one out of five were myopic (and did not have eyeglasses); and one out of four children had intestinal worms. Soil-transmitted helminth infections are a threat to the nutritional status of children and their cognitive development.[11]

Increasingly, studies recognise that early childhood (up to three years old) is a sensitive and critical stage, foundational for lifelong human development.[12] In the international literature, delays in early childhood development have been associated with decreased cognitive functioning and lower labour productivity in adulthood.[13] Empirical evidence from China specifically demonstrates that the rural/urban education gap in the country emerges during the first years of life, when rural children start lagging behind in their development.[14] A systematic review and meta-analysis calculated that the risks of delay to early cognitive development and language function for children younger than five years of age in rural study sites across China amount to 45 percent and 46 percent, respectively.[15]

Most of the workers who have fuelled the country's rise come from rural villages and have never gone to high school
Source: Wang Whale, Unsplash

A safe home environment with sufficient learning opportunities, healthy nutrition and responsive caregiving are essential for healthy development during early childhood. An optimal home is a clean and safe environment, sensitive to the nutritional needs of young children and equipped with developmentally appropriate objects, toys and books that provide opportunities for children to play, explore and discover. However, survey results have shown that parental investment in cognitively stimulating parenting practices and child nutrition in rural China is low. No more than 25 percent of the rural caregivers in large-scale field surveys in rural China report frequently reading or telling stories to their young children.[16]

Another study in China's rural areas found that no more than 30 percent of the caregivers provide a diet for their children that satisfies the WHO's minimum dietary diversity criterion.[17]

Parenting training programs focusing on cognitive stimulation can benefit the developmental opportunities of young children in developing countries.[18] Pioneering studies from the 1970s and 1980s, with long-term follow-up, include the Jamaican Nutrition and Cognitive Stimulation Program (or Reach Up and Learn). They found evidence of lasting positive impacts of small-scale parenting interventions on a range of adult outcomes, including lifetime educational attainment.[19] The promising results incentivised researchers and policymakers in the 2010s, in particular after the United Nations introduced Target 4.2 of the Sustainable Development Goals, which would 'ensure that all girls and boys have access to quality early childhood development by 2030', to replicate such interventions in resource-poor settings around the world.[20] Over the past decade, evidence from randomised controlled trials has confirmed the effectiveness of parental training experiments in resource-poor settings in a range of developing regions, including in rural China.[21] Therefore policymakers no longer debate the effectiveness of parenting programs, only how quality child and family services can be delivered cost effectively, sustainably and at scale.

China's government has announced its intention to steer China on a path of 'people-centred development' towards Common Prosperity. In 2010 China became the second largest economy in the world after the United States, and claims to have eradicated extreme poverty in 2020.[22] Despite achieving these milestones, 600 million Chinese had a monthly per capita income of US$140 or less in 2020,[23] and regional and rural/urban inequalities have widened over the past decades.[24] In the face of these remaining challenges, China's central leadership has promoted the phrase 'Common Prosperity' 共同富裕 since 2020.[25] This signals an intent on the one hand to curtail income inequality and excessive wealth accumulation by individuals and on the other to help people achieve a better standard of living.

Investing in the developmental opportunities of disadvantaged children is crucial to improve equality of educational opportunity and social mobility and to build the large, high-skilled labour force China will need to support a strong, innovation-driven economy in the future. Providing young children with a fair start in life is crucial to address the 'principal contradiction between unbalanced and inadequate development and the people's ever-growing needs for a better life' that China's society faces today.[26] This principal contradiction was highlighted as the main stumbling block that needed to be tackled for further social development by Xi Jinping during his report to the 19th National Congress of the Communist Party of China in 2017.

Why we should want China to succeed ... or at least not to fail

The risks of a stagnating China would reverberate far beyond its shores. China's sheer size—one-fifth of the world's population—means that what happens there will have outsized implications for foreign trade, global supply chains, financial markets and growth around the globe. There are political perils, too. An economically insecure China might boost nationalism to maintain legitimacy. No assessment of China's growth is complete without considering the implications of China having hundreds of millions of underemployed people in its economy for the foreseeable future.

FROM POVERTY

ELIMINATION TO RURAL

REVITALISATION:

THE PARTY TAKES CHARGE

Ben Hillman

Xi Jinping boosted the prominence of rural affairs when he came to power in 2013 and outlined his vision for China's future development.[1] That vision was built around the 'Two Centennial Goals': first, that China would become a moderately prosperous country by 2021, the year of the 100th anniversary of the founding of the Communist Party of China (CPC), and second, that China would become an advanced, high-income and strong country by 2049, the year of the 100th anniversary of the founding of the People's Republic of China.

To achieve the first centennial goal, the Party needed to address rural poverty since the highest concentrations of poverty were in the countryside.[2] In 2013 Xi Jinping launched the Targeted Poverty Alleviation Programme 精准扶贫, which shifted poverty targeting from regions to households.[3] Once target households were identified, each was allocated a government official who was tasked with lifting household members above the absolute poverty line of RMB 4,000 (US$620) per person per year. Their careers depended upon it. Assigned party members would try to help people find jobs and sell their produce, and sometimes simply gave people money. The Party also directed government agencies to invest in rural infrastructure and provide grants to rural areas where there were large numbers of poor households. Local government leaders who failed to eliminate poverty in their jurisdictions would not be eligible for promotion.

In 2021 Xi declared 'complete victory' in the struggle against extreme poverty, announcing that 99 million people had been raised above China's official poverty line as a result of the targeted poverty campaign.[4] The announcement enabled Xi to claim that his first centennial goal had been met, even though the livelihoods of many hundreds of millions of farmers remained very modest. China's official poverty line of 4,000 yuan (US$620) a year is equivalent to $1.69 a day, which is less than the World Bank's threshold of $2.15 a day, and far below the World's Bank recommended national poverty threshold for upper middle-income countries such as China, which currently stands at $6.85.[5] If applying this threshold, barely half of China's population would sit above it, as former Chinese premier Li Keqiang observed at a 2020 press conference (see 'Inequality in China: The Challenge of Common Prosperity', page 65).[6]

Following the 2021 declaration of victory against poverty, Xi Jinping raised the profile of the campaign to 'revitalise the countryside' 乡村振兴, which would become the Party's new catchcry for rural development and an essential component of China's march towards Xi's second centennial goal. As Document No. 1 (2023) noted, 'The most arduous and heavy task of building a modern socialist country in all respects still lies in the countryside.'[7]

Roadside billboard in Yunnan province: 'Where there is black, sweep it, where there is no black, eliminate evil, and where there is no evil, cure disorder'
Source: Ben Hillman

Since its launch in 2021, the significance of rural revitalisation for China's national development strategy has become increasingly apparent. Rural revitalisation matters for 'dual circulation': China's plan for future growth to be driven as much by consumer demand as by exports. It matters for employment—new rural enterprises are being touted as job-generators for new graduates. It also matters for 'common prosperity': the need to address the still wide gap between rural and urban incomes. And in the wake of US/China tensions and heightened concerns in Beijing about China's high dependence on food imports, rural revitalisation matters for food security. The program also intersects with the Xi Jinping administration's economic policy slogans 'green development', 'ecological civilisation' and 'beautiful China'. Rural revitalisation envisages beautiful and sustainable villages where people will want to live and visit.

Xi's second centennial goal includes a vision of China as an 'agricultural superpower' 农业强国. Party documents emphasise the need to modernise farming practices and develop new agricultural technologies. Document No. 1 (2023) outlined nine tasks for China's 'rural revitalisation', including the stabilisation of grain supply, increased domestic production of key agricultural products such as soybeans, and the expanded use of modern agricultural technologies.[8] Investments in rural infrastructure will continue under the program, but most government subsidies will be directed toward new local industries.

The Party's plan for achieving its ambitious rural revitalisation agenda is to put itself in charge, reasserting party authority in the countryside in much the same way the Party has expanded its control over other social and economic domains in recent years. Document No. 1 (2023) emphasises the important role of the Party in rural governance, calling for full implementation of policies empowering the village party branch to lead the village (in place of the elected village committee). Village party secretaries are now required to take over the formerly separate position of village leader under a party policy known as 'two burdens on one shoulder pole' 两副担子一肩挑. This policy requires township officials to orchestrate village elections to ensure that the village party branch secretary wins. Because the village party secretary frequently now stands unopposed in such elections, only minor positions, such as deputy village head or village accountant, are contested.[9]

The Party has also used a law-and-order campaign to chase 'undesirable' candidates out of consideration for village leadership. The campaign to 'Sweep Away Black and Eliminate Evil' 扫黑除恶 ran from 2018 to 2020 and has now been streamlined into local government and police work.[10] In rural areas the campaign targeted 'village tyrants' 村霸, who had built their own independent kingdoms and amassed power outside the state governance system. Villagers who had been 'dealt with' as part of the campaign typically became ineligible to run for village office.

During the week of 24–28 April 2023, the CPC's Central Party School organised its first nation-wide training program for China's village leaders. Offered via video link and run through 3,568 classrooms across the country, the training covered five main topics: 'developing and strengthening the village-level collective economy', 'party-building leading rural governance', 'doing in-depth and detailed mass work', 'strengthening village party organisation into a solid fortress', and 'building a beautiful, Red village'. A Xinhua news report of the training cited Kong Qingfan, party secretary of Tongfa village, Qing'an county, Heilongjiang. According to Xinhua, party secretary Kong 'believes that the village Party organization secretary must truly become the "leading goose" of rural revitalisation, and the grassroots party organisations must truly become the "backbone" of the people, shouldering their mission and responsibility in line with the [party's] original intention' (i.e. original revolutionary spirit, *chuxin* 初心).[11]

To further strengthen party organisation at the grassroots, the party has dispatched a plethora of cadres from government agencies and public institutions, including universities, banks and state-owned enterprises (SOEs). Xi Jinping has revived and expanded the position of first secretary 第一书记, an official who is deployed from outside the village and whose mission is to strengthen the leadership and management capacity of the village party branch and village party secretary. A first secretary is meant to serve as a trainer, mentor and 'missionary' of the Party.[12] According to the National Rural Revitalisation Commission, in 2023 more than 400,000 first party secretaries and supporting work team personnel were deployed across 26 provinces.[13] The first secretary is typically supported by a work team 工作队, a mechanism the Party uses to support the rapid adoption of major policy initiatives, which means that millions more public sector employees are being rotated into China's villages to forge ahead with the Party-led rural revitalisation agenda.

Rural revitalisation calls for innovation and entrepreneurship in agriculture and agribusiness
Source: qi xna, Unsplash

By putting the Party back in charge, the Xi administration's approach to governing the countryside is consistent with the Party's wider recentralising agenda. In the countryside, however, it represents a break with four decades of rural governance in which self-governing village committees and directly elected village leaders played a lead decision-making role in village affairs. While party secretaries remained a strong presence in some villages where they were known as the 'first hand' 一把手, the Party's influence was otherwise much diminished in the post-collective countryside.[14]

In reasserting its authority in China's villages, the Party has created new risks and challenges for itself. For one, it will not be able to shift blame for policy failures to village leaders or village committees since party representatives now control those positions. Although the Party has criticised corruption and cronyism by elected village leaders, it is not clear how village party leaders, working in the same social and cultural milieu and under similar pressures and constraints, will be immune to such behaviour.[15] Second, the costs of grassroots party building are staggeringly high: just the salaries of 400,000 deployed party functionaries in 2023 alone would cost an estimated 24 billion yuan (US$3.4 billion) before costs of deployment and administration.[16] Millions of first secretaries and work team members have been mobilised to strengthen the Party's grassroots capacity to lead the rural revitalisation agenda, but effective capacity-building will take years and the costs of deployment will place an increasing strain on fiscal resources, especially if China's economy continues to fall short of expectations, as it did through much of 2023. The strain is felt most acutely by local governments that are heavily indebted and unable to raise new revenue through land sales as they did in the past (see 'China's Local Government Debt', page 35).[17]

Most importantly, rural revitalisation calls for innovation and entrepreneurship in agriculture and agribusiness. The last time the Party inspired such innovation in the countryside was in the 1980s when it disbanded the communes and got out of farmers' way. Rural China then took off and kickstarted the Chinese economic growth miracle.[18] It is not clear how a centralised approach to governing the countryside will encourage private investment and cultivate innovation in rural business and technology. If the Party continues with the top-down grant-making schemes that were rolled out for previous rural campaigns, farmers will absorb the funds, but it will not necessarily generate sustainable new initiatives.[19]

In imagining China as an agricultural superpower, Xi Jinping and the party leadership have dared to dream big. But in sending the party in to take charge, they have followed a playbook that has become standard since Xi came to power. Whatever the political or policy problem—the Party organisation will fix it. To guide party functionaries in their work, in October 2023 the Party Publicity (formerly Propaganda) Bureau released yet another book of quotations by Xi Jinping. Titled *Extracts from Xi Jinping's Discourses on Grassroots Governance*, the book highlights the importance of party intervention to 'improve the system of governance in the countryside'.

With the Party in charge, the success of China's ambitious rural revitalisation campaign will likely mirror the success of the country's wider economic policies, over which the Party is asserting increasingly centralised control. It begs the same question that we might ask of the economy more broadly as China emerges from the ravages caused by COVID-19–related restrictions: can a centralised and tightly controlled political system provide the conditions necessary for a leap to high incomes and advanced economic development?

ARE THE *NONGGUAN* COMING? THE EVOLUTION OF THE RURAL COMPREHENSIVE ADMINISTRATIVE ENFORCEMENT TEAM IN CHINA'S RURAL GOVERNANCE

Tan Zhao

In April 2023, videos featuring uniformed rural enforcement teams known as *nongguan* 农管 forcefully confiscating farmers' livestock or taking down trees went viral on Chinese social media. 'The *nongguan* are coming!' 农管来了became a trending topic, often followed by the phrase 'the peasants are panicking' 农民慌了.[1]

Nongguan is the unofficial name for the rural comprehensive administrative enforcement teams 农业综合行政执法队 ('rural enforcement team' hereafter), whose responsibility is to supervise and improve law enforcement in China's vast countryside. People use the term *nongguan* to show they view these teams as the rural equivalent of the infamous *chengguan* 城管, the urban management and law enforcement force, which has been often criticised for harassing and bullying street vendors in urban areas, causing injuries and even deaths.[2] The fact that the *nongguan* wear similar official uniforms to *chengguan* further reinforces public concern that *nongguan* are overly empowered and bound to behave as negatively as *chengguan*. Subsequently, rumours such as 'the *nongguan* are collecting property management fees' or 'the *nongguan* are making peasants apply for licences to farm' began to spread online, expressing widespread anxiety over the extent of the *nongguan*'s power and jurisdiction over rural areas today.

In fact, rural enforcement teams are not new. When the 1993 Agricultural Law was revised in 2002, the revision indicated that 'the Agricultural Departments of county and higher-level governments shall, within their jurisdiction, improve the construction of administrative enforcement teams that shall practice comprehensive administrative enforcement and improve the efficiency and standard of enforcement'.[3] My field research reveals that many places have had rural enforcement teams for more than two decades. For example, in a county in China's coastal Zhejiang province, rural enforcement teams were established in 1998 under the county's Agriculture Department; their main task was to supervise the 'agricultural product shops' 农资店, ensuring that the products they sell, such as seeds and fertiliser, were certified. Other county bureaus, such as the Department of Water Resources and the Department of Forestry, also had their own enforcement teams whose tasks involved rural law enforcement. In one county in Anhui province, the task of enforcing rural laws was shared by the county's Agricultural Department, Forestry Department and Animal Husbandry Bureau, each of them forming their own independent enforcement teams. Hence, although rural enforcement teams have long existed in China, their bureaucratic affiliation and scope of enforcement has varied from place to place.

Many places in China have had rural enforcement teams for more than two decades
Source: Rod Waddington, Flickr

In 2018, following the Third Plenary Session of the 19th CPC Central Committee, the central government initiated a comprehensive reform of rural enforcement teams, which aimed to integrate the jurisdiction and forces relevant to rural enforcement that had been scattered among a variety of bureaus or departments into the rural enforcement team, highlighting the team's 'comprehensive' 综合 feature.[4] Earlier that year, the Ministry of Agriculture was replaced by the newly created Ministry of Agriculture and Rural Affairs, with the new ministry integrating some of the management responsibilities previously under the jurisdiction of other bodies such as the Ministry of Land and Resources, the Ministry of Water Resources and the National Development and Reform Commission, which also became directly responsible for managing rural enforcement teams.[5] Accordingly, the teams at the local levels were required to use the unified name of 'rural comprehensive administrative enforcement teams', and their jurisdiction and staff were adjusted in accordance with the reforms. A county government in Shandong province, for example, established a new rural enforcement team on the basis of the county's Agriculture Department's Office of Fertiliser Management and selected a team of staff from the county's Department of Comprehensive Administrative Enforcement to join the team.

Subsequently, the central government issued a series of documents to institutionalise the rural enforcement teams. In 2020, the Ministry of Agriculture and Rural Affairs issued the 'Catalogue of Tasks for Rural Comprehensive Administrative Enforcement' 农业综合行政执法事项指导目录 to clarify the teams' duties.[6] These run to a total of 251 items relating to fertiliser, seeds, animal husbandry, agricultural machinery, fishing and land use. Most items belong to the traditional duties of rural enforcement teams to maintain a healthy rural market and production environment, but supervising land use appears to be a new task. According to the catalogue, rural enforcement teams now need to supervise two types of rural land: farmland 耕地 and residential land 宅基地, and to focus on two types of illegal activity: (1) the illegal possession of farmland for non-farming purposes and damage to 'growing conditions' 种植条件 (Item 222) and (2) illegal possession of residential land by individual households (Item 223). Notably, the Ministry of Agriculture and Rural Affairs has, on several occasions, stressed that the rural enforcement teams must follow the catalogue and not overstep their jurisdictions.[7]

Other central documents have focused on the enforcement processes of rural enforcement teams. In 2021, the 'Regulations on the Process of Rural Administration Sanction' 农业行政处罚程序规定 were issued, which stipulated how rural enforcement teams should handle and impose administration sanctions.[8] In 2022, the 'Guidelines for the Basic Equipment of Rural Administrative Enforcement' 全国农业行政执法基本装备配备指导标准 listed five main categories: (1) 'basic equipment', such as law enforcement vehicles and agricultural product rapid inspection vehicles 农产品快速检

验车; (2) 'evidence collection equipment', such as body and other digital cameras; (3) 'emergency equipment', such as satellite phones and handheld megaphones; (4) 'self-protection equipment', such as protective clothing and first aid kits; (5) and 'other equipment', such as signal jammers.[9] The rural enforcement teams can also discretionally select some of this equipment 'depending on their work needs' 根据工作需要配备. In 2023, the 'Management Measures on Rural Comprehensive Administrative Enforcement' 农业综合行政执法指导办法 further elaborated on the process, standard and methods for the purpose of 'reinforcing the management of rural administrative enforcement organizations and staff' and 'regulating rural enforcement behaviors'.[10]

These new documents suggest that while the party-state sees rural enforcement teams as vital to rural governance, it also realises the importance of regulating them. This is indeed important considering the types of tasks rural enforcement teams carry out and how they deal directly with rural residents. As the catalogue indicates, the rural enforcement teams are expected to continue to play their traditional role in combating counterfeit rural products and maintaining a healthy market for rural products. According to the Ministry of Agriculture and Rural Affairs, between 2020 and 2022, they helped prevent economic losses to farmers of nearly RMB 1.5 billion.[11] At the same time, rural enforcement teams have been assigned more tasks that they previously did not need to carry out, such as supervising rural land. In the county in Zhejiang where I conducted fieldwork, the rural enforcement team did not need to deal with illegal construction on rural residential land before the reform, which used to fall under the jurisdiction of the county's Department of Land and Resources. When I visited in October 2023, it had become an essential part of their work.

It also appears that the party-state increasingly views rural enforcement teams as essential to strengthening food security, a top priority for the leadership. In March 2023, a nationwide campaign for guaranteeing food supply involving the administrative enforcement teams kicked off with a conference in Changsha, Hunan province. There, the Deputy Minister of Agriculture and Rural Affairs, Deng Xiaogang 邓小刚, stated that the campaign's goal was to mobilise the rural enforcement teams to devote themselves to 'safeguarding' 保驾护航 national food security.[12] An interesting coincidence is that while the comprehensive reforms around rural enforcement began in 2018, it was after April 2023, not long after this campaign launch, that videos of *nongguan's* intrusive actions went viral on the internet—leading to the widespread misunderstanding that the *nongguan* had just been created. Some videos purported to show *nongguan* destroying vegetable farms and cutting down fruit trees, although they came from unconfirmed sources. Some netizens attributed such actions to the 'Returning Forest to Farmland' 退林还耕 policy for increasing grain production. It remains unclear whether such actions are in line with central government expectations or whether they reflected arbitrary local government decisions. In September 2023, the Ministry of Agriculture and Rural Affairs published a report titled *Successful Cases of 'Guaranteeing Food Supply' Conducted by Rural Enforcement Teams* 全国农业综合行政执法'稳粮保供'典型案例.[13] All the examples were about the combating of fake or uncertified rural products. None involved land.

Rural enforcement teams are viewed as essential to strengthening food security
Source: Matt Briney, Unsplash

The party-state has clearly noticed the negative perceptions of rural enforcement teams among the general public. Also in September 2023, the Ministry of Agriculture and Rural Affairs held another conference on 'Constructing the Work Style of the Rural Comprehensive Administrative Enforcement Team' 农业综合行政执法队伍作风建设座谈会, which stressed the importance of following principles such as 'enforcement in accordance with the law' 依法执法 and using 'civilised methods' 文明执法.[14] However, to what degree the rural enforcement teams will abide by these requirements and rules remains a critical issue. In the management of *chengguan*, although the central government has also required them to conduct 'fair and civilised law enforcement' 公正文明执法, coercive and excessive enforcement actions still often occur, giving rise to intense social unrest. The causes are, of course, complex, including uneven qualifications 素质 among *chengguan* staff, weak supervision, and intensive pressure imposed by top-down evaluations. These issues may likewise exist for managing rural enforcement teams, with some of them even more difficult to tackle considering that they are enforcing laws that exist at the grassroots level of China, in other words, furthest from the central government. Hence the question: are the *nongguan* coming? The answer likely depends on whether the party-state can effectively develop its capacity to manage and supervise these enforcement staff, which often not only entails efforts from the state but also the empowerment of peasants.

CHAPTER 4:
DISGRUNTLED
COMMUNITIES

DISTURBING BUT NOT POLITICALLY THREATENING: VETERANS' ACTIVISM IN THE XI ERA

Kai Yang

In October 2016, more than 1,000 veterans rallied outside the Ministry of National Defence in Beijing in the People's Republic of China (PRC) to demand better government support. In February 2017, a similar incident occurred outside the offices of the Central Commission for Discipline and Inspection, also in the capital. The next year, more than 1,000 veterans from a dozen provinces gathered in Luohe city, Henan province, to support a fellow veteran whom they believed had been harassed by local police after petitioning Beijing over her husband's post-service job assignment. In June 2018, more than 2,000 veterans convened in Zhenjiang city, Jiangsu province, for a similar cause. In October that year, violence broke out in Pingdu city, Shandong province, when veterans armed themselves with wooden sticks and fire extinguishers and clashed with police.

These events highlight a growing sense of dissatisfaction among veterans 退役军人 (former members of the People's Liberation Army, including officers and soldiers) and frustration with the government's handling of their concerns. Such public displays of discontent on the part of veterans have gained the attention of international media, with the *Voice of America* describing such activism as a thorn in the flesh of the party-state.[1] A Hoover Institution report asserts that the ongoing activism 'must be a source of intense anxiety for [President] Xi Jinping and the leadership'.[2] Kevin J. O'Brien, a China expert at the University of California, Berkeley, cautions that when such 'disaffected insiders' feel that the system is not serving them well, their discontent could be a sign that the regime is corroding from within.[3]

Activist veterans are indeed a cause of concern to the Communist Party of China (CPC), as they possess unique features that make them more threatening than other protest groups. First, official propaganda hails veterans as heroes and defenders of the nation-state. Their public defiance of state authorities could signal declining solidarity among the groups considered to be in closest accord with the regime. Their contentious actions could also shake other people's faith in the system and embolden other protest groups. Second, veterans have exceptional disruptive capabilities, as they have acquired organisational, communication, and combat skills in the armed forces. The fact that they would have served with people from around the country makes them more capable than other social groups of organising cross-regional collective actions. When these well-trained personnel redirect their energies from external enemies to state authorities, their actions can have severe implications for grassroots stability.

Although veteran activism can be disturbing, they do not constitute a genuine threat to the rule of the CPC. As part of a group that is broadly sympathetic to the regime, activist veterans primarily focus on addressing defective policies and policy implementation, rather than toppling the regime or seeking structural political reforms. The Ministry of Veterans Affairs, established in 2018, may not be able to address veterans' concerns in full or straight away, but it does provide alternative institutional channels through which veterans can voice their grievances, such as petitions rather than street protests.

Disturbing but not politically threatening

Veteran activism is not a new phenomenon. There are accounts of veterans engaging in conflicts with low-level bureaucrats in the Mao Zedong era. For example, from January 1955 to February 1956, the Ministry of Interior (later the Ministry of Civil Affairs) received 43,363 petition letters, 90.9 percent of which were from veterans. Veterans also made 15,318 visits to the ministry. Half the topics raised in visits and letters related to job assignments, 20 percent to job changes or position adjustment, 15 percent to livelihood hardship, and 15 percent were about miscellaneous issues such as marriage.[4] Veterans also expressed their anger outside institutional channels, including by 'refusal to accept assigned jobs, surliness and uncooperative behaviour during and after assignment, or leaving their village to seek urban jobs through personal connections and other informal means'.[5] In the post-Mao era, veterans reliant on pensions that did not keep up with inflation and quickly lagged behind average wages in the expanding private sector struggled to adjust to the socioeconomic changes. Many found themselves left behind while other groups, such as private entrepreneurs, progressed. They complained about poverty, unresolved medical problems, and a lack of recognition for their service to the nation. Of course, veterans' grievances and claims varied by the location, duration, and types of service. For example, veterans who had been involved in wars and nuclear tests—collectively called 'two-participating veterans' 两参老兵—focused on demanding state compensation for their sacrifices. Former officers mainly demanded recognition of their status as 'state cadres'.

Since the 1980s, veterans have become one of the most prominent of all disaffected groups in Chinese society. They have employed a wide repertoire of tactics to make their voices heard, including writing letters to state leaders, petitioning, contacting journalists, publishing online blogs, and mounting street demonstrations. In some cases, they have established informal fraternal organisations and launched cross-regional collective actions. In the early 2000s, the party secretary of the Law School at China University of Political Science and Law noted that the central leadership viewed veterans' activism as the second-largest source of social instability. In 2012, a public security official ranked veterans' protests the third-largest source of social instability after dispossessed farmers and the unemployed.[6]

There is a growing sense of dissatisfaction among veterans
Source: Jens Schott Knudsen, Flickr

However, despite state authorities' concern, and the commentary of Western experts such as those quoted above, veterans have never constituted a substantial threat to the Party's rule. Why?

First, veterans-turned-protesters constitute only a minority of the veteran population in China. We get the impression that veterans are highly militant mainly because their actions are more disruptive than the actions of others and thus more likely to attract international media attention. Media bias has led to a distorted picture of state–veteran interactions in China. In fact, military service remains an important channel for upward social mobility, although its political and economic benefits are no longer as significant as in the Mao era. Zhang Chunni 张春泥, a sociologist from Peking University, has analysed the China Family Panel Studies 中国家庭追踪调查, a nationally representative social survey. Writing in 2015, Zhang found that military experience brought lifelong benefits, such as educational attainment, marriage, political credentials, economic advantages, and swifter career advancement.[7] Similarly, my fieldwork finds most elderly veterans are proud of their service. Many of those from lower-class families changed their destinies through service. For example, 'Wei', a veteran whom I interviewed for my research, was born into a poor rural family in a northern province and, due to hardships, his parents sent him to the army at an early age in the 1960s rather than to school. After service, he was transferred to a state-owned machinery factory and later appointed as a division head in his home county's Public Security Bureau, where he obtained an urban residence permit and CPC membership. He retired as a state cadre and is now entitled to a monthly retirement pension. His experience is common among the veterans I interviewed. They are largely grateful to the government, and some are willing to see their children and grandchildren join the armed forces as well. Although Wei revealed his sympathy for protesters in the Zhenjiang and Pingdu incidents, he characterised their actions as 'irrational and unacceptable' 不明智, 也不可接受.

Among the outspoken veterans, it is important to note that different individuals and groups have distinct grievances and claims, and their protests thus pose different levels of threat to sociopolitical stability. There are three types of veteran activism.

I. Individually specific activism

Some veterans' claims are particularistic, such as individual requests for recognition of status. For example, during the Cultural Revolution, many civil affairs offices were ransacked by Red Guards and veterans' dossiers were destroyed accidentally. In the post-Mao era, many veterans' and martyrs' families were hard-pressed to prove they deserved the preferential treatment due them for their service. For instance, 'Yang' served in a nuclear test unit but could not prove his identity or access regular subsidies until his former comrades-in-arms stepped in to help by petitioning the provincial government in 2019. In another case, 'Zhang', a 90-year-old veteran at the time of interview in 2019, revealed that he had repeatedly sent petition letters to different levels of state authorities about his political status, but received no response. He had defected from the Nationalist Party and joined the CPC during the Civil War and was later involved in the Korean War. He retired at the rank of platoon commander 排长 and was eligible for job placement in state institutions, but he was instead sent back to his village as an ordinary farmer in the 1960s for unknown reasons. He has since demanded the government recognise him as a 'state cadre' and provide him with a monthly pension. His case was not resolved at the time of interview.

Others have been similarly frustrated. In 2007, the Chinese government began to provide regular pensions to veterans who had taken part in officially listed wars and nuclear tests. However, not all battles or nuclear tests are recognised. In one case, a veteran from Beijing's Miyun county petitioned to be recognised as a combatant in the Battle of the Paracel Islands 西沙群岛自卫反击战 in 1974. The local Bureau of Civil Affairs at first denied this, saying there was 'no original record' in his dossier. In 2014, the veteran petitioned the municipal bureau, but was declined again as his affiliated unit was 'not included in the official list'. In other cases, such as during the Support Vietnam, Resist America 援越抗美 campaign, many soldiers were sent on to the battlefield in plain clothes and anonymously, frustrating the later verification of their identity.

This type of grievance is less likely to develop into collective action, as it is relatively difficult for any individual to find large numbers of people with similar grievances. In addition, such issues can be more effectively addressed through institutional channels than by disruptive means such as petitions. The government seldom perceives as threatening such isolated and individual activism for personal redress.

II. Locality-specific activism

Local officials' distorted policy implementations constitute another source of grievance. For example, volunteer soldiers 志愿兵 or non-commissioned officers 士官 used to spend at least one decade in service and the demand for job assignments was huge. From 1978 to 2011, most demobilised soldiers were entitled to posts in state enterprises or public institutions. However, as enterprise and administrative reforms progressed, many local authorities were unable to assign jobs to all eligible veterans. As a result, veterans with connections to civilian bureaucrats obtained decent posts, while others missed out. Moreover, there were cases where veterans' job quotas were misused or sold to third parties by corrupt officials. One of the most notorious cases was the 'fake veteran' incident in Daqing city, Heilongjiang, in 2001, in which 3,000 non-veterans were found to have bought veteran identity papers for fifty thousand yuan apiece. More than 2,000 had already assumed posts assigned by local bureaus of civil affairs.

Conscripts face similar problems. In 2013, the director of the Preferential Treatment and Resettlement Office 优抚安置办公室 in Taihe county, Jiangxi, was discovered to have embezzled more than two million yuan in pension funds earmarked for deceased and disabled veterans, conscripts' families, and demobilised soldiers.[8] In 2016 in Leizhou city, Guangdong, 300 of 529 recipients of war-related subsidies were found to hold fabricated credentials. A further investigation revealed a criminal ring within the bureaucracy, and the deputy chiefs of the Civil Affairs Bureau and its Preferential Treatment and Resettlement Office were later prosecuted. In 2018, in Rong'an county, Guangxi, twenty-nine pension recipients were found to be fake nuclear test veterans.

This type of grievance tends to trigger parochial protests or 'skip-level' petitions 越级上访 in which discontented veterans bypass local authorities and directly approach those at a higher level—usually the municipal or above. For example, in September 2017, 180 veterans in Hunan province protested fake veterans appropriating their employment quotas. Although such protests can disrupt local stability, they seldom develop into broader-based movements, such as cross-regional protests.

III. Category-specific activism

Policy changes have also frequently aggrieved some categories of veterans. The most typical case involved former officers who lost their cadre status in the 1990s. From 1993 to 1999, the government experimented with a policy that deprived military-transfer cadres 军转干部 of their cadre/administrator status in state enterprises, and downgraded them to ordinary workers. Meanwhile, for officers demobilised during this period, the state offered only a 'one-off compensation allowance' 一次性安置金, ranging from 30,000 to 100,000 yuan, but no further benefits such as job assignment and retirement pensions. These two groups were collectively labelled 'demobilised and transferred officers' (DTOs) 复转军官.

In 2011, the state annulled the trial policy and reinstated preferential benefits for newly discharged officers but refused to restore cadre status and benefits for DTOs. This aborted policy experiment created one of the most active veteran protest groups in China. A study based in a county in the Yangtze River Delta revealed that military-transfer cadres' petitions constituted nearly 60 percent of total petition cases from 2000 to 2002, and 85 percent from 2003 to 2006.[9] The state still consistently refuses to restore their cadre status, and these former officers remain one of the most vocal protest groups.

Category-specific activism is more disturbing to the party-state than that driven by individual or localised claims. This is because the grievances involved are widely shared across the country, and the protests primarily target central authorities. It is more likely to lead to the establishment of nationwide networks such as fraternal associations, and even coalitions formed with other groups of people within or connected with the regime, such as Maoist intellectuals, retired cadres, or senior People's Liberation Army officers. This is the most unsettling form of dissent for the ruling elites.

However, even these groups have no real intent to topple the CPC or the party-state, because their demands for compensation and privileges are only legitimate and recognisable under the current regime. Stressing that they have devoted their best years to it, they assert that the regime has a moral responsibility towards them. State workers laid-off in the late 1990s, when the CPC deepened its market-based economic reforms, could similarly claim that they had worked hard to build the country with little material reward, so the state had a moral responsibility towards them. Therefore, despite veterans' unique capacity for mobilisation at scale and significant disruption, they are not a threat to the regime.

The Ministry of Veterans Affairs was established in 2018 to supervise nearly all veteran-related matters
Source: Mingjia Zhou, Flickr

The rise of the Ministry of Veterans Affairs

In March 2018, Chinese President Xi Jinping commended military personnel as the 'Most Adorable People' 最可爱的人. He emphasised that military service should be respected and 'heroes should not have to shed tears after shedding blood' 不要让英雄既流血又流泪. In the same month, the Ministry of Veterans Affairs 退役军人事务部 was established, taking over responsibilities previously shared among different ministries, such as the Ministry of Human Resources and Social Security 人力资源与社会保障部 and the Ministry of Civil Affairs 民政部.

The new ministry now supervises nearly all veteran-related matters, including employment assistance, vocational training, retired cadre resettlement, preferential treatment 优待抚恤, and the commemoration of martyrs. By April 2021, 640,000 local branches of veterans' service centres 退役军人服务中心 had been created across the country. The ministry drafted the Veterans Protection Law 退役军人保障法 in 2020, which addressed issues such as entitlement to medical care. It has also initiated substantive actions to assist veterans. For example, in 2019, a rural veteran recalled that local officials had not visited him for more than a decade, but after 2018, they started visiting him on major dates, such as Chinese New Year and Army Day. On these visits they usually gave him gifts such as wall calendars, honorary medals, bags of rice, and slices of pork. The newly founded County Bureau of Veterans Affairs has also started organising vocational training and job introduction sessions for local veterans.

It is too early to judge whether the new ministry can achieve its stated goals, but such an institutional reform signals a strong state commitment to veterans' affairs and may temporarily appease discontented veterans. Many described the ministry as their 'maternal family' 娘家人 and chose to make claims via this institutional channel. For example, in 2019, the 'Minister's Mailbox' 部长信箱 received 25,601 letters, covering a range of issues such as employment, pensions, and disability assessments.[10] The soaring number of petition cases could create an excessive workload for frontline bureaucrats, but the new ministry itself provides an alternative channel for veterans to speak out about their interests, and could deter them from continuing street protests.

Conclusion

Veterans' activism should not be viewed as a significant political threat, given that even the most contentious veterans are not seeking political reform or regime change, and the new ministry is designed to systematically address their grievances. Where their grievances cannot be addressed institutionally, they are still likely to protest or reach out to potential allies, including active-duty military personnel and retired cadres; if they remain aggrieved, they pose a threat to the internal cohesion of the regime.

In 2023, the Chinese Government continued to pay special attention to veterans' affairs. During the Two Sessions 两会 in March 2023, the *Government Work Report* 政府工作报告 stated that different levels of government should continue providing support for veterans with social welfare, employment, and other benefits. Given the growing unemployment rate in the (post–) COVID-19 era, the report called for extra attention to the employment of college graduates, veterans, and migrant workers. The ministry and its grassroots service centres 服务中心 or stations 服务站 post their activities on their websites and social media, especially their efforts in providing employment assistance, commemorating martyrs, and glorifying veterans and their families. The government also initiated some innovative measures, such as inviting veterans to serve as village party secretaries 兵支书.

Moreover, to pre-empt veterans' protests, the ministry and its branches keep their online petition portals and service centres open to veterans. They also hire loyal veterans to work as part-time thought instructors 思想指导员, helping maintain regular contact with local veterans, detecting their grievances, and dissuading them from taking to the street. These measures seem to be working for the time being, as veterans' overt protest actions have not been so widely reported recently. However, this cannot be seen as the end of veterans' activism. Many fundamental grievances, such as military-transfer cadres' loss of status, have not seen any substantive policy changes. Therefore, the effectiveness of the new ministry in accommodating veterans remains to be seen.

WHY ARE CHINA'S

UNEMPLOYED GRADUATES

COMPARING THEMSELVES TO

LU XUN'S CHARACTER?

Annie Luman Ren

CHINA STORY YEARBOOK | Why are China's Unemployed Graduates Comparing
CHINA'S NEW ERA | Themselves to Lu Xun's Character?
| Annie Luman Ren

For graduates in search of a job in China, March and April are traditionally the busiest hiring season. This golden window of opportunity has even acquired the nickname 'golden March, silver April' 金三银四.[1] But this year's job-finding season proved exasperating for many, with the National Bureau of Statistics reporting that in March 2023, unemployment among urbanites between the ages of 16 to 24 had risen from 18.1 percent in the previous month to 19.6 percent.[2] By June, this figure rose further to 21.3 percent, meaning that more than one in every five young people living in cities was jobless.[3] Right before the National Bureau of Statistics suspended the release of unemployment figures for youth and other age groups in order to 'optimise labour force survey statistics' in August, an economics professor at Peking University, Zhang Dandan, published a report estimating that as many as sixteen million young people might be unemployed, bringing the real youth unemployment rate closer to 46.5 percent.[4]

At the same time, China is producing more university graduates than ever. An estimated 11.6 million students, the largest cohort ever, graduated in June 2023, and the number is expected to grow in the future.[5]

Faced with growing competition and slimmer prospects of finding a job, China's graduates have turned to the internet to vent their frustration and find support among those experiencing similar hardships. In early March, a video went viral on Douyin, the Chinese version of TikTok, of a graduate weeping and questioning the point of her university education after more than 800 job applications, 30 job interviews—and still being without a job.[6] In the same month, a comment on Weibo resonated with millions:

> People say education is a stepping stone towards something better, but lately I found it to be a high platform from which I can't climb down. It is the scholar's gown that Kong Yiji refuses to take off.[7]

Kong Yiji 孔乙己 is the title as well as the central character of a short story by Lu Xun 鲁迅 (1881–1936), who is widely considered to be the greatest Chinese writer, essayist and polemicist of the twentieth century. Writing as someone who was schooled in China in the early 2000s, 'Kong Yiji' was a text that we all had to read and memorise in the ninth grade, the last year of China's compulsory education. Set in a tavern in a fictional country town called Lu (modelled on Lu Xun's hometown Shaoxing in the coastal Zhejiang province), Kong Yiji stands out among the tavern's regulars for being the only customer who wears a scholar's 'long gown' 长衫—a symbol of his elite status—but who also drinks yellow rice wine standing up, something only poor manual labourers (the 'short-coated class' 短衣帮) would do. Throughout the story, Kong is mocked for his refusal to take off his dirty and tattered gown as well as for his sham morality—Kong maintains that stealing books doesn't count as theft. He is also ridiculed for his useless learning—Kong knows how to write one character in four different ways and can recite passages from the Confucian *Classics*, yet he was never able to pass the imperial examination and obtain stable employment. Pathetic as Kong Yiji might be, we were nonetheless taught in class that he was a *victim* of both the 'oppressive feudal society' and the imperial examination system that stifled individual creativity and perpetuated social inequality.

Visitors at Lu Xun's hometown in Shaoxing
Source: Gisling, Wikimedia

CHINA STORY YEARBOOK
CHINA'S NEW ERA

Why are China's Unemployed Graduates Comparing
Themselves to Lu Xun's Character?
Annie Luman Ren

'Kong Yiji' debuted in the April issue of *La Jeunesse* 新青年 (New Youth) in 1919, a magazine created by Chen Duxiu 陈独秀, one of the founders of the Communist Party of China (CPC). The goal of the magazine was to enlighten and educate a new generation of youth fit to create and govern a modern, democratic China. Strangely, however, this laughable character from China's inhuman past whom Lu Xun and his compatriots so vehemently mocked and sought to overthrow would resonate with millions of young Chinese today. Following that post, a new genre of internet writing arose under the hashtag #孔乙己文学# or 'Kong Yiji Literature', used by those who see their university education as a 'burden that prevents them from taking jobs seen as beneath their qualifications. 'Had I not gone to university, I'd be content to work at a factory, tightening screws at an assembly line ... but there's no "ifs" in life' wrote one netizen.[8] 'When I first read the story of Kong Yiji as a child, I didn't know its meaning. Now I realise that I am Kong Yiji!' exclaimed another.[9]

State media quickly attempted to change the new narrative around 'Kong Yiji', which, to their eyes, was overly negative in its depiction of opportunities open to educated young people in China today. On 17 March, China Central Television (CCTV) published an online commentary entitled 'We must look seriously at the anxiety behind "Kong Yiji Literature"'.[10] The commentary, while acknowledging the stress and competition young graduates face, stresses that 'Kong Yiji's tragedy lies not in the fact that he was educated, but in his refusal to take off the scholar's gown and work hard towards improving his circumstances. The gown is not just a garment, but "a shackle around his heart"' 心头枷锁. The piece ends with the usual boost of 'positive energy' 正能量, solemnly declaring that 'those with ambition will not remain trapped by their scholar's gown'.[11]

Two related news stories filled with even more 'positive energy' soon appeared on various state media: one of a 28-year-old graduate who quit her tedious white-collar job and who now earns more than 10,000 yuan (roughly AU$2,000) a month by collecting and recycling scrap. The other story was about a couple, both college graduates, making more than 9,000 yuan in one night as street food vendors.

Netizens were quick to question the validity of these stories. 'Surely the 9,000 yuan is their income, not net profit,' someone asked.[12] But it is the condescending tone of the CCTV commentary that caused emotions to run high. 'So [you're claiming] Lu Xun wrote the story to criticise Kong Yiji? Weren't we taught that it was to criticise old China?' one netizen retorted.[13] 'It was you who made me put on the scholar's gown in the first place, now you are telling me to take it off?' wrote another, referring to the fact that for years, the party-state has actively promoted success stories of young students from impoverished backgrounds improving their circumstances by studying hard and getting into a good university.[14]

Enraged by CCTV's commentary, Guishange 鬼山哥 (literally 'Ghost Mountain Brother'), a content creator and singer on China's video-sharing platform Bilibili, wrote a sarcastic song entitled 'Sunny, Happy Kong Yiji' 阳光 开朗孔乙己 in which he recasts Kong as a present-day patriot whose sanguine outlook is nonetheless a mask for his helplessness. As the modern-day Kong tells his audience in the tavern:

> I keep my face clean, but my pockets are empty
> So I put on my gown and scribe for the powerful 'n' wealthy
> I thought work would be easy, but it's 996
> Working six days a week, twelve hours a day
> When I had the nerve to ask for my pay, they called me malicious and the cops dragged my sad arse away
> …
> Optimism's my armour, but tears flow behind this mask
> I'm sunny, happy Kong Yiji; sunny, happy Kong Yiji[15]

The song attracted more than three million views before the censors took it down just one day later, while suspending Guishange's account. Posting on another platform, Zhihu, Guishange later said his only means of making money had been cut off; his savings were previously used up to pay for his mother's hospital bills. He had been planning to earn some money as a delivery driver, but his car broke down. 'They've forced me into a dead end, and for what? Just because I told the truth?' he asked.[16]

CHINA STORY YEARBOOK | Why are China's Unemployed Graduates Comparing
CHINA'S NEW ERA | Themselves to Lu Xun's Character?
Annie Luman Ren

Nearly a century ago, Lu Xun had already observed that 'When the Chinese suspect someone of being a potential troublemaker, they always resort to one of the two methods: they crush him, or they hoist him on a pedestal'.[17] The irony, of course, as pointed out by the eminent Sinologist Pierre Ryckmans (aka Simon Leys), is that Lu Xun himself was subjected to both treatments: 'When he was alive, the Communist commissars bullied him; once he was dead, they worshipped him as their holiest cultural icon.'[18]

A record number of 11.58 million students are expected to graduate and enter the job market in 2023
Source: ANU Image Library, Flickr

An even greater irony is the rich afterlife that Lu Xun's writing continues to enjoy—now through multiple media—for a writer who, when he was alive, was constantly tormented by suspicion of the act of writing. In fact, Lu Xun's dying words to his son were, 'Don't ever become a pseudo writer or artist'.[19]

The fact that 'Kong Yiji' is still widely discussed and debated more than a century after it was originally written can be seen as a vindication of Lu Xun's penetrating insight and the unrelenting frankness with which he depicted the China of his day. It is also, ironically, the consequence of the CPC's feverish canonisation of Lu Xun as its patron saint of literature. During the Cultural Revolution, Lu Xun was the only author other than Mao Zedong whose works were allowed to be read in public. The ubiquitous phrases 'Chairman Mao has instructed us ...' and 'Mr Lu Xun once said ...' were political slogans synonymous with continuous revolution and political correctness.[20] Even until recently, students in China had to study at least one text by Lu Xun per semester.[21] Both the text and its prescribed meaning also had to be carefully memorised and subject to repeated testing.

Lu Xun has been so forcefully drilled into the consciousness of multiple generations that it is no surprise people would turn to him for every new ordeal they experience. After the military crackdown on student-led protests against corruption and for democracy and free expression around Tiananmen Square in 1989, many recalled Lu Xun's remarks on the 18 March shooting of student protesters by Beijing security forces in 1926: 'Lies written in ink can never disguise facts written in blood.'[22] During the hunger strike that was part of those protests, supporters hung a banner next to the young people refusing food and water painted with a famous line from Lu Xun's short story 'Diary of a Madman' 狂人日记: 'Save the children!'[23]

Lu Xun is thus the voice of both official and unofficial China. During the COVID-19 pandemic, both state media applauding young volunteers trying to prevent rumours circulating about the virus as well as supporters of the 'Blank Paper' protests of late 2022 quoted the same message from Lu Xun to China's future generation: 'Ignore what the cynics have to say. Make your voice heard and your actions seen, like a firefly glowing in the darkness of night.'[24]

Unlike other writers of the 'leftist canon', Lu Xun never painted a future utopia in his writing; he was far too sombre to indulge in any form of daydreaming or to embrace any sect or ideology that made promises of a brighter future. He wrote only about the China he knew. At first, this was

CHINA STORY YEARBOOK | Why are China's Unemployed Graduates Comparing
CHINA'S NEW ERA | Themselves to Lu Xun's Character?
Annie Luman Ren

the China of his childhood, a small country town within a giant empire that was crumbling into pieces, filled with pitiful characters like Kong Yiji and strange tales of ghosts and murders told by his nanny, A-Chang. Later, it was the nominal republic plagued by civil unrest and tyranny as well as a cultural and literary tradition that, in Lu Xun's eyes, was not only irrelevant but also thwarted China's modernisation. A true iconoclast, Lu Xun went as far as calling for the eradication of the Chinese writing system, declaring: 'If Chinese characters are not exterminated, there can be no doubt that China will perish.'[25]

To make way for a better, modern China, Lu Xun was painfully aware that his own writing would be doomed along with the rest of the tradition he so detested. As he wrote in 1919,

> Let the awakened man burden himself with the weight of tradition and shoulder up the gate of darkness. Let him give unimpeded passage to the children so that they may rush to the bright, wide-open spaces and lead happy lives henceforth as rational human beings.[26]

In this scenario, the gate of darkness eventually drops, crushing the weight-bearing hero into pieces.[27]

The self-effacing aspect of Lu Xun's thought produced some of the most haunting and passionate images in his writing. For instance, there are the nihilistic flames that reoccur in his collection of prose-poems, *Wild Grass*:

> A subterranean fire is spreading, raging, underground. Once the molten lava leaks through the earth's crust, it will consume all the wild grass and lofty trees, leaving nothing to decay[28]

Then, in the same collection, there is the image of a self-devouring serpent:

> There is a wandering spirit which takes the form of a serpent with poisonous fangs. Instead of biting others, it bites itself, and so it perishes[29]

Had he been alive today, Lu Xun would have been horrified to discover all the 'museums, plaster busts, spin-off books, dedicated journals, plays, television adaptations, wine-brands' operating in his name.[30] He would have been even more shocked that young people still felt the need to evoke his work. After all, a China that clings to the culture and language of its past was a *wushengde Zhongguo* 无声的中国, a 'voiceless China', as Lu Xun famously told an audience at the Hong Kong YMCA in 1927.[31] Although he was mainly speaking about the need to move away from classical Chinese, an outdated mode of expression permeated with Confucian authoritarianism, Lu Xun, who had received a traditional Confucian education, saw himself as part of that decaying tradition when he urged the youth to 'push aside the ancients, and express their authentic feelings' so as to transform China from its state of 'voicelessness'.[32]

When asked about Lu Xun in 1990, the exiled Chinese writer Zha Jianying 查建英 said: 'The fact that he's so relevant is very sad.'[33] More than thirty years later, in 2023, Lu Xun's legacy endures—a poignant reminder that the struggle for a liberated, authentic voice persists under Xi Jinping's China.

CHINA STORY YEARBOOK | Why are China's Unemployed Graduates Comparing
CHINA'S NEW ERA | Themselves to Lu Xun's Character?
| Annie Luman Ren

CHINESE 'INCELS'?

MISOGYNIST MEN ON

CHINESE SOCIAL MEDIA

Qian Huang

In 2020, Yang Li 杨笠, a Chinese female stand-up comedian, rose to national fame with punchlines addressing China's gender inequality and biting jokes about Chinese men, most famously: 'How can some men look so ordinary yet be so confident?' While her piercing humour resonated with many Chinese women, it was not so well received by many men. A male user on Chinese social media claimed Yang 'was repeatedly insulting all men and preaching hatred, inciting internal conflicts among the masses, and creating gender opposition'.[1] An endorsement deal with Intel fell through due to threats to boycott the brand by many Chinese men on social media platforms such as Sina Weibo. She also received death threats via social media.[2] These men's resentment of Yang Li is part of the general pushback on Chinese social media against women who support feminist causes and criticise deep-seated patriarchal attitudes and widely accepted misogynistic male behaviour.[3]

Such collective, aggressive attitudes towards women's rejections and criticism resemble the dominant sentiments in the Incel Movement in Western countries. Incel refers to 'involuntary celibate'; the term started life as the name of an online safe space for women struggling to find romantic partners, but later became a self-referential term among young men who express rage at women for denying them sex.[4] Incels discuss their misogynist beliefs in online forums, where they might become radicalised by the manifestos of 'incel heroes' like Eliott Rodger, the son of a Hollywood filmmaker who killed six people and himself in 2014, and injured fourteen others, declaring himself 'the true victim in all of this'. Andrew Tate, the American–British self-proclaimed misogynist influencer currently facing trial in Romania for rape, human trafficking and forming an organised crime group to sexually exploit women, is another exemplar.

Incels have developed their own memetic narrative system, categorising women as either Becky or Stacy, while men who have no difficulty finding sexual partners are Chads.[5] Chad represents the supposedly desirable masculinity in American society: muscular and sexually attractive due to their genetically masculine features. Stacy is hyperfeminine, attractive and only dates Chads, while Becky is the average-looking feminist. These categories originated on Reddit but have been popularised in recent years.[6]

Online misogyny has been on the rise in China due to a number of factors. A crucial one is the underlying strong patriarchal attitudes and an increasingly gender-conservative media and educational system under Xi. This trend is signalled by Xi's speech on the Women's Congress in November 2023, in which he emphasised the importance of 'love and marriage, fertility and family' without discussing women as members of the work force.[7] Another factor is the gender imbalance caused by the one-child policy and preference for male heirs, leading to uncounted female infanticides and nearly 34 million more males than females (the general sex ratio being 105.07 male to every 100 females).[8] Social and economic stagnation over the last decade means that many have no hope of finding a girlfriend or wife, especially given that prevailing ideas around gender and marriage still uphold men as the main breadwinner, and women are perceived to prefer men with wealthy backgrounds, higher education and property.

Research has shown that men from prefectures with a greater gender imbalance, and under pressure in the competitive marriage market to be able to offer a woman financial security, are more likely to commit crimes with financial reward such as robbery, burglary, drug dealing and illegal business dealings.[9] China's most gender-skewed cohort—in 2021, the 15-to-19-year-old age bracket, with a male:female ratio of 116:100—coincides with those most inclined to misogynistic and anti-feminist views similar to those of Western incels.

While there is no equivalent Chinese term for 'incel', some comparable terms include the relatively outdated, playful and self-deprecating term *diaosi* 屌丝 (literally 'pubic hair'), referring to young men who are disadvantaged in romantic or sexual relationships compared to those who are *gaofushuai* 高富帅 ('tall, rich and handsome'), a term with echoes of 'Chad'. Misogyny, including the blanket sexualisation and objectification of women, can be observed in the *diaosi* narrative and public discussion—such as scoring women based on their appearance, feminine traits and sexual experience—but the violence that characterises Western incel culture is mostly absent, with some exceptions, discussed below.

After Yang Li's popular punchline 'so ordinary yet so confident', many Chinese women started using *pu nan* 普男 ('ordinary men') or *pu xin nan* 普信男 ('ordinary yet confident men') to describe average, misogynist and overly sensitive men. For example, a female user shared the screen shot of her WeChat conversation with a blind date, captioned 'Let me show you a *pu xin nan*'. In the conversation, the man listed the traits he deemed attractive about himself, and after the woman did not reply to him for a few days, he asked her: 'Are you worried that you don't deserve me?' Similarly, Chinese women have also used words like *zhi nan ai* 直男癌 ('straight-men cancer') and *guo nan* 国男/蝈蝻 (literally 'this country's men'; the second way of writing the characters further belittles Chinese men as insects 虫) to criticise misogynist men.

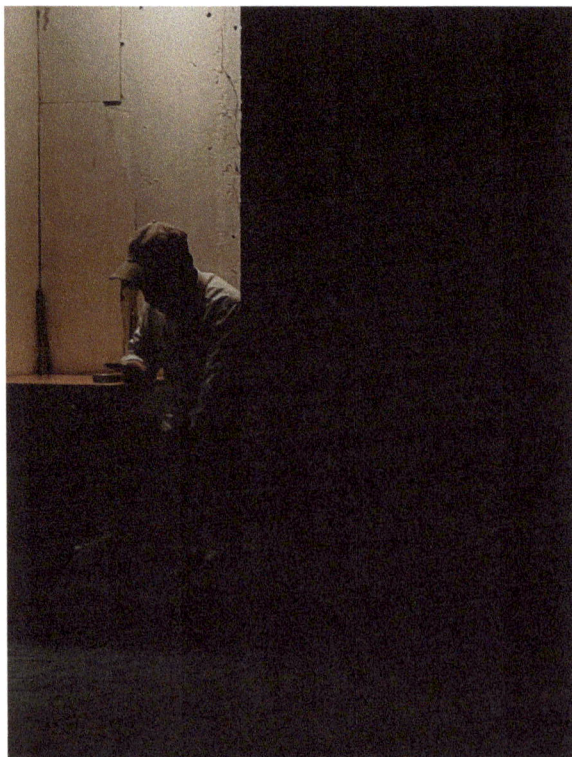

Online misogyny has been on the rise in China
Source: Ewan Yap, Unsplash

Unlike in the United States and other Anglophone countries, there are no specific forums or platforms where misogynist men in China gather for the sole purpose of discussing their hatred of women. Instead, they manifest themselves on most of China's social media platforms, including Sina Weibo, in different ways and for different reasons, often in response to reports of gender-related violence or other incidents. On Zhihu, the most popular user-generated question-and-answer website in China, questions related to gender issues tend to generate polarised debates, with misogynist answers and responses often dominating.[10] For example, many users use 'easy girl' or 'slut' to answer the popular question 'How do you feel about or understand the women who date or marry foreigners?' Other sites where misogynistic discussion and interaction is common include the video-sharing site Bilibili, which hosts a subculture around Japanese anime consisting largely of young men, and Hupu, China's most popular forum for sports fans, with more than 90 percent male users, who rank female celebrities on their appearances and discuss relationship issues in addition to chatting about sports. All of these platforms accidently evolved into sites with a significant presence of misogynist men because of their large male user bases and the attention economy; that is, a tendency for the most extreme or sensationalist content to attract the most attention.

There are high-profile KOLs (key opinion leaders) among the anti-feminist influencers and incel heroes. One is Zhu Zhou 煮肘 (often referred to as Teacher Zhu 煮老师 and Teacher Precious 宝宝老师). Zhu Zhou had around 495,000 followers on Sina Weibo in 2023.[11] In his posts, he shows off his wealth, criticises feminists and the idea of female independence, promotes the practice of 'successful men' spreading 'good genes' by producing children with as many 'high-quality' women (younger than 23 years old, B-cup breasts, model-level beauty, more than 165 centimetres or pretty virgins more than 162 centimetres tall) as possible and, worst of all, claims that men should attack women who do not fulfil their 'reproductive duties' with sulphuric acid. Such violent threats against 'non-cooperative' women are not censored by platforms unless there is a mass reporting from platform users.

Different from the Western incel narrative begrudging women's preference for the physical masculinity of 'the Chads', misogynist men on Chinese social media begrudge women for their desire to date or marry wealthy men, yet typically express envy rather than hatred against such men.

The combination of sexual and economic frustration is illustrated in comments made after the suicide of Su Xiangmao 苏享茂, founder of a successful Beijing IT company. Men on social media quickly shamed Su's ex-wife Zhai Xinxin 翟欣欣 as 'greedy and vicious' for demanding a large divorce settlement; they blamed her for Su's suicide, doxing and harassing her online. Such narratives of 'gold-diggers' harming 'innocent men' support their argument that Chinese women are greedy and evil.

Misogynist men on Chinese social media also take issue with feminists and the rise of feminism in China (despite acknowledging that at least feminists don't ask for a bride price). They regard feminists' speech and campaigns as 'stirring conflicts between two genders' 挑起性别对立 and 'organised by "foreign agents"' 境外势力 to subvert China'. Such antagonism against feminism is conveniently combined with nationalism and chimes with the Communist Party's hyper-vigilance against social instability, its tendency to blame dissent on foreign agents and its own hostility to feminism. Influencers on Sina Weibo such as 'God's Eagle' 上帝之鹰 and 'Meridian Knight' 子午侠士 repeatedly use such narratives to justify their trolling, harassment and reporting 举报 of feminists.[12] For example, Meridian Knight wrote a series of posts accusing Chinese feminists, including Lü Pin 吕频 and other #MeToo activists, of being manipulated by 'Western forces' to destablise and destroy China.[13] Due to their close alignment with the party-state's nationalist, anti-Western and anti-liberal narrative, such speech is usually condoned and even promoted by mainstream state-run media outlets. For instance, in 2020 April, *Beijing Evening News*—an official media outlet operated by the Publicity Department of the Beijing Municipal Committee—issued an editorial that called out feminists as toxic and harmful to Chinese society.[14] The state's efforts to keep Chinese society stable in its family-based social structure and solve the issue of low birth rates also provides a supportive environment for sexist and misogynist opinions and statements.

As elsewhere, cyber bullying and online aggression also encourage offline violence. In 2020 December, a male university student attacked three female classmates with sulphuric acid in a class.[15] While the exact reason for this attack was never publicised, in the comments section under the relevant news story, many assumed the victims were to blame for being 'unattainable'—meaning refusing their attacker's advances—and celebrated the 'punishment' they got. Then there was the incident in June 2022, where four women were violently assaulted by a group of men in a barbecue restaurant in Tangshan, Hebei province, after these women rejected one of the men's sexual advances. Similarly, in September 2023, two women were violently attacked by a drunk man in Yiyang, Hunan province, after they refused to share their contact information with him.[16] In both cases, the violent and graphic security footage where these men repeatedly and brutally dragged down, hit and kicked the women was shared widely on Chinese social media and shocked many Chinese citizens, especially women.[17] Online public discussions demonstrated Chinese women's anger and fear when facing the rise of misogynistic male violence.[18] Due to the obvious brutality, there were few comments supporting the attackers, but the attackers were blamed for their gangster-like violence instead of the gendered violence they imposed on the women. However, there were comments blaming the women for 'being stupid to fight back and infuriate the attackers'.

Chinese social media incel narrative stems from sexual and economic frustration
Source: Kaihao Zhao, Unsplash

An increasing gender imbalance, decreasing social mobility and the dominant misogynist ideologies and discourses left to flourish by the party-state means that more young men are likely to express their grievances online in misogynist discourses and that there will be more conflict around gender issues on Chinese social media. This is alarming because the social consequences are real and severe. While there is an official attempt to tamp down online violence in general, the misogynist discourses do not receive any special attention. Xi's crackdown on civil society and the mainstream narrative of fearing 'feminism as Western ideology' means that feminist voices in opposition to misogyny are either silent or silenced. More research is needed to investigate this phenomenon, and government and civil society should work together to slow down, stop and reverse this trend.

五

CHAPTER 5: VOICES OF THE ORDINARY PEOPLE

The following translations are excerpts from two episodes of the popular Chinese-language podcast *StoryFM* 故事FM. With a subscriber base of over two million, the podcast, hosted by Kou Aizhe 寇爱哲, is celebrated for inviting Chinese people from different regions and backgrounds to tell their own story, in their own voice.

The editors

LONELINESS, DEATH AND DESOLATION: WHY I RETURN TO ANTARCTICA TIME AND AGAIN

Translation by Peishan Yann

Kou Aizhe: The short happy Antarctic summer ends too soon and is followed by a long winter.

Many scientific researchers return home to China at the end of summer as most Antarctic research can only be done in the summer months. Only a small number of staff are left at the research station for what is known as 'winter-over' 越冬.[1] Cao Jianxi used to be one of the team members wintering over at the research station, responsible for ensuring that the research station operated normally during the winter months.

'Wintering over': A gruelling experience

Once we are wintering over, everyone's workload is much lighter. Someone like me, who is in charge of the kitchen, only has to make sure meat and vegetables are brought in from the storeroom and ready for cooking the next day.

We rise much later in winter as the sun only rises after ten o'clock in the morning, when it is almost time for lunch. Between lunch and dinner, we have plenty of time to ourselves.

I'd often sit by my bed, wrapped up in a warm blanket to play online games or watch movies. There was a particular actress, I can't remember whether I saw her on TV or in a movie, but I was very fond of her at that time, and thought her very beautiful.

She has very oriental features, with a delicate 'melon-seed' oval face. She appeared wearing a crimson veil and appeared against a red background.

I took a photo with my mobile phone and would often stare at it, my heart heavy with loneliness and the yearning for a companion.

Although there were other people at the station, our interactions were minimal. In this sort of closed environment, the longer we stayed together the more silent and withdrawn we became, with no desire to connect with anyone, just amusing ourselves alone in our rooms.

Exploring the Frozen Frontier in Antarctica
Source: Cassie Matias, Unsplash

Those who are more extroverted, especially the older ones, seemed less affected by the isolation. The younger team members tended to be more quick tempered, and would ignore the others if they were in a bad mood.

At times an older team member would walk into the dining hall and, sensing the negative vibe, would attempt to lighten the mood by telling jokes or asking people how they were going.

But the strange thing is, they would get no response from the others. As you can imagine, under such circumstances, that made most team members feel even more depressed.

It was also common to see conflict among team members. I personally experienced this: as the period of isolation grew longer, the more my relationship with my direct superior deteriorated. At the start, we got along well because we were polar research centre co-workers.

But later, because of the nature of our working relationship, he made more demands on me than others. Sometimes it was over small things like cigarettes or alcohol. I would get annoyed and feel like he was mistreating me or that he wasn't looking after me. As time went by, our relationship worsened with every such incident.

As a result, my relationship with the station master deteriorated as well. Even when winter was over, we could not repair our relationship. In normal life, if we run into problems at work, we can always go home or go for a drink or a meal with friends after work to relieve our stress. But in the extreme conditions of the Antarctic, that isn't an option. We are always together. If something goes badly today, tomorrow we still have to continue working together. Frustrations build up and never go away.

Food

> Kou Aizhe: In Antarctica, growing crops is strictly prohibited.[2] All crops are considered 'exotic species' that risk damaging its unique environment. Of course, the harsh conditions in Antarctica are not conducive to growing crops either, so supplies of food and other necessities are completely dependent on infrequent transport links to the station.
>
> The popular Chinese saying goes, 'Food is the people's heaven'. Even when they are at the 'end of the world', those stationed in Antarctica are determined not to compromise on their enjoyment of food. It is at times like this when culinary creativity is at its most prolific.

My job as a manager at the research station means I am like the 'housekeeper'. I manage all the storerooms, especially the kitchen store. Every day, I would go to the kitchen to prepare supplies, like alcohol, other drinks, rice and flour. Our dishes mostly consisted of dried goods from the north-east of China because they could be kept for a long period of time. It was rare to have green leafy vegetables. Usually we'd eat bean curd strips, seaweed and other dried goods that had to be soaked in water first.

Among the twelve of us who stayed behind in the winter months, there was a chef by the name of Old Zhu. He used to be the main chef on board the [icebreaker and resupply ship] *Xue Long*.

Before each meal, one of us rang the bell outside the dining hall. Sometimes it was me, sometimes the chef himself or one of the kitchen hands, and then everyone would come to eat.

At the station, big steel trays were used for serving meals, which usually consisted of three dishes, such as chicken or black fungus stir fried with sliced pork belly, and a soup, typically egg-based with seaweed, which was vacuum packed; all we had to do was to steep it in hot water first.

We also had desiccated vegetables, but no matter what we did with them, they were flavourless.

Sometimes we would have barbeques outdoors using large steel plates and long iron skewers. Barbeques were fun, especially after the tide receded and lots of abalones were left stranded on the rocks. We would barbeque abalones on a large metal plate as if they were lamb on skewers. Those abalones were the best I have ever eaten—extremely tender.

When celebrating festivals or birthdays, we would prepare more dishes, sometimes a dozen or so, in smaller portions and served on white porcelain plates. We would lay them out on a table covered with a white tablecloth, plus flowers for decoration. The flowers were plastic, but it looked pretty.

To celebrate the birthdays of our teammates, Chef Zhu would also bake a cake. The station manager would pass a birthday card around for everyone to sign. On each card would be twelve signatures, making it something worth keeping.

On special occasions like the Mid-Autumn Festival, I would also make banners that read 'China's 22nd Antarctic Scientific Expedition Team at the Great Wall Station Celebrating Mid-Autumn Festival'. I would print out the Chinese characters individually on A4-size sheets and pin them together on a scroll of red cloth to make a long banner.

End of winter

Kou Aizhe: The first time Cao Jianxi spent the winter at the polar research station, he had a calendar pinned up in his room and he would stare at it for ages every day, studying it minutely, counting down the days until his return home.

But as the end of wintering over drew nearer, Cao had mixed feelings. On the one hand, he was dying to see his family and friends. Over and over, he'd imagine the scenes of meeting them all again in detail.

On the other hand, human society became like a beautiful dreamscape. The long separation from society instilled a sense of anxiety in Cao, who worried whether returning to a normal life would ever be possible.

After more than a year's wait, the day finally came for Cao to finish wintering over.

When I was in the Antarctic, I never thought I'd go back again. But back in China, I found myself having difficulties adapting to society. Like a prisoner who has been released after a long jail term of more than a decade or so, I found it hard to get used to a life of freedom and was nostalgic for the prison environment.

After many months of trying to adapt, I decided to return to the South Pole. Society was a little hard to fit into.

Life and death

Kou Aizhe: In 2007, Cao Jianxi boarded the icebreaker *Xue Long*, to join China's 24th Antarctic Scientific Expedition to the South Pole. The first destination was Zhongshan Station. If Cao's first 'wintering over' at the Great Wall Station had only subjected him to mental anguish, venturing into the interior of Antarctica was a severe ordeal that tested both his body and spirit.

Zhongshan Station was the second scientific research station that China built in the Antarctic. It is located in East Antarctica and is 4,986 kilometres away from Great Wall Station, making the distance between the two research stations even greater than that from Shanghai to Urumqi. What's more, the climate in Zhongshan Station is much harsher.

It was during the 24th Expedition that Cao had the most dangerous experience of his life.

In Antarctica, you never know where the danger lies until you come face to face with it. The further you travel into the interior, the more dangerous it becomes. Accidents are common, especially for those venturing onto the endless plateau of snow, ice and glaciers for the first time.

When the icebreaker *Xue Long* arrived at Zhongshan Station with our research team, we had to start unloading 10 to 20 nautical miles from the station. This is because the *Xue Long* could only drive through ice up to 1.1 metres thick. We had to use snowmobiles and sledges to transport our cargo from the vessel to the station.

This zone is notorious for its haphazard formation of ice sheets, resulting from huge blocks of old ice bonding together and refreezing. This makes the structure of the ice non-uniformly thick, with some places thick and others thin.

As a precaution, having two drivers (a pilot and a co-pilot) operate an oversnow vehicle is the norm. This boosts safety because in an emergency, one person can radio in a report.

At the time, a very experienced chief mechanic, Mr Xu Xiaxing, decided to drive an oversnow vehicle on his own, so as to allow the other members of the team to rest. He didn't take a sledge, which signified it was an empty vehicle. We'd put caterpillar treads on it while it was still in the hold, and it was the best equipped of all the vehicles. The crane moved it from the hold onto the ice.

Mr Xu wanted to move the vehicle to another spot and began driving.

Our assistant expedition guide Wang Hailang was on duty in the control room of the *Xuelong*. He witnessed the whole episode. The vehicle began moving forward when it suddenly stalled and began spinning. Then, suddenly, it started sinking.

When Mr Xu discovered his oversnow vehicle had stalled, he thought all he had to do was pump the accelerator to get the vehicle to lurch forward, as he had done before. But this was a totally different situation: the area's ice layer was too thin. Underneath, it was already broken into ice debris. The vehicle started sinking rapidly, as if the wheels were shovelling up ice from below.

When the oversnow vehicle first started sinking, Mr Xu didn't panic. He still thought that hitting the accelerator would solve the problem by propelling it forward and freeing it from the ice. But before he realised it, the vehicle had sunk to a considerable depth and a stream of bubbles began to burst forth from its interior. Only then did terror enter his heart, and he thought of his family. He realised the peril he was in and feared this would be the end of him.

Water gradually flooded the car. He prepared to escape but couldn't open any of the windows or its sunroof owing to the pressure of the water. Pushing open the door would be futile for the same reason.

However, the window on the driver's side could slide back and forth. By chance, Mr Xu managed to push that window open. Water rushed into the car and completely flooded the interior.

He then tried to escape through the sunroof.

The sunroof was like that of a family car, except it was not able to open fully. It could only be cracked open to a 5- or 10-degree angle at most.

Mr Xu decided to stand on the vehicle's middle console and push up as hard as he could to force the sunroof open. The connecting rod of the sunroof gave way completely, opening the only possible escape route for him.

He tried to float to the surface, but he continued to sink. His boots were caught.

Those boots were specially designed to withstand a temperature of around minus 30 degrees Celsius so they were extremely bulky and heavy. But he eventually managed to free himself from them. He'd used up almost all his energy and swallowed another mouthful of ice-cold sea water.

After he had made his escape from the sunroof, he swam upward with all his might, until he heard his head bump against the ice debris, and knew he'd reached the top. He raised his hand and ascertained he'd found the ice hole.

The rescue team still hadn't reached him, but he climbed his way out onto the dry ice all by himself. He managed to make two steps before collapsing.

As a result of this, all the work of the research team came to a temporary stop. Everyone was at a complete loss. The whole team's spirit sank to an all-time low.

Return to Antarctica

Kou Aizhe: After his fourth expedition to Antarctica, Cao Jianxi resigned from the Polar Research Centre. Not long after, he moved to Australia and began a new phase of his life.

After leaving China, I didn't think about returning to Antarctica. I threw myself into an entirely new life. I got married and devoted my time and energy to raising a family.

At first, I wasn't nostalgic or keen to think about those days. Nor did I want to dig out old photos and videos. However, with the passing of time, I began thinking more and more of the memories of those events.

In Antarctica, under such harsh conditions, a small group of us still managed to work together using our own skills to complete our mission. There is a sense of camaraderie in having been through thick and thin together, akin to that of having been comrades-in-arms on a battlefield.

CHINA STORY YEARBOOK | Loneliness, Death and Desolation
CHINA'S NEW ERA | Translation by Peishan Yann

I feel like this deep connection is too precious to be discarded or forgotten. It is so rare in one's life to have relationships built on shared experiences of life and death.

By chance, a friend asked if I was interested in working on board a cruise ship specialising in tours to Antarctica. The steep increase in the number of Chinese tourists in recent years has raised the demand for people like me, who know Antarctica and speak English and Chinese.

At first, I didn't take this opportunity seriously, but when night came, I thought more deeply and got very excited. Things big and small that happened when I was living and working in Antarctica, the friendship and connection with teammates, started to play out in my mind. If I returned, I would be return to my old circles.

I felt an urgent desire to go back, a bit like how I felt the first time I was bound for Antarctica after college. But before I ventured back, the cruise company decided that I should travel to the Arctic a few times first. As a result, I visited Iceland and Greenland several times. Some six months later, I was finally on my way back to Antarctica.

When the cruise ship arrived at Antarctica, the sight of the snow-capped mountains and glaciers in the far distance made me extremely emotional, and tears welled in my eyes.

Penguins in Antarctica
Source: Martin Wettstein, Unsplash

When I went ashore, I felt that every rock and stone was familiar. I also ran into a teammate who once wintered over in the same year with me at the research station. He was very happy to see me and cooked some noodles for us. I felt extremely happy and excited. I really hadn't expected that.

In that distant place, I returned to where I first started, as if some mystical power was at work, or perhaps this is just what is meant to be. When Heaven opens a door for me, I linger hesitantly at the doorway, but when I finally decide to cross the threshold, I keep going.

HOW AI CHANGED THE WAY WE WORK

Translated by various

Kou Aizhe: Late in 2022, ChatGPT, an artificial intelligence (AI) chatbot, made a sudden yet impressive debut, sparking a wave of discussion in 2023. Suddenly, the spotlight was on the world of generative AI technologies, which use artificial intelligence to generate speech, images, videos and more. These technologies, often referred to as AIGC (Artificial Intelligence Generative Content), have also gained attention across various industries alongside ChatGPT's skyrocketing popularity.

In the first six months of 2023, a wave of new technological advancement swept into the workplace. But what changes has this wave brought to the professional landscape? And how have these changes affected individuals within the workplace? We've invited four people from different industries to share some of the transformations they've experienced at work.

Our first speaker today, 'Big Dragon' (Da Long), is the founder of a small company. He was proactive in introducing AIGC tools to the workplace, which has already become the norm.

AI saves us money

Hello, everyone. My name is Zhu Bolong, and people around here call me Big Dragon. I'm the founder of a tech company, and we currently have about 20 employees. Our main business centres around dance-related fitness, games and training. Back in 2016, we switched from teaching dance offline to online. In 2020, we directed our focus towards motion-sensing dance games that could be played on home TVs.

I majored in computer science at university. Although what I learned was not related to algorithms, I've always been interested in the tech industry. After just a week or two experimenting with ChatGPT, my business partner and I realised the huge potential of AI drawing tools.

We worried about facing competitors who could utilise AI more effectively and potentially push us out of the market. So, starting in February 2023, we made it a requirement for all our employees to start exploring the use of these AI tools. They had to learn even if they needed to put aside their regular tasks.

My business partner's office is a few cubicles away from mine. One day, I was in my office when suddenly I heard him yell, 'This is amazing!' along with the F-word. I went over to his office to find out what was happening. I couldn't see his face at first because his dual-monitor set-up blocked my vision. But as I got closer, I saw him kneeling in front of his computer.

Still facing the screen, he said, 'You see this? It's way better than what I can draw.' My business partner started his career as a cartoon artist, and he's worked as an animation director. He takes a lot of pride in his artistic ability. But on that day, it was like AI completely 'broke' him. He said, 'There's no way I can compete with this. I might as well team up with it.' I told him, 'All right. In the coming months, you can put most of your focus into exploring it and making it even better.'

Over the next month and a half, my business partner spent roughly 6 to 8 hours every day studying these AI drawing tools, often staying at the company until around 10 or 11 in the evening. They excited him immensely. Sometimes, I would also be in the office in the evening, and I'd hear him eating while the computer was busy creating pictures. He would often exclaim with surprise mid-mouthful.

Even before he familiarised himself with the use of prompts, plug-ins and so on, he achieved an impressive 50 percent or so increase in work efficiency. Now, several months on, we can almost generate what we want instantly, which is truly astonishing.

Initially, our colleagues from the technical team were quite dismissive of ChatGPT. When they heard that ChatGPT could assist with coding, they felt there were plenty of open-source codes online and that the code of ChatGPT didn't necessarily adhere to coding standards better than theirs. However, once they mastered it, they realised that it could replace at least 30 percent of their workload, which is quite significant.

Our colleagues in the operations department initially attempted to use Chatgpt for writing, including articles for WeChat pages and video scripts. Similar to the initial experiences of our technical colleagues, when they didn't know how to communicate effectively with ChatGPT, the generated content turned out overly artificial and formulaic. It lacked depth and substance.

I then showed them how to use AI to write about China's 5,000 years of dance history with a summary of several important periods. I first used their method to ask AI to write on the topic and showed them the copy. Then I said: 'This is your way of thinking. Let's try it my way.' I gave ChatGPT the prompt 'Imagine you're a stand-up comedian. Please summarise China's dance history in a stand-up comedy style', then it generated something quite different. My colleagues immediately understood that you can get ChatGPT to role-play, to write in a certain style and to word-count, paragraph and other requirements. This experience transformed their understanding of AI. It actually functions like a real human assistant. Once my colleagues learnt to communicate with it in the same way we communicate with humans, they were able to quickly put AI into effective use.

After that, my business partner and I have put ourselves in the position of the company's managers and applied AI tools to our daily work to see what problems it can solve and how much efficiency it brings. Then we had to take action.

There was someone in our company who was responsible for design-related work. This does require a certain degree of originality, but his main job was to make poster images, characters and background effects. In February 2023, we discovered that AI could do this very well, and, unlike when using creativity tools such as Chuangkit, we don't need to consider copyright issues with AI. When a colleague in the operations department discovered that he could complete this part of the design work through AI without designers, I contacted him directly to confirm whether he could complete the work by himself. After getting a definite answer, I went to the designer.

I called him to the stairwell to have a chat. At first, he thought I wanted to talk about something related to his current work. I said: 'No. You know we are using AI now, and your position is consumption-oriented, not a revenue-generating one. What we need are employees who can bring in web traffic or profits to the company.' Considering the optimisation of the personnel structure, I said to him, 'I'm sorry. Your current position is no longer required. You can either transfer to another position or you can leave.'

He said that he needed some time to think. A day later, he came to me and said that he wanted to try a position in operations. But after another day, he said he'd decided to give up. He said, 'I feel like even if I put in a lot of time on this new job, I still may not make much progress. I'd rather leave.' The whole thing was brutal, and it was the first time I made a lay-off decision so quickly. Nonetheless, I still believe I made the right call because it was AI that replaced him.

Later, I heard from someone in the operations team that the sacked colleague was hit hard by the experience. He couldn't find a new job for several months and stayed in his apartment every day. He was aware that he had been replaced by AI. Moreover, the apartment he rented was in the same building as our company, only a few floors above us, and he had just paid the rent. I felt really sorry, but there was nothing that I could do. We didn't save a lot of money from his salary, but it was enough for a subscription fee to Midjourney [a generative artificial intelligence program], so now everyone else in our company can use it freely.

Later, we realised that we still needed a full-time UI designer to monitor the computer. It does seem cruel that we hired someone exclusively for the purpose of assisting the computer.

Only one week after the job was posted, we received close to 150 résumés, which was pretty scary. Our colleague responsible for recruitment interviewed approximately 20 to 30 of them. Almost all were high performers, but they lowered their salary expectations themselves. AI gives us advantages in recruiting people and negotiating salaries.

During the interviews, we told them that there was the possibility that their positions would be replaced by AI. Our current focus is on recruiting individuals who aren't at the A-level but are at the D-level with the potential, with AI's assistance, to do A-level work. In this way, our costs can be greatly reduced.

One of the candidates lowered his monthly salary requirement from RMB 12,000 to 8,000. He had previously worked in Beijing, where he could earn about RMB 15,000. Returning to Chengdu, he was hoping for RMB 12,000. I asked. 'What is your salary expectation now?' He replied, 'RMB 8,000.'

Our colleagues' PCs always have ChatGPT open, as they have become accustomed to using it as a search engine. Colleagues in the animation department always have Stable Diffusion or Midjourney open. As everyone's productivity rises, it frees up a lot of time for breaks and even a little loafing on the job.

The first area we're looking forward to is AI-generated animated videos, although the quality isn't yet up to commercial standards. We think that will take three to six months.

Second, for dance-related products, we normally have to pay for the use of copyrighted music, a relatively big investment. There is a lot of music for which we cannot track down the copyright holders, and we have faced lawsuits in the past. But we expect that within the next three months AI will be able to produce any style of music we want. We do respect copyright, but when the creators charge an astronomical price for use of their work, say RMB 200,000, there's no way we can use it. But AI can replicate their style, and it's actually the musical style we're after. So we hold great expectations for the ability of AI-generated music to subvert the music copyrights market.

My client is not at fault, and neither am I

> Kou Aizhe: Our second speaker, A Li, works in the music industry. The law of demand and supply means that when companies like Big Dragon's turn to AI-generated music, someone like A Li will begin losing customers.

My name is A Li. I'm 29 years old and live in Xi'an. I've been working in the music industry for six or seven years, doing things like soundtrack creation and song customisation.

I have a coding background and have always enjoyed learning new technologies. After I returned to work when the COVID-19 pandemic [restrictions] ceased at the end of 2022, I noticed a surge in AI-related content on the Internet. At the time, I was most interested in the emergence of AI 'singers': AI that could be trained to mimic perfectly a recorded human voice.

I joined a chat group on the subject. The shared document in the chat group was so long, even for someone like me with some coding experience, that it was tough to follow. I had to refresh my knowledge of coding, but after a week or so, I got the program running. I tried inputting my own voice first. I've done a lot of recording jobs in studios, so I uploaded the materials to the cloud processor for 20 hours of memory training. I kept the computer running overnight.

Many have turned to AI to write songs
Source: James Owen, Unsplash

The next morning, I downloaded the generated voice. Both my partner and I were in shock because it sounded exactly like mine. My mind was racing, and the next thing I knew, I was sending it to my mother, who heard it and said, 'You still sing so badly!' It chilled me that my own mother couldn't differentiate my voice from AI.

It was thrilling and terrifying at the same time. It occurred to me that AI singing is so developed that there must be AI-generated content and product in all fields related to music.

I'm self-employed. Normally, I get commissions from clients, and there's a collaborative process. This part of the business has not been lost. The area where I have experienced a greater loss of business is in the customisation of songs and soundtracks. I used to get a dozen or so orders a month, but now I get none. After asking around, I discovered that [AI] is so cheap that human labour simply cannot compete. What would have cost thousands of yuan in the past now cost only hundreds or less. This is a very natural market selection process.

When I first began experimenting with AI for work, I couldn't use it effectively. After a client heard a demo I sent, he asked, 'Who wrote this song? It sounds like it's by someone who has little experience arranging music.'

After a week of using AI, I sent the client a new demo, and he said, 'That's pretty good. Can you sell it to me?' The transformation was interesting and scary. He couldn't tell the difference between human and AI any more. When I told him that the demo was made by AI, he was so shocked that his pupils dilatated. 'This is AI?!' he asked. I told him it took only 30 seconds to produce, and he fell silent. He was struggling to process this shocking piece of information.

What the market pursues is efficiency. Although what we produce [as humans] may be better, it is inefficient. If our clients can't tell if a song is written by a human or not, it just proves that AI-generated content has reached commercial standards.

After showing the demo to the client, he stopped contacting me. When I asked him why, he was honest and said that he had found someone else who was willing to use AI to generate content. After all, he wants to receive products in the fastest and most efficient way. What I aim for is higher-quality content, so it's all right for him to stop cooperating with me.

The impact of AI is comparable to the Industrial Revolution. Textile workers stormed the factories and smashed the steam engine, but progress cannot be reversed. If you can really get the unit price down through AI, it's not necessarily a bad thing for the individual consumer. While it's painful for us in the music industry, and our profits will go down, it's actually a boost for the consumer to be able to get the product they are looking for at a lower price.

In the past, if the client didn't like our demo, we had to start from scratch and rewrite everything. Now if we use AI to make a demo, and the client thinks the style and content is OK, I only have to customise it further based on the client's demand. This reduces communication costs and improves productivity.

This situation will force us to step up our game. If we don't raise the quality of our work and create something artistic and original, we'll definitely be replaced in the future.

My boss asked us, 'You're using AI. How come you're still slow?'

Kou Aizhe: Our third speaker, Xiao A, is a rookie with only a year of work experience.

Hi, my name is Xiao A, and I'm 24 years old. I work as a game concept designer in Xiamen. I design characters, patterns and special effects for online games. The company I work for specialises in art and design, with more than fifty employees in the design team.

I have been fond of drawing since I was a kid, and considered becoming an art student. However, I came from a less developed region, and there's a preconception that only students who fail academically studied art. I ended up studying engineering. I didn't enjoy the courses at university. After graduation, I learned about game concept design and enrolled in several training courses. About two years after graduation, I started to work in the industry.

I joined the company last March, just over a year ago. Early this year, I began hearing about AI-generated paintings, and thought 'Here we go again'. Starting from March, I began seeing a lot of AI-generated paintings on the Internet. At that time, it was less developed—people drawn with a dozen or so fingers. But it learned really fast and corrected mistakes, so that after a short while most people couldn't tell which paintings were generated by AI.

Back then I was involved in a project. The demand for illustrations suddenly surged. All my other colleagues were busy, so the company hired another person. He was given a draft sketch that had already been approved by the client, and was asked to refine it into a full version. The new colleague asked me, 'How long would it take for me to finish refining the drawing?' I said, 'A week or so.' He sent me an emoji meaning 'Wow', and I wondered what he meant. Did he think a week was too short for the task?

Game designers have been impacted by the rise of AI
Source: Sean Do, Unsplash

The new colleague used AI. I was right next to him. After he finished, he showed me the drawing and asked, 'Is this OK?' I didn't want to be overly critical, so I just pointed out a few problems and told him, 'Change this and that, and then send it to the manager.'

The manager told him frankly that the quality of the drawing was bad. It was not a particularly difficult task. Since the clothing in the picture was single-layered, at the beginning it worked quite smoothly with AI. However, some of the finer accessories tended to trip up AI. After the colleague had his work rejected, he asked me, 'What should I do now?'

I said, 'Didn't I send you a bunch of guidelines and reference drawings? Why don't you revise it according to those?'

'Do you mean I need to draw it by hand?' he asked. He was in disbelief. 'What about AI? Can AI help me?' I was speechless.

We use an AI image generator called Stable Diffusion, and I've been learning how to communicate with it. But I never get what I want. I think the quality is still pretty poor. There is also a very serious issue: characters drawn by AI don't seem to have genuine human emotions. Their facial expressions are so dull, and there is always some inexplicable blush on their faces, probably because people have been inputting a lot of images of this kind.

Most gamers now are quite averse to seeing traces of AI in the games they play, so after using AI to generate the illustrations, we have to erase the traces of AI manually. It's like putting the cart before the horse. People say AI is here to assist humans, but in fact I feel like it's quite the opposite. It is humans who now have to wipe AI's arse.

I think our boss's judgement has already been clouded by AI. He thinks that what it does is good and what humans draw is bad. It is fine for him to criticise young team members like me, but he even criticises our team leader. Our team leader is a relatively senior artist who's been in the industry for almost eight years. Sometimes when the team leader is editing AI's work, the boss comes up and says, 'I think the AI's drawing looks better' Our team leader must be furious, but he doesn't dare to say anything. When the boss isn't busy, he just sits in the office and uses AI. Because of this, he thinks he can draw too and that he can teach others how to draw.

Editing is a huge workload for us. AI has not reduced our workload by much. Yet our boss has laid off a few people. As a result, my colleagues and I had to work overtime until 10.30pm for more than 20 consecutive days!

The overtime work made everyone very depressed, and we all felt like we were on the verge of collapsing. Our team leader was also working overtime, and he said to us, 'If you want to quit, make sure you have another job lined up. The job market is really bad.'

I have a couple of colleagues who left their previous jobs, and their job-searching journeys haven't been smooth. They are all much better at game illustrations than I am. If you search the hashtag #failedinterview on social media, you will see many talented artists and designers struggling to find employment. Browsing these posts has been making me increasingly depressed; for a while, I was staying up until two or three in the morning scrolling. Honestly, I have no idea what my future holds. What if I quit my job and can't find another one and am forced to change careers? Truth is, I don't have the courage to resign because of this economic environment. I hope that my company fires me because at least I could get some compensation.

Anyway, I have never stopped drawing all these years. After work, before AI and now, I draw for myself. I still hope that my drawing skills can improve.

We want to be 'preachers' of Artificial Intelligence Generated Content (AIGC)

> Kou Aizhe: Initially, the introduction of AI tools was meant to improve efficiency, but who actually benefits from this high efficiency? There is another group of individuals who have profited from the enormous technological transformations. The fourth speaker, Hu Bo, is one of them.

Hi, everyone. My name's Hu Bo. I am a lead instructor of the AIGC program at Qieman Education. Our team is based in Beijing and consists of five members.

We discovered AIGC at the end of last year. Some AI drawing tools within the industry suddenly made headlines, and we believed at the time that this would affect the entire design industry in the future.

We already were doing online training, specialising in training graphic designers. So, initially, we integrated new materials, whether it's how to use Midjourney or Stable Diffusion, as module supplements within our existing employment courses. It was only later that we separated them into a short course.

We stayed up for two nights and came up with the materials for the foundational course on AIGC: writing lesson plans, filming, recording and editing, all in two days. We needed to rush it because if we waited until everyone started doing this, we would have missed the boat.

At the beginning, the foundational course was relatively cheap, around RMB 300. We usually do live Q&A sessions with students on Douyin, and explain the contents of our courses on live stream. During one live session, we casually mentioned the pre-sale of this stand-alone foundational course, and in only about an hour and a half, nearly 80 people signed up for it.

Kou Aizhe: In the following month, Hu Bo gradually expanded and improved the course content, initially consisting of eight sessions focusing on the AI drawing software Midjourney. Eventually, this course was priced at RMB 1,099 and comprised more than 20 video lessons, a collection of software operation manuals and related materials, as well as guides on how to monetise contents on social media platforms like Xiaohongshu and Douyin.

Over the past few months, this new AIGC business line has generated several million yuan in additional revenue for his training institution.

Many companies have swiftly added proficiency in AIGC tools as a requirement in their job postings. But where do the eligible candidates come from? When universities are not responsive enough to provide new graduates with necessary skill training, after-school training institutions like Hu Bo's seize the newly emerged opportunity and bridge the gap.

Many universities have invited him to give lectures on AIGC to students who are about to graduate.

For those big tech companies, the first requirement in their job descriptions is that candidates should be able to use Midjourney or Stable Diffusion. This means that AI operation skills have become a must. For example, a former student of mine worked for the ride-sharing app Didi. He told me that Didi is no longer hiring traditional designers; they only hire AIGC designers who can train AI using keyword descriptions. These positions are completely new. I'm not afraid of sharing what we teach: we study the job descriptions of companies and teach whatever the employer needs. To gain employment, students only need to complete their study accordingly.

Universities are forcing their students to learn about these new developments because they want their students to gain employment. This is brand-new and highly sought after. The students may have heard of things like ChatGPT or Midjourney yet have no idea of what they are.

My job is to get my students interested in AIGC. To achieve this I'll have to keep up with industry developments. For instance, at Osaka University in Japan, researchers have successfully combined Stable Diffusion with MRIs in the hospitals to create a 'human eye camera'; that is, AI can directly re-create what people see by reading their brain scans. The tremendous potential of AI is very intriguing for my students. This is also a topic for them to discuss in job interviews to give the interviewer the impression that they have a deep understanding of the industry. We pay attention to what is being researched in companies and universities, then we pass on the information to our students. Companies also see our students as 'geeks' who won't need to be retrained after recruitment.

> Kou Aizhe: According to Hu Bo, the employment rate of their students this year has increased by 30 percent compared to previous years thanks to the new AIGC content. He is so busy he now has time to research new developments in the industry only when travelling on trains and planes.

Translated by Master of Translation students Yuan Cai, Zhirui Chen, Yurun Dai, Yifan Li, Wenjing Liu, Jiaqi Tan, and Ke Wu at the University of Melbourne, under the guidance of Mr Yahia Ma. This translation has been edited by Annie Luman Ren and Linda Jaivin for clarity and length.

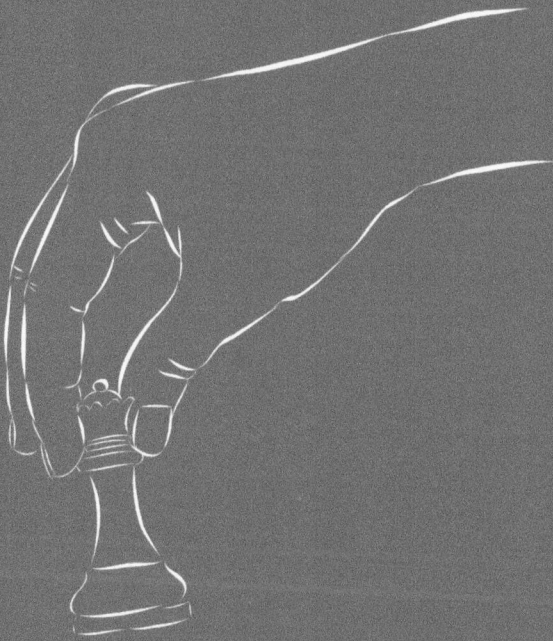

六

CHAPTER 6: CHINA'S GLOBAL AMBITIONS

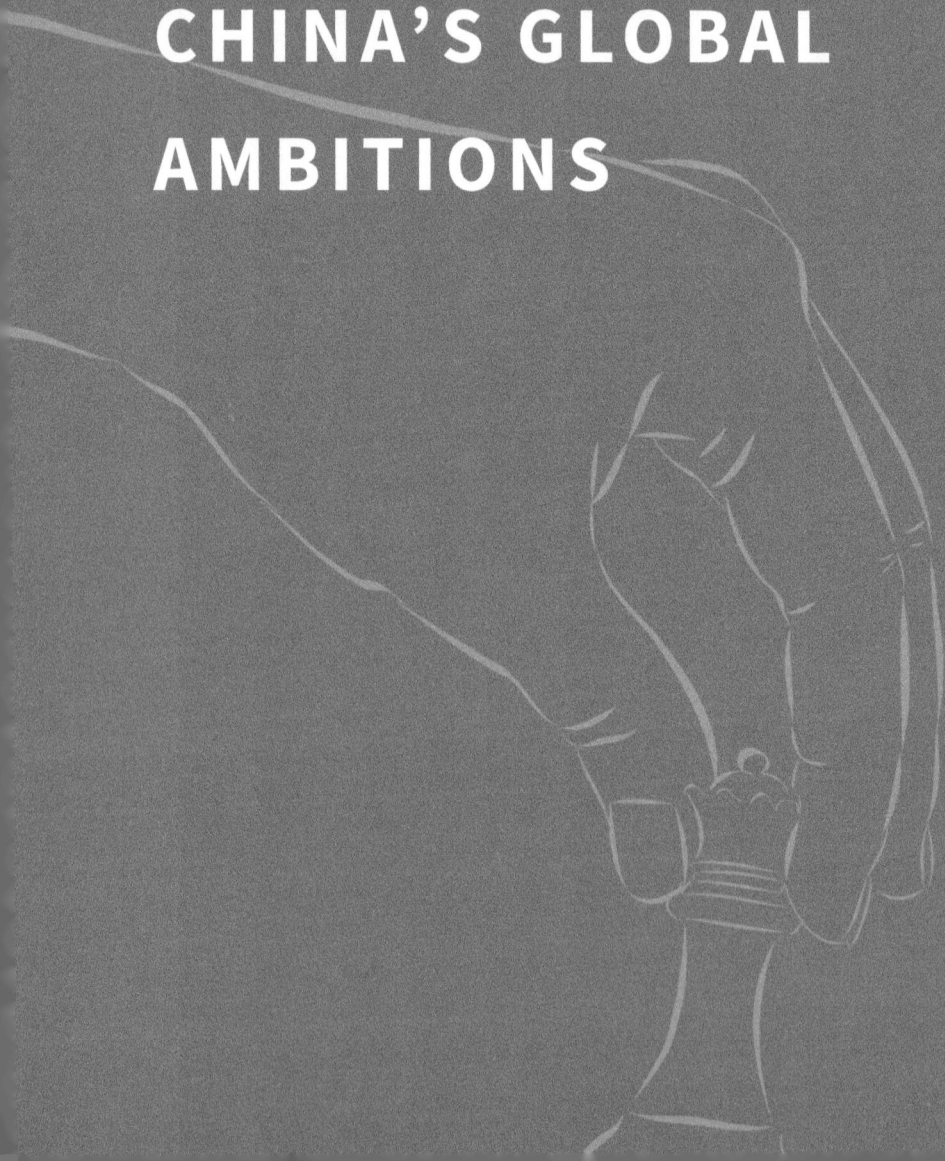

FROM RIYADH AND TEHRAN

TO BEIJING:

CHINA'S DIPLOMATIC ROLE

IN A CHANGING WORLD

Kevin Magee

In Moscow on 22 March 2023, Chinese President Xi Jinping told Russian President Vladimir Putin: 'Right now there are changes—the likes of which we haven't seen for 100 years—and we are the ones driving these changes together.'[1] Leaving the hyperbole aside, there is evidence that many certainties of the Western-led world and the 'rules-based order' are changing and, with this, so is China's role in the diplomatic world. Since emerging from its zero-COVID period, Beijing has launched a significant series of diplomatic initiatives in areas where hitherto China has played little or no diplomatic role.

Chief among these was brokering a deal between Saudi Arabia—a long-time staunch US ally—and Iran on 10 March 2023 in Beijing for the two countries to restore diplomatic relations. This achievement shocked Washington. The United States had long been the dominant external force in the Middle East and had brokered key developments there from the Camp David Accords in 1978 to the Oslo Agreement between Israel and the Palestinian Liberation Organisation of 1993. The last three years had seen the Abraham Accords whereby the United States brokered the establishment of diplomatic relations between Israel and Bahrain, the United Arab Emirates, Morocco and Sudan.

China, a long-time observer and trader in the Middle East, is now suddenly a key player and peacemaker in the region, a mark of its rising position and influence in the world. The Saudi–Iran deal signals that the United States cannot take its dominance in the diplomatic sphere for granted. Many other countries are prioritising good relations with Beijing and hedging their diplomatic strategic bets.

This has been most marked in the Global South, particularly in the Middle East, Africa and Latin America. In South-East Asia, much of ASEAN seeks to avoid choosing between China and the United States as tension has developed between the two major powers. For the majority of countries in South-East Asia, China is not an adversary or enemy but a vitally important neighbour with whom they have problems from time to time. Other regional players, including Australia and Japan and increasingly the Republic of Korea (ROK) and the Philippines, have strengthened their alignment with

US strategic goals while continuing to build and stress the importance of economic and other ties with China. In the case of the Philippines, tensions have been building with China over the Scarborough and Second Thomas Shoals in the South China Sea, which both countries claim. Although China's role as a de facto supporter of Russia in the Ukraine war has strained relations with much of the European Union, during his visit to China on 5 to 7 April 2023, French President Emmanuel Macron said that Europe should not automatically follow the United States and get 'caught up in crises that are not ours'. On the subject of Taiwan, Macron advocated a course of 'strategic autonomy' for the European Union.[2]

BRICS has been expanding with the admission of new members
Source: GovernmentZA, Flickr

A second significant example of the development of an alternative non-Western grouping is the BRICS, comprising the large developing countries Brazil, Russia, India, China and South Africa. At the BRICS meeting in South Africa in late August in 2023, the BRICS grouping announced the admission of six new members in a decision widely interpreted as an attempt to reshape the international order and provide a counterweight to the United States and its allies. From January 2024, Egypt, Ethiopia, Iran, Saudi Arabia and the United Arab Emirates will join the grouping in a move described by China's President Xi Jinping as 'historic'.[3] The significance of this expansion is the development of a non-Western grouping with significant political and economic power and with China as one of its central members. According to the International Monetary Fund (IMF), the BRICS grouping will collectively account for 32.1 percent of global Gross Domestic Product (GDP) in 2023, more than the G7's share of 29.9 percent of global GDP.[4] With the addition of the six new members in January 2024, the GDP of BRICS will grow to 36 percent of global GDP.[5] The grouping, with its focus on de-dollarisation, promotion of local currencies for global trade and finance, and the admission of new members, mostly accords with Beijing's agenda.[6]

China's diplomatic initiatives

A suite of major initiatives serves as the basis of China's new approach to diplomacy. These include the Global Security Initiative (GSI), the Global Civilisation Initiative (GCI), and the Global Development Initiative (GDI), as well as the Belt and Road Initiative (BRI). The GSI opposes Western 'hegemonic' dominance in the area of international security, promoting instead a central role for the United Nations and emphasising non-interference in other countries' internal affairs and sovereign equality under international law. The multibillion-dollar BRI launched by Xi Jinping in 2013 aims to improve China's connectivity with the world through infrastructure and investments. The United States and other Western countries have criticised the BRI as merely a mechanism to spread China's geopolitical and financial influence throughout the world. The success of many of the projects has been mixed, but it is certain that the BRI has expanded China's influence, especially in the Global South (see "The Belt and Road's Midlife Crisis: Perspectives from Latin America and the Caribbean" on page 163). Of the 152 countries that have signed BRI memorandums of understanding, fifty-two are in Africa, forty are in Asia and the rest in the Middle East, Latin America and Europe. The BRI also appears to have increased Chinese exports to the member countries.[7] The Third BRI Forum was held in Beijing on 17 to 18 October 2023. Leaders from twenty-three countries attended the event, including Russian President

Vladimir Putin. This was a lower number of leaders than attended the 2017 and 2019 forums, but the large turn-out from the Global South indicated that the BRI retains strong currency and support in the developing world.[8]

Taken together, these initiatives aim both to enhance China's global influence and to build a diplomatic and security architecture to rival the US-led system of multilateral alliances and institutions.[9] They also aim to enhance China's role as mediator or peacemaker in regional conflicts.

Other important bodies that are non-Western focused in which China plays a significant role include BRICS Plus, the Shanghai Cooperation Organisation (SCO),[10] and a range of summits that China holds with groupings such as the China–Arab League Summit, the China Gulf Cooperation Council (GCC) Summit and the China–Africa Summit. In 2016, China also opened the Asia Infrastructure Investment Bank (AIIB); by 2023, it had more than a hundred members (including Australia), a Triple-A rating and some US$100 billion in capitalisation.[11] These are all part of a suite of organisations and initiatives that are beyond US and G7 influence. The GSI and the other initiatives, together with the BRI, provide an alternative to the US-led rules-based order and are attractive to many countries, especially in the Global South.

Riyadh and Tehran to Beijing

In the past, China was satisfied to trade and observe in the Middle East, an area where US influence was politically and militarily dominant. However, China is now the largest trading partner of most GCC countries, including Saudi Arabia.[12] China has backed this economic influence with active diplomacy. Xi Jinping made a high-profile visit to Riyadh in December 2022, during which he participated in the first China–GCC Summit on 9 December and the first China–Arab States Summit that same afternoon. Most participants at these meetings were expressly focused on building relations with Beijing as a hedge against dependence on the United States.[13] Most countries, however, were conscious that the United States was still the most significant defence partner in the region. Iranian President Ebrahim Raisi went to Beijing from 14 to 16 February 2023.[14] There have also been several announcements of large-scale Saudi–Chinese investment deals worth more than US$10 billion.[15] On 5 September 2023, the Bank of China (BOC) opened its first branch in Saudi Arabia in a move to expand the use of yuan in the growing number of economic deals between the two countries. Saudi Arabia is China's largest source of crude oil imports, with 87.5 million metric tonnes (641 million barrels) shipped in 2022. BOC is the second Chinese bank to open branches in China after the Industrial and Commercial Bank of China (ICBC), which has branches in Riyadh and Jeddah.[16]

Many Middle Eastern countries, including Saudi Arabia, admire China's four-decade record of deploying state capital to achieve profound economic change while tightly managing social and political change. China's experience challenges US insistence that only liberal systems can produce economic growth and stability. As Saudi Arabia's largest trading partner, with growing economic influence in the Middle East and friendship with Iran, China was a logical partner for the mediation process.

Saudi Arabia is seeking a more independent foreign policy under Crown Prince Mohammed bin Salman
Source: Dimitris Papamitsos, Flickr

China the peacemaker?

Chinese officials describe facilitating the rapprochement between Saudi Arabia and Iran as a successful example of the GSI at work. The discussions that led to the 10 March 2023 accord began in the Middle East. Iraq and Oman hosted talks between 2020 and 2022, but the accord needed China's imprimatur to finalise the deal. It was impossible for Washington to play its traditional role of mediator in this case because, after four decades of mutual hostility, the United States still does not have diplomatic relations with Iran. Another factor was that, under Crown Prince Mohammed bin Salman, long-time US ally Saudi Arabia is seeking a more independent foreign policy and is rebalancing its relations with the major powers, including China.[17]

Additionally, in contrast to the Trump administration and family's close relations with and support for the Saudi royal family, which did not waver even after evidence linked the crown prince to the killing of journalist and US resident Jamal Khashoggi in 2018, the Biden administration has hardened its policy towards Saudi Arabia. While campaigning in 2019, Biden said he would make Saudi Arabia a 'pariah'. When the Saudis cut oil production after Russia's invasion of Ukraine, fuelling global inflation, Biden threatened 'consequences'. US policy and rhetoric only helped to open the door for Beijing.[18] Iran has good relations and a strong economic relationship with China. A close economic relationship with both countries based both on economics and on China's new ambitious foreign policy made China the natural partner to secure the deal. In addition, China's new influence in the region was achieved without the use of military coercion, in contrast with the US record of the use of military force and coercion to resolve differences with Iraq, Iran, Lebanon, Yemen and other countries. Saudi Arabia has used its growing links with China to leverage its interests with the United States. These new links with China, together with the tentative steps by the kingdom before the Gaza crisis to establish diplomatic relations with Israel, had brought the United States around to consider providing the Saudis 'Non-NATO Security Guarantees', armaments and nuclear technology it had not agreed to provide before.

China has relished its role bridging the gap between Saudi Arabia and Iran. Beijing continues to seek to pay the role of mediator and peacemaker. It has put forward a peace plan for the Ukraine war and is seeking to play a role in the Israeli/Palestinian conflict, although there are serious doubts it can achieve much in either case.

A Chinese emissary, Ambassador Li Hui, visited Kyiv and Moscow from 14 to 18 May 2023 with a plan announced by Beijing in April to end the fighting between Russia and Ukraine.[19] As the plan did not call for the withdrawal of Russian troops from Ukrainian territory, Ukraine rejected the proposal. The proposal was politely received in Moscow but not accepted by President Putin.[20] Although the Chinese intervention was broadly welcomed, it did not provide a way forward for the ending the war. Nonetheless, it was another example of China projecting itself on the global stage as a positive player.

On 18 April 2023, China offered to broker peace talks between Israel and Palestine.[21] The gesture is undoubtedly aimed at strengthening the positive perception of China in the Arab World and Global South. On 13 to 15 June 2023, Palestinian National Authority President Mahmoud Abbas visited Beijing, where he welcomed China's involvement.[22] China, in contrast to most Western countries, has taken a position sympathetic to the plight of the Palestinians in Gaza and has not specifically condemned Hamas for its 7 October attacks on Israel. Foreign Minister Wang Yi has said that Israel's actions have 'gone beyond self-defence'. In a conversation with the Saudi foreign minister, Wang said Israel should stop its 'collective punishment of Gaza's citizens'. China has increasingly aligned its response to the Gaza war with the Global South.[23]

Israeli Prime Minister Benjamin Netanyahu had announced on 26 June 2023 that he would make his fourth visit to China as prime minister at the invitation of Beijing before the end of 2023. Following the Gaza war and the position that China has taken on Gaza, the visit has not gone ahead. China's position means that Israel is also very unlikely to engage in the near future in any Chinese attempts to broker peace in the Middle East.

China's power is rising globally

China's power and influence power is also rising in Central Asia. On 18 May 2023, at the inaugural China–Central Asia Summit attended by the leaders of Kazakhstan, Kyrgyzstan, Turkmenistan, Tajikistan and Uzbekistan, Xi Jinping announced 26 billion yuan (US$3.8 billion) of loans, financial support and non-reimbursable funds for the five Central Asian republics and a new gas pipeline to China from Turkmenistan. Xi also met individually with each of the five presidents. Each of the five republics are active members of the BRI. Bilateral trade between China and the Central Asian republics reached US$70.2 billion in 2022.[24] As China's power has risen in Central Asia, it has remained careful not to cut across vital Russian interests. China's centrality to the power structure in Central Asia is also ensured by the Shanghai Cooperation Organisation (SCO) and the fact that both Russia and China face competition from the US-led West. China's partnership with Russia is based on common interests and economic complementarity, which has become even more important to Russia since the start of the Ukraine war. Russia is increasingly becoming a junior partner in what is proving nonetheless a durable relationship.[25]

From 12 to 17 April 2023, Brazilian President Luiz Inácio Lula da Silva visited China and called for an end to US dollar dominance of the world's financial systems.[26] This reflected a growing trend towards countries moving to reduce their dependence on the dollar as a reserve, exchange or accounting currency in certain areas of the world. For countries in the Global South including Brazil, this is driven by efforts to avoid US sanctions and the Biden administration's control over microchips. In reality, however, only a small percentage of the world's financial system uses the Chinese yuan and other non-Western currencies as the basis for reserves and exchange. Nonetheless, there is some appetite in parts of the world for moving beyond control of the US dollar and to adopt the yuan.

China has not surpassed the United States yet

Chinese activism is based on a sense that the global role of the United States is declining and China's is rising. Although there is some evidence of shifting strategic power balances, it would be wrong to discount the remaining power and influence of the United States. President Biden has made it clear that the United States is determined to compete with China for influence and strategic power.[27] In terms of military power and economic and financial heft, the United States remains the world's leading power despite the rise of China, the multipolar world and groupings like the expanded BRICS. Although the United States remains the single most powerful country in the world, the global strategic environment is increasingly multipolar and de-dollarisation is increasing—facts recognised by much of the world. China, with its Global Security Initiative and its suite of other projects and initiatives, has become a significant challenger to the United States and Western hegemony in the Global South and in long-time US-dominated regions like the Middle East.

Despite the increasing multipolar nature of the world, both Beijing and Washington see their great power competition as the fulcrum of international relations as countries are increasingly encouraged to line up with one side or the other. Australia and regional countries like Japan and the Philippines have clearly declared their adherence to Washington. Many other countries, especially in the Global South, seek to maintain a balance between China and the United States and to hedge against both countries. Other rising powers such as India seek to follow their own independent strategic and economic paths and are wary to a degree of both Beijing and Washington. With a period of competition and uncertainty ahead, much of the world, especially the Global South, would welcome a world without US primacy. Perhaps the accord between arch rivals Riyadh and Teheran is a harbinger and a foretaste of the future Chinese role in the contested strategic world.

THE BELT AND ROAD'S

MIDLIFE CRISIS:

PERSPECTIVES FROM

LATIN AMERICA AND

THE CARIBBEAN

Ruben Gonzalez-Vicente

China's Belt and Road Initiative (BRI) turned 10 in 2023. Assessing its progress to date is challenging, given the persistent lack of consensus on its true nature. Few global initiatives evoke such disparate perceptions. To some, the BRI epitomises the People's Republic of China's (PRC) audacious foray into twenty-first-century grand strategy, a bold vision for a new era of global connectivity bankrolled by an endless supply of state resources, and the cornerstone of a China-centric world order.[1] To others, the BRI registers as little more than an exercise in branding, dovetailing a variety of pre-existing, disjointed and uncoordinated ventures by various Chinese businesses and state entities.[2] In this essay, my assessment of the BRI zeroes in on the infrastructural shift witnessed in the PRC's international development outlook in the years that followed the Global Financial Crisis of 2007–08. Therefore I focus explicitly on the materiality of Belt and Road encounters rather than on the rhetoric and diplomacy enveloping this new era of global economic engagement.

In Latin America and the Caribbean (LAC), something started to change around 10 years ago. After a decade marked by surging Chinese investments in the region's natural resource sectors—financed by the 'Going Out' policy, which offered soft loans for Chinese corporations to acquire new projects—the landscape of Chinese economic engagement evolved to include infrastructure development. Even as early as 2005, the Export-Import Bank of China and the China Development Bank had been actively involved in the region, extending loans to sovereign nations for diverse projects. However, the emphasis on infrastructure became particularly pronounced in the aftermath of the Global Financial Crisis. In response to the global economic downturn, the Chinese government pumped money into domestic infrastructure projects, which sustained robust economic growth amid the crisis. These were the infamous three years (2011–13) when China consumed more concrete than the United States had done throughout the entire twentieth century.[3] Soon, China's construction capacity began to outstrip domestic demand, prompting a global quest for new profitable markets for Chinese contractors. This would mark the beginning of a new chapter in China–LAC relations, in which loans for infrastructure projects executed by Chinese firms became a cornerstone of the trans-Pacific connection, particularly within LAC countries with strained relations with Western-based international financial institutions. Chinese contractors have also made inroads into some LAC countries through open bids for public works that have not involved government-to-government agreements or financial backing from Chinese policy banks. Although some analysts like to set the start of this era in a speech by Xi Jinping in Kazakhstan in 2013, where he officially announced the BRI, the underlying currents of change had been set into motion much earlier.

Road leading to the JISCO Alpart bauxite refinery in Nain, Jamaica
Source: the author

Over the period from 2008 to 2019, China's development finance rivalled the lending capacity of the World Bank, with both entities nearing the half-trillion dollar mark for lending globally.[4] In Latin America, the volume of Chinese loans in some years surpassed the combined lending of the World Bank, the Inter-American Development Bank and the US Export-Import Bank,[5] although not all these loans were allocated to infrastructural projects. The distribution of both the number and the volume of loans across the region exhibits disparities. Countries such as Venezuela, Brazil,

Ecuador and Argentina emerged as primary recipients of Chinese financial support, whereas others such as Jamaica and Trinidad and Tobago have also secured considerable loans in proportion to the scale of their economies. In contrast, Chile, Peru and Colombia remain notably absent from the roster of nations with sizeable debts to China, although Chinese contractors have successfully secured bids for significant public works in these countries, such as the Bogotá metro project in Colombia. By 2023, 21 LAC countries had become signatories of the BRI, although formal membership does not correlate with eligibility for funding. Many of these countries were already beneficiaries of loans from Chinese policy banks before joining the BRI. Furthermore, several LAC countries that have not yet formalised their BRI membership are recipients of Chinese infrastructural loans. Indeed, some researchers have contended that the BRI in LAC represents a 'repackaging of existing relations' and economic trends set in motion by the Global Financial Crisis.[6] In this context, it is more useful to conceptualise the BRI as a distinct economic moment in China's developmental trajectory, marked by overaccumulation and the global expansion of Chinese construction firms. Through this lens, a clearer depiction of the developmental impact of the BRI in LAC begins to take shape.

Now often taken for granted, one of the crucial ways in which Chinese development finance reshaped the political landscape of development in LAC was by introducing an (optional) end to unilateral conditionality. For decades, at least since the debt crisis of the early 1980s, the region had been subject to structural adjustment programs as a condition for financing. Certain aspects of conditionality might have yielded benefits—others clearly did not, as illustrated by the World Bank's acknowledgement that the 1980s were a 'lost decade of development'.[7] A fundamental critique has focused on the undemocratic nature of structural adjustment. Sovereign nations were forced into liberalisation trajectories that in occasions diverged from their electoral mandates. In this context, the absence of political conditionality in Chinese developmental finance, whether BRI-branded or not, was welcomed by those critical of the US-centric global development system. But it is important to note that even though Chinese loans do not come with political conditions such as liberalization and governance reforms, they often include particularly stringent conditions aimed at ensuring repayment, inspired by commercial lending contracts rather than typical development finance.[8] Nevertheless, China's emergence as a major lender has afforded LAC countries additional options to finance their development agendas, consequently providing them with more political leverage to reimagine development beyond the conventional template provided by Washington-based institutions—even if some might have found themselves 'doubly trapped' between two mighty lenders.[9]

By focusing on infrastructure, the Belt and Road Initiative has addressed a regional gap that the World Bank estimated to necessitate investments equivalent to 6.2 percent of annual GDP.[10] But by lending to this sector the BRI has waded into turbid waters. Across LAC countries, major infrastructure works have been a source of contention and conflict as land use changes and authoritarian methods and practices have threatened sustainability and community rights.[11] In this regard, evaluating individual BRI projects requires a consideration of their economic and social returns, alongside an assessment of socioenvironmental costs. Economic dividends are relatively straightforward to measure. In essence, some BRI projects have acted as economic multipliers, generating sufficient economic activity eventually to offset the initial investment. Examples include the expansion of airports in tourism-dependent countries like Antigua and Barbuda, the financing of a national broadband network in Suriname, and investments in road and railway construction and repair in places like Bolivia and Argentina.[12] However, some projects fall short of meeting this multiplier criterion. Examples include 'white elephants' like the Montego Bay Convention Centre in Jamaica or, more broadly, underutilised infrastructure such as the North-South highway in Jamaica, which has high toll prices that have deterred many Jamaicans from using it.

There are examples of Chinese-funded projects that might have not been intended as economic multipliers but which have added social value. Examples include the construction of hospitals and healthcare facilities in Ecuador and Trinidad and Tobago. Similarly, the construction of convention centres or sport venues has often been criticised as a wasteful enterprise in the developing world—but some might wish to challenge the notion that sport and cultural facilities should remain a luxury exclusive to the developed world while the poor should focus on productivity. Nevertheless, not all these initiatives have yielded the anticipated outcomes. For example, the Couva Hospital in Trinidad and Tobago fell short of its envisaged role as a children's hospital, owing both to structural limitations and to neglect of capacity-related challenges.[13] The proposed construction of a new stadium in El Salvador has also garnered attention, raising questions about scale (if built it will be the largest stadium in Central America) while also triggering geopolitical anxieties in Washington—a matter that arguably diverges from developmental considerations.[14]

Sir Vivian Richards Stadium in Antigua, built with a grant from the Chinese government
Source: the author

Related to the above, concerns have also emerged regarding the processes through which BRI projects have been implemented. A salient feature of projects financed by Chinese policy banks is that they invite limited or no participation from stakeholders and the general public. The development of the National Academy for the Performing Arts in Trinidad, for instance, faced criticism from local artists who lamented the lack of consultation regarding the needs of the local artist community.[15] In a broader perspective, the construction sector both in the region and beyond has developed a dubious reputation on issues of corruption and accountability. Brazilian and Spanish contractors, for example, have established a low standard in LAC.[16] Chinese enterprises in this sector, too, have faced their share of scandals in such countries as Guyana or Peru.[17] In doing so, they stand on the shoulders of the giants that preceded them, rather than representing isolated anomalies. However, Chinese development finance for infrastructural works stands out for its poor record on issues of transparency, participatory approaches, and consultation. Chinese policy banks typically confine their interactions to central government authorities, thereby distinguishing themselves from such organisations as the World Bank, which, in recent decades, has endeavoured to foster participatory approaches and transparency standards, although not without controversy over whether these initiatives genuinely aim to empower local populations or merely to co-opt them.

Chinese infrastructure projects have also, at times, the distinctive characteristic of relying on an imported Chinese labour force, although the degree to which this has happened varies across the region, with some countries placing severe limitations on the importation of labour. Central American and Caribbean governments have shown a higher propensity for accepting the influx of Chinese labour, a phenomenon less prevalent in South America. For Chinese contractors, the use of Chinese labour is an aspect that might be negotiable, with local authorities being presented with varying price tags depending on the percentage of local workers engaged in the construction process. Employing Chinese workers allows for a more economical and expedient delivery, thereby reducing costs for both parties involved. This efficiency stems from the greater ease with which contractors can exploit Chinese migrant labour.[18] Host countries find themselves at a crossroads, having to decide the extent to which infrastructure aims to generate local employment versus prioritising the swift and cost-effective delivery of projects.

Furthermore, a considerable number of BRI projects in Latin America and the Caribbean grapple with environmental challenges. Some fall into a grey area; for instance, the Coca Codo Sinclair hydroelectric dam in Ecuador has locally significant environmental impacts but could contribute to an overall reduction in carbon emissions.[19] In contrast, others, like the Santa Cruz River Hydroelectric Complex, blend labour violations with inadequate environmental impact assessments that downplay the substantial damage they could inflict on local ecosystems.[20]

While many debated the BRI's merits and characteristics, few doubted it had become a cornerstone in LAC's developmental landscape. As various Chinese-funded projects proliferated throughout the region, the prevailing belief was that the rise of China was unstoppable, inevitable and exponential, and that China seemed destined to challenge US regional hegemony. However, by 2018, a shift had begun. Reports from the Dialogue and Boston University's Global Development Policy Center highlighted a substantial reduction in Chinese loans to the region. Having consistently surpassed the US$5 billion mark annually since 2009, the figure plummeted to US$2.1 billion in 2018 and US$1.1 billion in 2019.[21] This was not merely a hiccup but rather a new trend, consolidating in 2020 as the first year in which Chinese development banks issued no loans to the region. Subsequent years saw the total loan figures not reaching the US$1 billion mark per year.[22] This new normal coincided with increasing caution on the part of some of China's borrowers. The Jamaican government, for instance, announced in 2019 that it would refrain from taking on more Chinese loans for the time being.[23]

A decade since its inception, the BRI finds itself grappling with a midlife crisis. There is insecurity in a model that once inspired certainty, hesitance where success once appeared inevitable. Notably absent from recent Xi Jinping speeches, the BRI has seemingly been supplanted by less China-centric branding, such as the Global Development Initiative.[24] In material terms, China confronts its first overseas debt crisis, renegotiating US$52 billion in loans in the 2020–21 period.[25] This suggests significant miscalculations in China's overseas development lending, especially in the case of Venezuela. At the same time, while Chinese loans have been rescaled, investments by individual firms not backed by policy banks continue unabated, many of them increasingly under public–private partnership frameworks.[26] This suggests that, at the very least, the BRI has served as a successful mechanism for the internationalisation of many Chinese state-owned and private firms, enabling them to operate with increased autonomy. Furthermore, the BRI has helped to generate a multitude of bilateral and multilateral agreements designed to facilitate new commercial activities in the years to come,[27] including most recently a free-trade agreement with Ecuador, or a yuan-settlement deal with Brazil.[28]

Over the past decade, the BRI has come to represent a significant moment in China's development trajectory—one that is characterised by state support for the internationalisation of Chinese construction and engineering firms, of which China now has an oversupply. From the perspective of LAC countries, the BRI has reshaped the politics of development and bolstered the developmental agency of policy elites in the region. At the same time, from the vantage point of communities and activists across the region, the BRI has often reinforced existing developmental hierarchies and introduced new barriers for non-elite populations' influence in national and local development projects. As the Chinese government recalibrates its commitment to the BRI in light of the successes and failures of the last decade, along with changing global geopolitics and domestic economic challenges, the relationship between China and LAC is entering a new phase, gradually taking shape.

CHAPTER 7:
NEW FRONTIERS

CHINA: THE NEW NO. 2

SPACE POWER

Brad Tucker

On 4 October 1957, the USSR launched Sputnik, the world's first artificial satellite, and with it the Space Age itself. In February 2023, China's National Museum put on a grand exhibition marking thirty years since the start of the Chinese human space program.[1]

The environment in space is very different from that of Earth. The extremes in temperatures, from less than −150 degrees Celcius to more than 150 degrees, the lack of atmospheric pressure, and other issues mean that the margin for error to achieve success is zero. Even the most experienced space powers, the United States and Russia, can fail. Luna 25, Russia's first probe to the Moon in nearly fifty years, crashed there in August 2023.

The difficulties of space travel are challenging for countries and companies relatively new to the space race. China, during a period of about thirty years, has not just overcome these hurdles but also surpassed many other countries, including Russia, to become the world's number 2 space power.

Launching rockets

One way to measure the progress China has made is by the number of rocket launches. The US National Aeronautics and Space Administration (NASA), which put the first people on the Moon, now primarily relies on private companies to launch its spacecraft, including crewed missions. SpaceX is one of the companies doing most of this work for NASA. SpaceX can launch multiple rockets per week, sometimes every day, while having the rocket boosters return to Earth to be refuelled and reused.

In 2022, the United States achieved a total of seventy-four orbital launches, sixty-one by SpaceX; China boasted sixty-four. Far behind was Russia at twenty-one, and fourth was New Zealand's RocketLab at nine.[2]

SpaceX rockets often take multiple, and in some cases, nearly a hundred satellites into space whereas Chinese rockets usually only carry one or two. This is not because China lacks the capability but because it is sending larger satellites and only one or two can fit. However, China is rapidly developing the capability to do these missions that take multiple satellites, called ride-share.

The Tiangong Space Station: Building in space at speed

Space exploration is not only a hard journey but also a long one. Missions take years to design and develop, and the equipment must be tested, and often the process repeats. It is common for missions to run over time and over budget.

The two issues—time and money—are related. Most costs are related to paying hundreds to thousands of highly skilled people. The longer they work on a project, the more that project will cost. Famously, NASA's James Webb Space Telescope ended up being more than ten years late and US$9 billion over budget.

When the China Manned Space Agency (CMSA) announced that it would need six additional major missions to complete China's first space station, Tiangong 天宫太空站 (literally 'Heavenly Palace Space Station'), the goal of finishing in one year seemed ambitious. It involved launching and preparing two modules (sections), multiple crewed missions and associated launches. But in the end it only took eleven months, with the space station beginning operation in late October 2022. The Chinese space program is one of the few that not only meets its deadlines but also beats them. In the case of Tiangong, early cooperation and knowledge-sharing with Russia saved China time and effort.

Even when the United States was spending 7–9 percent of its GDP to get the Moon, delays were experienced. China is only the third country to operate its own space station after the United States and USSR/Russia, which has since cooperated on the International Space Station (ISS). However, the ISS is ageing and has an uncertain future. Russia has not committed to partner on it beyond 2024. The United States is planning for private companies to build and operate commercial stations around the Earth that NASA can use.

At the same time, NASA is focusing on the Gateway, a space station that will orbit the Moon. The Gateway, built and operated with commercial and international partners, will be able to support four astronauts at a time for a few months—much like the International Space Station. It will specialise in research, exploration and resource extraction on the Moon. Russia has said it will build its own. However, it is doubtful that Russia has the financial and other means to do so, especially in light of the Luna 25 failure. They are also planning on collaborating with China on efforts on the Moon, which will further diminish their limited budget. It might eventuate that China has the only national space station orbiting the Earth.

China's race to the 'dark side' of the Moon

Landing on the Moon requires probes to decelerate from tens of thousands of kilometres per hour on leaving Earth's orbit to thousands of kilometres per hour around the Moon to zero. Adding to the difficulty of a Moon landing, the surface is rocky and the soil fine and adhesive. Just over half of missions to the Moon have succeeded.

Yet the race to the Moon is heating up. Since late 2022, a number of countries have sent probes and satellites to the Moon for the first time including South Korea, the United Arab Emirates and New Zealand. A private Japanese company, ispace, unsuccessfully attempted a landing while the US company Intuitive Machines will attempt a landing in 2024. India became the fourth country to land on the Moon and operate a rover in August 2023, while Japan became the fifth, with JAXA landing SLIM on the Moon in January 2024.

China was the first country, and is still the only country, to land on the far side of the Moon, sometimes misleadingly called the dark side, as it does receive sunlight; it is called the far side because it always faces away from the Earth. The Moon does one orbit around the Earth every 27.29 days. Since the orbit around Earth occurs at the same rate as its rotation, it means the same side is always facing towards Earth. Likewise, every spot on the Moon has about two weeks of continuous sunlight and daytime, followed by two weeks of continuous night-time and darkness.

What makes landing on the far side tricky, is that if you are facing away from Earth, you cannot see Earth or communicate with it. Landing a probe on the Moon is hard enough, harder when you are cut off from communications. To solve this problem, China launched two satellites in orbit around the Moon to act as communication relays between Earth and the rover.

China has already landed two missions, Chang'e 3 and Chang'e 4, on the far side of the Moon. Chang'e 3 conducted experiments including successfully growing plants in a biosphere. Chang'e 4 extracted samples of the Moon's rocks and soil, and carried them back to Earth—only the third country to do so.

China is planning a mission to the Moon nearly every year for the rest of the decade. Its lunar ambitions will culminate in landing taikonauts (what China calls its astronauts) on the Moon in 2030. Given the current pace, it should have no trouble making the timeline.

The new Moon race—resources in space

The new Moon race centres around the utilisation of resources on the Moon. It started when India's Chandrayaan-1 discovered vast amounts of water ice there, in particular at the Moon's South Pole. Through a simple process, water (H_2O) can be broken down into hydrogen (H_2) and oxygen (O_2), providing astronauts with water, air and ingredients for rocket fuel. There are other potential fuel sources on the Moon as well—in particular Helium-3: an isotope of Helium. The Helium used to inflate balloons is Helium-4, which has two protons and two neutrons. Helium-3 only has 1 neutron. You can smash, or fuse, a neutron on to it—creating a nuclear fusion reaction, which creates Helium-4 and, more importantly, a lot of energy. It is not yet known whether Helium-3 exists on the Moon, especially in any useful or accessible quantities. China is examining the samples brought back to Earth from Chang'e 4 mission to the Moon for Helium-3.[3]

The weaker gravity on the Moon means spacecraft need less energy to leave the surface of the Moon than to leave Earth: about twenty times less. Take NASA's new, gigantic Space Launch System (SLS) rocket for the Artemis missions, which is bigger than the Saturn V in the 1960s and 1970s. Most of the rocket is fuel to lift and fly a lander, along with a tiny amount of fuel to reach the Moon, so there is enough fuel to leave the Moon's surface.

The possibility of refuelling on the Moon will significantly lessen the limitations of space travel. This is part of a broader discussion around in-situ resource utilization—living off the land, so to speak. By using resources in space, rather than taking them up from here, it will be cheaper and more effective in the long term.

Space exploration and astronomy

The name NASA conjures up images from the Hubble Space Telescope, missions to Mars, and asteroids. Its space and astronomy explorations set it apart from other such bodies, which are focused on human space flight, like building space stations or landing on the Moon.

Increasingly, China has been doing the same. It has its own Mars exploration program, landing its first rover on Mars—Tianwen 天问 ('Heavenly Questions')—in February 2021, only the second country to do so after the United States. In late 2024, China is planning to launch its own space telescope: Xuntian 巡天 ('Heavenly Exploration').

Telescopes are measured by how big their mirrors are. The bigger the mirror, the more light they can collect. China's telescope will be nearly the same size as NASA's Hubble: two metres in diameter compared with Hubble's 2.4 metres, and therefore will be able to see in similar detail. Its field of view, moreover, will be about 300 times wider than that of the Hubble. It will be capable of taking a highly detailed picture of a much larger area at the same amazing resolution as Hubble.

It will also take a page out of NASA's playbook. The Hubble Space Telescope is more than thirty years old. The US Space Shuttle program had four missions to Hubble: upgrading, fixing and servicing the space telescope. This kept Hubble at the forefront of science until the shuttle program came to an end. Once it is in orbit, the taikonauts on Tiangong will be able to dock with Xuntian, and therefore service and upgrade Xuntian with the best technology available, keeping it at the forefront of science.

Space telescopes are not the only thing China is building. In 2022, NASA with Johns Hopkins University launched the Double Asteroid Redirection Test (DART). This probe deliberately crashed into an asteroid to see how much energy could be directed into an asteroid to alter its orbit. It was built so that if an asteroid was heading for Earth, we could divert it, avoiding the sort of impact that put an end to the dinosaurs.

Chinese space suit display
Source: Shujianyang, Wikimedia Commons

China will launch its own asteroid redirection mission in 2025, a year earlier than originally planned, and to a different asteroid. They will also launch Tianwen-2, which will be sent to an asteroid, land, extract samples and return to Earth—much like Japan's Hayabusa-2 did in 2020 and NASA's OSIRIS-Rex did in 2023. These samples have revealed exciting features like amino acids, nucleobases (which go into making DNA) and organic compounds.[4]

China also operates the largest single-dish radio telescope on Earth, the Five-hundred-metre Aperture Spherical Telescope, or FAST, nicknamed Tianyan 天眼 ('Heavenly Eye'). This telescope is built into a natural depression on top of a mountain in remote Pingtang County, Guizhou. In Australia, by way of contrast, the largest single-dish radio telescope is 70 metres in diameter.

Commerce and defense in space

Like the United States, Europe, and Australia, China has commercial and military infrastructure in space, and is massively expanding its footprint there. China is second in spending on space projects and infrastructure, spending nearly four times what Russia spends annually.

SpaceX through its Starlink service, soon to be joined by Amazon with Kuiper, operates thousands of communications satellites to provide global high-speed internet. China has started building its own rival network this year, called Guo Wang 国网, or 'National Network'.

Since 2000, China has maintained its own Global Navigation Satellite System (GNSS)—the generic term for GPS. GPS is the US version of a GNSS network. China's is BeiDou, Russia operates GLONASS and Europe has Galileo. While all are similar in operation, GPS is still the most accurate. However, due to the importance and dependency of countries on these networks, in particular for defence, they operate their own.

China is also developing cutting edge space technology for government and defense purposes. China has also now built and flown what can only be described as a space drone. In the mid-2010s, Boeing built the X-37B for the US Space Force. Not much is known about it, but it is about a quarter the size of the old US Space Shuttle, can stay in orbit for more than four years and can land remotely.[5] It appears that China has also developed and launched its own space drone to do so.[6] Like the US versions, knowledge of the details of it and its capabilities are limited; however, it is most likely for flying and testing military payloads in orbit.

China will also soon enter the space tourism race. Blue Origin and Virgin Galactic have built dedicated space vehicles for short tourist flights. SpaceX and Axiom Space have also flown tourists into orbit and to the International Space Station. A Chinese company with mixed private and state ownership (partly funded by the Chinese Academy of Sciences), trading as CAS Space in English but actually called Guangzhou Zhongke Aerospace Exploration Technology Co. Ltd 广州中科宇航探索技术有限公司, is developing a system similar to that of Blue Origin: vehicles that will go about 100 kilometres above the surface of the Earth for a few minutes before returning.[7] Their aim is to start operations in 2025.

China, Russia and money

With only twenty years since the first Chinese taikonaut ventured into space, how has China caught up? There are a few reasons, two of which are money and Russia. The Russian space program itself, despite its long and proud history, is falling behind. A lack of investment and exciting projects, and a failure to embrace the private sector, has meant that Russia is no longer the power in space it used to be. However, it does have the experience and knowledge China has needed.

While China is rapidly developing its own expertise, its space scientists have taken advantage of Russian space heritage since 2000, most notably in the development of China's Tiangong Space Station. Agreements have led to the sharing of detailed knowledge, classified information, and technical advice.[8] As a result, Russia's scientists and space program can work on exciting projects, at the forefront of space exploration, without footing the whole bill. The two countries have worked on twenty missions together already.[9]

Just as the United States spent more than US$180 billion (in today's dollars) during the Apollo era, China is now rapidly increasing its spending, on space exploration and infrastructure. In 2020, it spent around US$10 billion, and in 2022, it spent US$12 billion.[10] As a result of investment and cooperation, China has now surpassed Russia in all measures of space exploration. When looking at the amount, sophistication and sheer variety of missions and programs China is leading compared to Russia, it is clear who the number 2 space power is.

The two countries have agreed to work together on Moon exploration—including building a Moon colony and a semi-permanent presence on the Moon. However, judging from such evidence as Russia's failed Luna 25 mission, Russia needs China more than China needs Russia.

View of Earth and satellite
Source: NASA, Unsplash

A decade ago, India was working with Russia on the Luna 25 probe, not having had its own experience with Moon exploration. Due to a lack of progress and the belief it could do it faster and better, India stopped working with Russia and worked alone. Its first attempt, Chandrayaan-2, failed three and a half years before Luna 25 reached the Moon. Its second attempt, Chandrayaan-3, succeeded in the same week as Russia's failed attempt to land Luna 25. The question is whether China will similarly outgrow its need for Russia.

As mentioned above, Russia will leave the International Space Station after 2024. The United States banned China from participation in the International Space Station in 2011. Fuelled by worries that cooperation would lead to technology that benefits China's military, the United States passed the Wolf Amendment. Russia announced plans to build its own space station during the early days of the Ukraine invasion, amid other political ploys involving space exploration, such as propaganda videos showing that they would leave an American astronaut in space[11] or even hold a UK company's satellites hostage.[12] However, it is unlikely to be ready in the next couple of years, if ever, due to the limited resources Russia's space program is suffering from. One option is for Russia to build modules and attach them to Tiangong—or work with China some other way. Tiangong was built in a modular fashion, like the International Space Station, allowing for new modules in the future. It would be another situation where Russia needs China more than China needs Russia.

The race to the top

Will China become the number 1 space power? The United States claims that title thanks to investment and cooperation between NASA, the United States military (e.g. Space Force) and private companies (Lockheed Martin, Boeing, SpaceX and so on), which has accelerated the US space program. The progress, spending and pure diversity of projects, whether for exploration or commercial purposes, is truly astounding: missions to the moons of Jupiter and Saturn, satellite networks that will use lasers instead of radio waves to transmit gigabytes of data per second, as well as dozens of small exploration missions planned every few years.

However, this model is not drastically different from what China is doing. The biggest point of difference is the way private companies operate in the two countries. The independence of US companies, which is greater than those in China, has spurred innovation and reinvigoration in the US space program. To challenge the United States for the top spot, China must continue the pace of its progress and find the right balance with the private space sector and innovation.

US companies have a level of independence that allows them to pursue innovation and seek new directions and technology that might not be the priority of the US government. As an example, the drive of private space travel from SpaceX, Blue Origin and others forced US companies to design systems that were cost effective and profitable. NASA frowned on private space travel for a long time. To accomplish it, private companies developed reusable rockets and capsules, making the cost of launching significantly cheaper—twenty-five times cheaper—than NASA's Space Shuttle. This cheaper access to space benefited not just private companies but also the research sector and the government itself. Until China has truly private companies that can determine their own directions, investments and subsequent priorities, the United States will remain top of the pecking order.

THE FRONTIERS OF HISTORY:

CHINA DISCOVERS

THE PACIFIC'S DARK

COLONIAL LEGACY

Graeme Smith

On a scorching hot afternoon in July 2023, the Prime Minister of Solomon Islands, Manneseh Sogavare, met with President Xi Jinping in the Great Hall of the People for the mandatory grip and grin for the cameras. China's official media had made much of Sogavare's visit, and he did not disappoint, remarking upon his arrival in China, 'I am back home' in a clip posted to Twitter by CGTN,[1] and later giving a fulsome interview on the same network in which he pronounced Xi a 'great man' and urged everyone to read all four volumes of *The Governance of China* 习近平谈治国理政, a collection of Xi's speeches and writings.[2]

Less noticed was what Sogavare—and the Pacific more broadly—received in return. A host of memorandums of agreement (MOAs) was signed, including the controversial security agreement, which was first leaked online by a provincial government adviser in 2022, but the final text, which covers military and police cooperation, has never been made public. China–Pacific relations also got their first policy slogan: the Four Fully Respects 四个充分尊重.[3] Much of it was boilerplate doggerel around 'win–win results' and 'shared benefits', but it also touched on 'cultural traditions of Pacific Island nations' and the need to support the 2050 Strategy for the Blue Pacific Continent—a regional strategy agreed on by Pacific Island Forum nations in 2019 to tackle climate change against the background of geostrategic competition.[4]

Unpromising beginnings

Less than a decade ago, China's knowledge of and interest in the Pacific was rudimentary at best. Back in 2013, I worked with a team of researchers from the Chinese Academy of International Trade and Economic Cooperation (CAITEC), a think tank affiliated with China's Ministry of Commerce (MOFCOM). One of their team was tasked with coming up with China's five-year plan for its relations with the Kingdom of Tonga, which would map out China's strategies for aid, investment and trade with the one Pacific nation never to have been colonised. It looked to be a sensitive mission.

Tonga already figured large in fears about China's intent in the region, with some analysts arguing that the kingdom might 'fall' to China as a result of debts owed to Export-Import Bank of China dating back to 2006.[5]

Beowa National Park, formerly Ben Boyd National Park
Source: Michael Dawes, Flickr

I had expected the researcher, fresh from a posting in Pakistan, to be familiar with the history of China's engagement with the kingdom, which switched its diplomatic allegiance from Taiwan in November 1998 as part of its confusingly named 'Look East' policy.[6] There was no shortage of entertaining detail for him to become familiar with: a 1996 deal brokered by the Tongan princess Pilolevu to lease Tonga's satellite spots to China after the kingdom—with the help of a colourful American businessman—had acquired the world's last 16 unoccupied orbital slots. Another deal that should have caught his attention was the origin story of China's 'debt trap diplomacy' in the Pacific, where the construction company China Civil Engineering Construction Corporation (CCECC) brokered a Export-Import Bank of China loan to rebuild Tonga's capital, Nuku'alofa, following anti-Chinese riots in 2006, breezily promising (never in writing) that the debt would be forgiven one day. China still holds nearly two-thirds of the kingdom's external debt.

To my disappointment, the researcher, flown out on the tab of the United Nations Development Program (UNDP) China to write his country report and assess sectors where Australia and China might team up on aid projects,[7] was not fully familiar with his brief. A week before heading to Shougang Airport for the long trip via Australia and New Zealand, he expressed surprise that he was not heading to Africa. He had assumed that he was off to Togo (*duoge* 多哥) rather than Tonga (*tangjia* 汤加).

Ten years since this unpromising start, a transformation has taken place. The Chinese government has invested in the teaching of Pacific languages— at Beijing Foreign Studies University, it is possible to study all the languages of China's Pacific diplomatic partners, even Cook Islands Maori. The field of Pacific studies is still relatively small,[8] although there are already six main research centres, led by the early mover: Sun Yat-sen University's Center for Oceania Studies, and the heavily funded Research Centre for Pacific Island Countries at Liaocheng University. The last benefits from a whole-of-university approach—even the vice chancellor at Liaocheng is engaged in Pacific studies—and institutional links to both the Shandong Provincial Government and the International Liaison Department, a Party agency charged with managing relations between the Communist Party of China (CPC) and foreign political parties.[9]

The quality of historical and political research coming out of China on the Pacific is still mixed. At one end, there are serious scholars equipped to engage in extended archival and field research in the Pacific and to conduct sophisticated analysis of how the Pacific is portrayed in China.[10] At the other end, I can recall an international conference in 2015 where participants sitting in the shade of the Great Hall Fale at the National University of Samoa silently exchanged incredulous glances as a senior academic from Liaocheng University shared her knowledge of an alleged secret plan by Banimarama's Fijian military to invade New Zealand.

Weaponising Pacific history

Despite such misfires, Chinese research on the Pacific has laid the foundations for strengthening ties with Pacific Island countries.

The Chinese state—and particularly its propaganda organs—is beginning to apply Mao's famous aphorism 'using the past past to serve the present' (*gu wei jin yong* 古为今用) to the Pacific. Alternatively, and more specifically, since the Chinese state had very little to do with the Pacific before the 1970s, it is using the West's Pacific colonial past to serve the present.

Although the Pacific was once relatively neglected, PRC academics with knowledge of it are in high demand to provide comment for outlets like the *Global Times*, China's influential nationalist tabloid. Such researchers as Yu Lei 于镭, from Shandong University, provide critical commentary about Western colonialism in the Pacific. In 2023 Australia agreed to resettle the entire population of Tuvalu under the Australia–Tuvalu Falepili Union treaty,[11] which had neocolonial overtones,[12] particularly Article 4, which stated: 'Tuvalu shall mutually agree with Australia any partnership, arrangement or engagement with any other State or entity on security and defence-related matters. Such matters include but are not limited to defence, policing, border protection, cyber security and critical infrastructure, including ports, telecommunications and energy infrastructure.' Commenting in the *Global Times*, Yu Lei argued the treaty demonstrated that 'former colonial powers' wanted these countries to remain 'politically subservient ... and economically reliant' on them through 'instructions and manipulation'.[13]

Although in its early stages, the popular deployment of historical narratives is likely to provide focus to China's discovery of Pacific colonial histories, as China—which has no historical baggage in the Pacific—looks to 'tell its story well' 讲好中国故事 in the Pacific. Part of that story is that unlike three of the other permanent members of the UN Security Council (the United States, the United Kingdom and France), China has not conducted any nuclear tests in the Pacific.

Chen Hong 陈弘, another prominent academic at East China Normal University and who gained the distinction in Australia of having his visa cancelled for allegedly trying to influence a NSW government backbencher,[14] was among the first to examine the deplorable nuclear legacy of the United States. His work has highlighted Operation Castle Bravo, the first of a series of tests on Bikini Atoll in the Marshall Islands, the first fusion nuclear bomb tested anywhere and still the most powerful nuclear device ever detonated by the United States.[15] The United States, the United Kingdom and France detonated 315 nuclear devices in the Pacific over three decades, including twelve in Australia.[16]

There are entire swathes of colonial history that China's commentariat have yet to exploit, presumably because they have yet to come across them. The practice of blackbirding, whereby Pacific islanders were often taken either by force or under false pretenses to provide slave labour for Queensland's sugar plantations, has yet to feature in the *Global Times*.

The frontiers of China's narrative competition

Future Chinese criticism of blackbirding, which began in the 1840s and was banned by law only in 1904, might not cause many current Australian politicians to lose sleep. But it would not hurt our standing in the region to make an official apology for the practice. The renaming of New South Wales's Ben Boyd National Park—named for Australia's first blackbirder— as Beowa National Park in 2022 was a good first step. But apologising for running a slave trade that tore tens of thousands of Pacific islanders from their families should not be a hard sell in Australia's parliament.

Australia's relations with Pacific Island countries have begun to evolve. If there is a moment we can look back on as a shift in Australia's relationship with the region, it might well be 18 October 2023, when the Pacific Engagement Visa (PEV) finally passed the Australian Senate with the support of the Greens and the crossbench. Bipartisan support for the PEV once looked likely, but the Coalition walked away from an initiative they once championed, objecting to the use of a lottery system.[17] The lottery element is why New Zealand's Samoa Quota and Pacific Access Visa (which the PEV is modelled on) are so popular—everyone can agree a random lottery is fair.

The significance of the PEV lies in its potential to transform Australia into a nation that looks more like the Pacific. When politicians turn their minds to the needs of Pacific constituents, as we see in New Zealand, the game will change. That is some way down the track, but the PEV is a start. Reams of research show that access to permanent migration is more effective than development assistance for Pacific islanders—and the gains to Pacific families are almost immediate. As Fiji's Deputy Prime Minister Biman Prasad argued, 'This is part of a broader strategy to integrate the region in the long term. And given the geopolitics as well, uniting the region in this way will benefit the whole of the region.'[18] Welcoming Pacific migrants is something that China cannot and will not do.

Despite the easy win represented by the PEV, bilateral competition in defence, economic ties and aid will continue to frame China and Australia's relations in the Pacific, with Australian governments of both stripes vying to be the 'partner of choice' for Pacific nations. Yet all three fields of contestation come with historical complications. Military needs—be they an airfield, a naval base or semi-automatic weapons—can be acted on much more quickly than economic or developmental needs. Nonetheless, Australia's military spending in the region continues to be shaped by historical concerns about the presence of a hostile power in its immediate vicinity, raised by political leaders as far back as 1883, and the need for Papua New Guinea to be a 'shield' against Asia, be it imperial Japan or newly independent Indonesia.[19] This reinforces a longstanding perception that Australia is more interested in securing the region's territory for its own safety than contributing to the well-being of Pacific peoples.

The American public might romanticise the United States' defining Pacific conflict, the battle of Guadalcanal, but it reminds Solomon Islanders of the problem of unexploded ordinance—a danger that remains to this day. This critique was made by a Solomon Islander who, as reported in the *Global Times*,[20] responded to US Ambassador to Australia Caroline Kennedy's declaration, 'We're coming back' with the words, 'But for what?'

Despite the tendency of the Australian and American publics to view our World War II engagement in the region positively—with Australian tales of the Kokoda Trail or the US focus on the battle of Guadalcanal—the conflicts of the past provide ammunition for China's anti-colonialist barbs.

Unlike China, Australian and US governments cannot direct their companies to invest in the region, even though this is what Pacific leaders from Rabuka to Sogavare are most keen on (Telstra's purchase of Digicel Pacific is the lonely exception[21]). While much ink has been spilt on the leverage provided by China's 'sky high debts',[22] the source of Beijing's sway over Pacific leaders is past and present investment and the promise of future projects. Qian Bo, China's abrasive special envoy to the Pacific, is known to regale his Pacific counterparts with derisory observations about Australia's economy and its inability to meet the Pacific's needs, either as a destination for Pacific exports or as a source of investment.

Although China's Pacific aid has plateaued since 2016,[23] China grounds its critique of other powers competing for influence in the region in its self-image as a developing nation, the provider of 'South–South cooperation' rather than 'aid'. On this front, Australia has a history of jumping at shadows. In 2021 the then foreign minister Marise Payne flew to Daru in Papua New Guinea in response to a (highly unlikely) proposed Chinese state-backed investment in a fish-processing plant on Australia's northern border. After this, China's representatives in Papua New Guinea suddenly started to mention the project in their talking points, having previously said nothing about it. With some glee, the *Global Times* cited a Facebook post by local governor Taboi Awi Yoto in the wake of her visit, claiming Australia wants 'us to be subsistence farmers and fishermen and maintain the status quo'.[24] With a bit of due diligence, the fuss could have been avoided. There was a reason MOFCOM had said nothing about the project. The company, which consisted of a couple of guys from Fujian kicking around Port Moresby, had no capacity to get the project off the ground.

The uptick in Australia's diplomatic relations with China might offer some protection from China's envoys snarking about Australia's colonial history, but China's political winds can change quickly (see 'Caution and Compromise in Australia's China Strategy, page 209). The best way to brace for a future narrative assault on Australia's Pacific history is to deal with it honestly, make reparations where appropriate, and encourage the United States, the United Kingdom and France to do the same. More importantly, Australia should continue on the path of becoming a nation that looks more like the Pacific. When Australian history becomes Pacific history, doing right by the region will not seem such a big ask.

八

CHAPTER 8:
THE POINTY END OF AUSTRALIA–CHINA RELATIONS

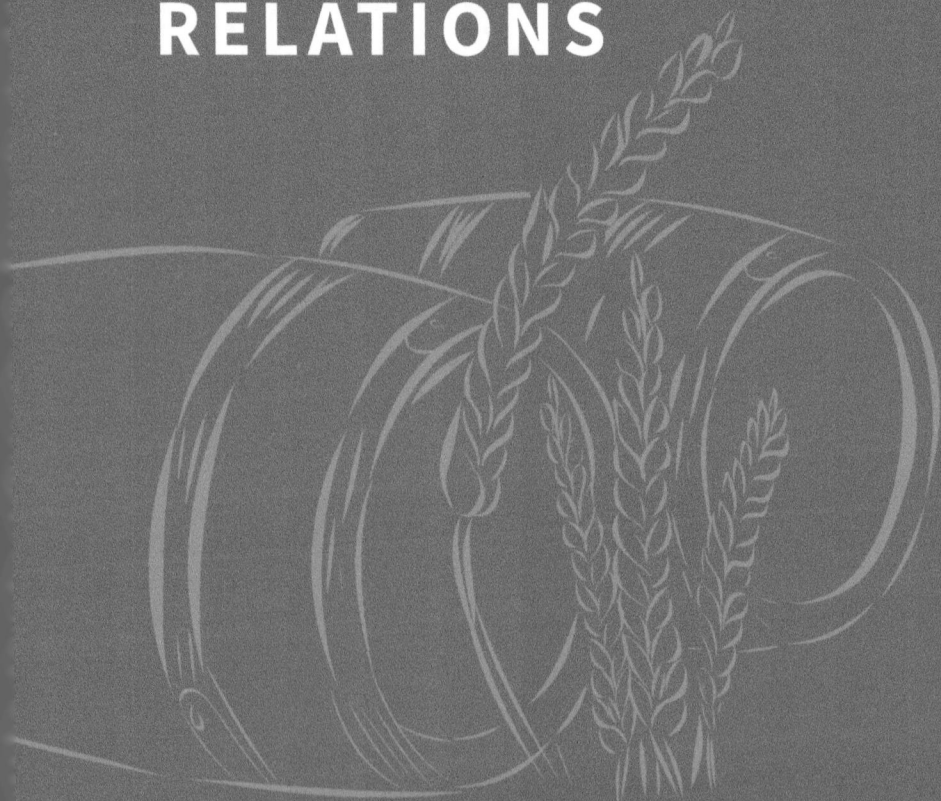

HOW FEARFUL IS CHINA'S

MILITARY RISE?

Edward Sing Yue Chan

During a meeting with delegates from the People's Liberation Army (PLA) and the People's Armed Police Force at the Fourteenth National People's Congress in March 2023, Xi Jinping called for the improvement of China's 'integrated national strategies and strategic capabilities' and to 'accelerate the modernisation of the army as a world-class armed force'.[1] His speech was seen as a signal of China's intention to speed up its military transformation. Indeed, in the new government budget announced in March 2023, Beijing revealed a yearly budget of RMB 1.55 trillion (US$224.8 billion), marking a 7.2 percent increase from the 2022 budget.[2]

Australia is increasingly concerned about China's military ambitions. The *Defence Strategic Review 2023*, released on 24 April 2023, suggests that 'China's military build-up is now the largest and most ambitious of any country since the end of the Second World War'. Whether or not the statement is true, it warns that China's military rise, 'without transparency or reassurance to the Indo-Pacific region … threatens the global rules-based order … that adversely impacts Australia's national interests'.[3] According to the Lowy Institute Poll 2022, 75 percent of Australians believe that China is very likely or somewhat likely to become a military threat to Australia in the next twenty years;[4] 88 percent said they were either very or somewhat concerned about China potentially opening a military base in a Pacific Island country.[5]

The governments of the United States and its allies are certainly responding to China's military rise. The Quadrilateral Security Dialogue (QUAD), a diplomatic and security network consisting of Australia, the United States, India and Japan, was revived in 2017 to promote 'an open, stable and prosperous Indo-Pacific that is inclusive and resilient'.[6] Since 2015, the US Navy has been patrolling in the South China Sea. By 10 April 2023, the US Navy had conducted forty-four reported freedom of navigation operations in the area. Particularly during the Trump administration, it navigated once every two months between 2018 and 2020 in the South China Sea.[7] Moreover, in September 2021, Australia, the United Kingdom and the United States announced a trilateral security pact, known as AUKUS. On 13 March 2023, the three countries agreed to increase nuclear submarine (SSN) port visits and training in Australia. More significantly, Australia will purchase at least three *Virginia*-class SSNs from the United States in the 2030s and build its first SSN with technical support from the two countries in the 2040s.[8]

Some media outlets are hyping up the possibility of war with China, suggesting that China will invade Taiwan by 2026 or engage in a war with the United States over freedom of navigation in the South China Sea.[9] However, many China analysts have argued that these claims are exaggerated and 'devoid of concrete analyses on China's intention and capability'.[10] So how much should Australia and its allies fear the PLA? Although numerous intelligence and defence reports are available, mostly from Washington, the public needs more context to understand China's military rise.

The US Navy has been patrolling the South China Sea since 2015
Source: U.S. Pacific Fleet, Flickr

Military transformation under Xi Jinping

Amid China's economic development, it has steadily increased its defence spending and military capability over the past three decades. According to the Stockholm International Peace Research Institute (SIPRI), China's military budget has increased by an average of 13 percent annually, with spending around 5 percent of the government's total budget throughout the last decade.[11] The PLA has developed numerous new types of military equipment, including the *J-20* fighters, *Jin*-class nuclear-powered ballistic missile submarines (SSBNs), *Shang-II*-class nuclear-powered attack submarines (SSNs), aircraft carriers, *DF-41* Intercontinental Ballistic Missiles (ICBMs) and other matériel researched, designed and built in China.[12]

China's military rise appears to have become more ambitious during the mid-2010s. The country has been in the thrall of the 'strong army dream' 强军梦, an integral part of the goal of national rejuvenation.[13] Xi Jinping, who chairs the Central Military Commission, also made a few speeches on China's military modernisation. For instance, in 2013, he advocated building armed forces that would 'obey the Party's command, that are able to fight and to win, and that maintain excellent conduct' in order to 'safeguard national sovereignty, security and development interests'.[14] In a series of speeches around 2016, he described the goal of PLA modernisation as being to 'achieve the goal of a strong army' and 'build a world-class military'. In 2017, he set out the three milestones for PLA development: basic mechanisation and major progress in 'informatisation' 信息化 by 2020, modernisation of national defence by 2035, and building an all-round world-class military by mid-century.[15] As political rhetoric, the military's three milestones echo the Party's 'Two Centennial Goals';[16] as military objectives, Chinese commentators and scholars describe a world-class military as having world-class operational theories, personnel, training, weapons and equipment, law-based management, combat power and innovation abilities.[17] Some also use these milestones to address the military's shortcoming in mechanisation, informatisation, intellectualisation and operation.[18]

The PLA has undergone several significant reforms during this period. In 2015, the People's Liberation Army Rocket Force (PLARF) was established to coordinate China's arsenal of land-based ballistic missiles, including nuclear weapons. In 2016, the PLA reorganised its seven theatre commands into five, each designed to counter different security threats: Eastern Theatre Command is responsible for Taiwan, Southern Theatre Command for the South China Sea, Western Theatre Command for the Sino-Indian border, and Northern Theatre Command for North Korea. In 2019, the Central Military Commission adopted a new military strategy for the PLA titled 'Military Strategic Guidelines for the New Era' to address the shift of strategic assessment outlined in the 2019 National Defence White Paper aimed at countering growing threats from the United States and Taiwan.[19] These structural reforms, according to the 2023 Pentagon Report, have strengthened the PLA's joint operations and capabilities.[20] However, as Joel Wuthnow and M. Taylor Fravel have suggested, this 'new' strategy was proposed against the backdrop of Xi's ideological consolidation and indicated little operational or strategic change.[21] Concepts from previous military doctrines, such as 'near sea active defence', 'informatisation war' and 'integrated joint operations', are still included in the 2019 military doctrine.[22] Indeed, after undergoing these military reforms, the PLA still lacks capabilities and combat experiences in amphibious operations, especially in the course of actions against Taiwan.

Xi's speech at the Two Sessions merely summarises China's continual military development, rather than signifying substantial changes in the timeline of national defence modernisation. The PLA is still gradually addressing its technological and operational limitations. The State Council Institutional Reform Plan 2023 unveiled significant steps to restructure the Ministry of Science and Technology, including the establishment of a Central Commission on Science and Technology 中央科技委员会 to enhance the party's leadership over scientific and technological development.[23]

The reform intended to '[push] forward the building of a national innovation system and structural scientific and technological reform, [study] and deliberat[e] major strategies, plans and policies for the country's sci-tech development, and coordinat[e] efforts to resolve major issues of strategic, guiding and fundamental significance in the sci-tech sector'.[24] Although the PLA's structure is not affected by the reform, the goal of the reform, including addressing the limitation of technological self-reliance and promoting integrated research between the civil and the military, falls in line with some of the PLA's objectives in its military modernisation.[25] Defence science and technology has been crucial in China's technological innovation,[26] so institutional reform in science and technology is relevant to national defence modernisation. Following the State Council reform focused on the sci-tech sector this year, we should see further reforms within the PLA to ground force, logistics and maintenance support, military staff training, and integrated warfare.

Will China wage a war?

The large-scale military exercises around Taiwan in early April (as a response to President Tsai Ing-wen's meeting with US Speaker of the House Kevin McCarthy) suggests that the PLA has become more capable in integrated warfare and deployment of aircraft carriers.[27] Nonetheless, military capability building is a gradual process. While the PLA has the budget and resources for research development, personnel training lags behind technological advances. For instance, a report from the US Naval War College suggests that the Chinese navy has 'faced tremendous pressure to keep pace with the rapid expansion and modernisation of the [naval] surface fleet and its growing mission set'.[28] According to an article published in a Chinese military magazine last year, the PLA Navy needs at least 200 pilots for its aircraft carriers, but it lacks a fighter trainer specifically designed for carrier-based operations.[29] Therefore, although the PLA Navy built its third aircraft carrier last year, construction of the fourth one was stalled.[30] More importantly, apart from a border skirmish with Vietnam in 1979 and a minor naval battle at the Johnson South Reef in 1988, also against Vietnam, the PLA has not fought in a war for more than four decades. It still lacks experience in warfare.

Multiple organisations in the United States, including the US Air Force, the Center for International and Strategic Studies (CSIS) and the Center for a New American Security (CNAS), have already simulated a few war games of the PLA pursuing military operations against Taiwan but with varying results.[31] Some suggest that in a war between China and Taiwan, China would likely win. However, we should factor US domestic political consideration into the hype of a war scenario. The outcome of war game simulations needs to be weighed against the fact that they are often intentionally skewed in favour of US forces in order to strive for more resources for national defence.

Whether China has the capability to wage war and whether China will go to war are two different questions. As the US Director of National Intelligence Avril Haines told the House Intelligence Committee, 'It is not our assessment that China wants to go to war.'[32] The concept of a world-class military, as Taylor Fravel, an expert in Chinese military strategy, argued, does not 'illuminate the PLA's global ambitions or how it envisions using force'. It has limited geopolitical implication of where China would project its military power. Rather, it expresses 'China's aspiration to become a leading military power in the world'.[33] It is essential to distinguish the differences between China's military ambition and policy outcomes.

Launching a war in the Indo-Pacific is complicated. Strategically as well as politically, the PRC would prefer to win Taiwan without fighting.[34] It needs to consider the consequences of sanctions and sea lane supply blockages from the West if there is a war across the strait.

Will AUKUS help to deter China's use of force?

There is no doubt that China's military capability is on the rise. The AUKUS security pact has been described as a 'demonstration of unity and ... [a] powerful deterrence signal to the region'.[35] To the United States, AUKUS indicates its commitment in maintaining its pivotal role in the Indo-Pacific. To Australia, AUKUS suggests that Australia is more likely to rely on 'the US committing to the "integrated deterrence" approach that the Biden administration set out in its 2022 Indo-Pacific strategy'.[36] As Ben Herscovitch suggests, 'If Australia chooses to deploy its nuclear-powered submarines in support of a US-led effort to defend Taiwan, then AUKUS will have made China's military goals harder to achieve.'[37]

However, it is important to note that the submarines themselves do not serve as a deterrent. The AU$368 billion deal is a long-term process, and the first of the new submarines is not expected to be delivered until at least the 2040s. By that time, it is likely that the PLA will have developed sufficient means for countering the AUKUS-class submarines, such as anti-ship missiles, SSNs, ballistic missile nuclear submarines, as well as other anti-submarine capabilities, which China is currently building. In fact, the US Congress Research Service report suggested in 2022 it is likely China will have a new class of SSN by the mid-2020s.[38] Furthermore, China's naval development consists of an aspiration to expand its influence globally, beyond the close waters of Taiwan, in which a submarine deal is simply incapable to deter.[39]

AUKUS submarines themselves do not serve as a deterrent
Source: Royal Navy

In addition, it is dangerous to have naval procurement driving the state's grand strategy. Traditionally, a grand strategy articulates clear security goals for a state to set all aspects of foreign policy, ranging from trade agreements to defence budget.[40] It is true that AUKUS is beyond a military exchange; it is also an investment in ideas, education, research, and community ties for Australia.[41] However, rather than establishing distinct security and strategic goals and generating a range of policy alternatives, experts warn that AUKUS, as a singular policy, has now manifested Australia's security decision-making. This could potentially limit Canberra's array of security choices.[42] In a worse scenario, it might draw Australia into a nuclear war because its continual support of US deterrence against China.[43]

What, then, is AUKUS for? Since the deal was announced in March 2023, Australian experts have debated its strategic implications.[44] As the Lowy Institute's Sam Roggeveen submits, there is a bigger question the Albanese government must answer: 'how exactly will these submarines make Australia safer'?[45] Australia must take China's military rise seriously, but it is not helpful to assume that this will inevitably lead to war. Instead, Canberra should approach this comprehensively and cautiously, and develop a clearer understanding of China's military rise under Xi Jinping as well as its strategic goals and institutional reforms. There also needs to be a wider and more constructive public debate about the best ways to respond to China's rise and to safeguard Australia's security in the broadest sense of the term.

CAUTION AND COMPROMISE

IN AUSTRALIA'S

CHINA STRATEGY

Benjamin Herscovitch

Policy consistency and diplomatic decorum have been the dominant themes of Canberra's publicly advertised approach to Beijing since the May 2022 federal election. The Albanese Labor government has reaffirmed all its Coalition predecessor's major China-related national security and defence priorities. Among other areas of policy continuity, Australia under Albanese is still trying to minimise China's security role in the Pacific, expand US military presence at Australian ports and airfields, combat Chinese government interference in domestic politics, and acquire nuclear-powered submarines through the AUKUS security partnership with the United States and the United Kingdom (see 'How Fearful is China's Military Rise?', page 199).

This broad policy continuity has been combined with a significant shift in Australia's diplomatic messaging. Gone is the talk of it being 'inconceivable' that Australia would not support the United States if it was involved in military conflict, including with China over Taiwan.[1] Meanwhile, Australian ministers no longer make historical comparisons between the challenge posed by China today and the threat of 'belligerent autocrats' in the 1930s.[2] Instead, Prime Minister Anthony Albanese and his ministers have sought to 'engage diplomatically, without a loudhailer' and guide the relationship 'with all the nuance that is required'.[3]

It is not wrong to say that the Albanese government's approach to China combines policy continuity and conciliatory rhetoric. But it is also far from the full story. This characterisation glosses over two central elements of the Albanese government's China strategy: caution and compromise. Although Canberra has not sought to advertise these aspects of its China strategy, they have been integral and enduring features since the election of the Albanese government.

Tactical caution

Despite sharing many of the China policy objectives of its predecessor, the Albanese government has taken a cautious approach to implementation. This is apparent in its handling of Confucius Institutes and Chinese investments in critical minerals. Like the Coalition before it, Labor has sought to mitigate the perceived security risks associated with exposure to Chinese investors and education links. But, unlike its predecessor, the Albanese government has pursued this objective in ways that minimise Beijing's ire.

Under the Foreign Relations Act (FRA) legislated in 2020 by the Morrison Coalition government, Minister for Foreign Affairs Penny Wong could have expelled Confucius Institutes from Australian universities. The Albanese government instead sought to achieve its national security goals without diplomatic fallout by opting for ongoing scrutiny. With the Albanese government 'concerned about foreign interference and potential risks to academic freedom', it pledged to 'keep these arrangements under review' and ruled out the establishment of new Confucius Institutes.[4]

The Albanese government has ruled out the establishment of new Confucius Institutes
Source: Matt Brown, Flickr

Likewise, the securitisation of the critical minerals industry appears to have been finessed to avoid antagonising Beijing, which has longstanding concerns about Australia's treatment of Chinese companies.[5] The Albanese government twice rejected investments from Chinese or China-linked firms in Australian rare-earth elements and lithium mining companies in 2023.[6]

Yet both decisions coincided with Canberra approving large Chinese investments in parts of the mining industry deemed to be less sensitive, including iron ore and nickel.[7] Coincidence cannot be ruled out. But the pattern of rejections coinciding with approvals and the influence of senior cabinet members over investment decisions suggest that the Albanese government is seeking simultaneously to keep Chinese and China-linked companies out of the critical minerals industry while also sending a welcoming message to Chinese investors more broadly and thereby reducing the likelihood of getting Beijing offside.

Might the Coalition have charted such a tactically cautious course on Confucius Institutes and investment decisions had they retained government? Maybe, although the Coalition's use of the FRA to veto Victoria's Belt and Road Initiative agreements in 2021 and their criticisms of the Albanese government's conditional acceptance of existing Confucius Institutes suggest not.[8] On two sensitive bilateral issues, the Albanese government has acted tactically: opting to put Confucius Institutes on notice and yet avoid the blunt trauma of expulsion, and soothing the sting of critical minerals investment rejections with the balm of approvals in other industries.

Policy compromise

The Albanese government's approach to China is defined not just by the tactics employed but also the decisions not taken. Most conspicuously, the Albanese government has decided not to sanction Chinese officials and entities implicated in severe and systematic human rights abuses.[9] Although the power to impose Magnitsky-style sanctions was legislated in 2021, Australia has declined to use these powers against China as the United States, Canada, the United Kingdom and the European Union have done. Despite 82 percent of Australians supporting such targeted sanctions against China and credible reports of ongoing mass incarcerations, forced removals of children, and cultural erasure in Xinjiang, Tibet and other regions, the Albanese government is unwilling to deny the perpetrators the freedom to travel to Australia and take advantage of financial opportunities there.[10]

Morality aside, the case for sanctions is far from clear-cut when viewed from the perspective of the Australian national interest. Imposing sanctions on officials and entities implicated in human rights abuses seems unlikely to change the Chinese government's behaviour. It might also have unintended negative implications for a wide range of Australian priorities. It is likely that China would respond with reprisals such as tit-for-tat countersanctions, arbitrarily detaining Australian citizens, prolonging the detention of Australians already imprisoned in China, and stalling or perhaps even reversing the progressive normalisation of the bilateral diplomatic and trade relationship.[11]

Still, not only did Minister for Foreign Affairs Wong tentatively support targeted sanctions against China when in opposition but also the Albanese government has committed to 'employ every strategy at [Australia's] disposal towards upholding human rights, consistent with our values and with our interests'.[12] Despite this and having levelled numerous targeted sanctions against Iran, Myanmar and Russia since taking office, the Albanese government has shied away from taking similar actions against China.[13] Taken together, this makes the Albanese government's unwillingness to sanction Chinese officials and entities look like a calculated compromise.

The responses to Beijing's anti-dumping and countervailing duties on Australian barley and wine similarly point to the role of policy compromise in Canberra's China strategy (see 'Ending Economic Sanctions: The Role of Chinese Industry Associations in the Removal of Barriers on Australian Barley and Wine', page 217). Rather than pursuing Australia's World Trade Organization (WTO) cases against China to their likely successful conclusions, Canberra chose to suspend and in the case of barely also discontinue proceedings in exchange for the review and eventual removal of duties.[14] Although Australia thereby lost opportunities to highlight China's trade malfeasance via the outcomes of these WTO processes, these decisions likely helped Australian barley and in all likelihood wine exporters once again to access the Chinese market. These decisions probably secured the quicker negotiated removal of trade restrictions, which pursuing the legal route might not have delivered. But these cases remain textbook definitions of compromise, involving as they did mutual concessions from both Canberra and Beijing to settle disputes.

The Albanese government has decided not to sanction Chinese officials and entities
Source: Michael Lieu, Flickr

Canberra might have compromised in other less clear-cut cases as well. According to the Chinese government, the process for the expected eventual removal of wine duties in March 2024 was made possible by the Australian Anti-Dumping Commission's preliminary finding that anti-dumping measures on Chinese wind towers should expire in April 2024.[15] Meanwhile, despite Prime Minister Albanese decrying Chinese company Landbridge Group's 99-year lease of Darwin Port when he was in opposition, his government decided to leave the lease in place.[16] This decision was welcomed by China and publicly announced in the immediate lead-up to Prime Minister Albanese's visit to Shanghai and Beijing in November 2023.[17] In another apparent compromise, the Albanese government used language in early October 2023 that gave the impression of legal rigour regarding the Chinese government's eventual release of long-detained Australian journalist Cheng Lei, despite her detention most likely having been an example of Chinese government hostage diplomacy.[18]

None of these recent cases are unambiguous compromises. The Albanese government insists that the Australian Anti-Dumping Commission is independent and has not shifted recommendations to please China.[19] At the same time, the review of Landbridge Group's Darwin Port lease was classified, and it is therefore not possible to determine whether it amounted to a decision to keep China happy by not annulling the lease.[20] Still, this series of China-friendly decisions suggests that the Albanese government's policy compromises might extend beyond not imposing targeted sanctions and suspending WTO proceedings.

Invidious choices and the costs of compromise

Some looming policy decisions do not seem to permit the kind of supple tactical gymnastics that the Albanese government has pulled off to date. These include whether to join proposed US measures to restrict foreign capital flows into select Chinese technology companies, and the choice between the Chinese and Taiwanese bids to join the Comprehensive and Progressive Agreement for Trans-Pacific Partnership (CPTPP) trade pact. But Canberra could still avoid being wedged by binary choices on these issues as well.

Building on the October 2022 export controls on semiconductors and related equipment to China, in August 2023 the United States proposed outbound investment restrictions to limit access to foreign capital for select Chinese technology companies.[21] As a minor player in the global semiconductor market, Australia was not pushed to join the export controls. But now the United States is sounding out the willingness of significant investors in China, including Australia, to participate in the proposed outbound restrictions on capital flows.[22]

These mooted capital restrictions seem to put Australia in a bind: either comply with Washington's request and deeply frustrate Beijing or not restrict capital flows into select Chinese technology firms and rebuff a request for support from Australia's most powerful ally. The former decision would likely damage Australia's bilateral relationship with China, while the latter might be diplomatically untenable, especially while the United States is sharing some of its most sensitive military technology with Australia. But even on this seemingly fraught policy dilemma, it is not clear that Canberra will be forced to make such an invidious choice—at least for now. The Biden administration's outbound investment restrictions have only been proposed, and the path for this kind of policy by executive order is likely to be long and uncertain given the vicissitudes of politics in Washington, especially in the run-up to the 2024 presidential election. So, with any luck, Australia will be insulated for some time yet from having to decide whether to sign up to this adversarial financial element of US China policy.

Canberra is also likely to be shielded from making any tough CPTPP choices. Yes, Beijing will heap pressure on Canberra and other capitals to back its bid just as Taipei lobbies for support for its candidature.[23] Yet the slow-moving and consensus-based CPTPP decision-making process and the trade pact's diverse membership mean that Australia might be able to sidestep taking any public positions on China's and Taiwan's competing bids.[24] With Japan, among others, wary of China's membership and smaller CPTPP members unlikely to back Taipei's accession for fear of frustrating Beijing, there is every chance that Canberra will be able to avoid having to cast the deciding vote.[25] Australia might even be able to secure better diplomatic and trade treatment from China thanks to Beijing's bid to get into the CPTPP. For as long as China is trying to work its way into this trade pact, Beijing will have an added incentive to play nice with CPTPP members like Australia.

The Albanese government's formula of China policy consistency and diplomatic decorum combined with a side of tactical caution and policy compromise will continue to be pressure tested. Reports of Chinese state-owned firms sending dual-use technology to sanctioned Russian defence companies point to how much strain the formula might come under as the case grows for punishing Beijing's support for Moscow's war effort in Ukraine.[26] But if Canberra's shrewd manoeuvrings to date are a guide, there is good reason to think that the Albanese government will continue to find ways to combine broadly tough China policy settings with ongoing relationship repair.

Still, as China's systematic and severe human rights abuses continue, past policy compromises will become difficult to defend. Statecraft does not allow much space for saintliness. Principled measures to punish human rights abusers might simply entail too much risk for the national interest. But we should at least honestly and openly recognise the moral impost of the Albanese government's so-far successful China strategy.

ENDING ECONOMIC

SANCTIONS:

THE ROLE OF CHINESE

INDUSTRY ASSOCIATIONS

IN THE REMOVAL OF

BARRIERS ON AUSTRALIAN

BARLEY AND WINE

Scott Waldron, Darren J. Lim and
Victor A. Ferguson

Under what conditions does China terminate politically motivated barriers to trade? In August 2023, China announced it would remove tariffs on Australian barley that were imposed amid bilateral tensions in May 2020. The removal was widely celebrated for enabling the resumption of a trade that had been worth up to US$1 billion annually. Barley was one of the most prominent of at least nine Australian export commodities targeted by China in an apparent sanctions campaign.[1] Although barriers on barley and five other commodities were removed by the end of 2023, three others remained in place, most notably for Australian bottled wine.

One possible explanation for the progress on barley focuses on foreign policy drivers. The barriers might have been removed due to warming bilateral relations under a new Australian government and a transition to a bargaining phase in the relationship. Another possibility is that Beijing dismantled the tariffs to avoid the potential reputational costs that might stem from the public release of a panel report adverse to China by the World Trade Organization (WTO).[2] Here, we consider the logic of these two arguments, and introduce a third underexplored explanation: the vested interests of groups within China, both government and non-government, and especially industry associations.

Examining the factors driving the removal of the barriers to Australian barley imports provides insight into a wider question that has received scant attention: when and why China removes sanctions. Although a burgeoning scholarly literature examines the termination of Western economic sanctions, it has not considered China.[3] New insights on this issue could have significant policy implications. Most immediately, they are relevant to ongoing negotiations about the removal of China's barriers on Australian wine. Many expect that the 'template' used in the barley negotiations—combining warming diplomatic relations with the concession of withdrawing a WTO case—will be successfully applied a second time.[4] This appears to be playing out at the time of writing. On the back of some recent Australian decisions that might have sweetened the deal,[5] Beijing has agreed to conduct a five-month review of its wine tariffs due to conclude in May 2024, and Canberra has temporarily suspended its WTO case.[6] Unlike the case for barley, however, Beijing's review may be complicated by substantially different underlying domestic political economy dynamics in the wine industry, which could well determine whether the tariffs ultimately stand or fall.

The imposition and removal of the barley tariffs

The origins of China's barriers on Australian barley go back to 2018. In October that year, the China Chamber of International Commerce (CCIC 中国国际商会) requested that the Ministry of Commerce (MOFCOM 商务部) investigate the dumping of Australian barley on the Chinese market.[7] MOFCOM began its investigation in November. On 28 May 2020, after China–Australia relations had slipped into free fall, MOFCOM handed down its ruling and applied tariffs of 80.5 percent (73.6 percent anti-dumping, 6.9 percent anti-subsidy) on the import of Australian barley.[8] The barriers reduced a trade of US$1 billion in 2018 to zero in 2021.

Although cautioned by some commentators,[9] the then government took the matter to the WTO dispute settlement system in December 2020.[10] After two and a half years of deliberation, the WTO issued its draft panel report confidentially to the parties. This appeared to expedite bilateral negotiations for a resumption of trade, whereby Australia agreed to suspend its WTO complaint in April 2023 while MOFCOM undertook to conduct a three-month review of its tariffs.[11] After extending the review from three to four months, China removed the barriers in August 2023.[12] The WTO case was subsequently settled,[13] and within weeks large shipments of barley set sail from Australia for China.[14]

What enabled this to happen?

Explanation 1: Warming bilateral relations

The first explanation focuses on the state of the bilateral relationship between Australia and China. If imposition of the barriers—or at least a failure to negotiate their removal—stemmed from a range of political grievances on the part of Beijing,[15] something was needed to enable a warming of the relationship. In this case, a change of Australian government following an election in May 2022 created the opportunity for both sides to move beyond positions hardened over the previous two years, first to resume high-level talks (previously rebuffed by Beijing) and later to negotiate the tariff's removal. Critical of their predecessors' rhetorical hostility towards China, the incoming government under Prime Minister Anthony Albanese stressed a change in tone even as it made clear there was no change in underlying interests. The goal was to 'stabilise' the relationship without making substantive concessions on any of the grievances believed to be motivating China's sanctions.[16] The Albanese government would, however, refrain from adopting new policies[17] that may have been seen by Beijing as provocative, and which would have disrupted relations and the resolution of the trade disputes (see 'Caution and Compromise in Australia's China Strategy', page 209). A change in government and tone, and the resulting resumption of high-level contact, were likely major factors in causing Beijing to remove sanctions. However, the stabilisation of the political relationship alone cannot explain the removal's timing and sequencing, nor does it alone offer decisive indication that the remaining barriers will be removed.

Explanation 2: The WTO dispute and aversion to hypocrisy costs

A second explanation is specific to barley itself and relates to the confidential draft panel report that was released to the Chinese and Australian governments shortly before the parties announced the suspension of the WTO dispute and Beijing's review of the duties.[18] The content of the draft report is not known and unlikely ever to be released. However, the decision was likely favourable to Australia due to significant weaknesses in China's arguments that Australia had been dumping barley on its market.[19]

This explanation, also rooted in foreign policy logics, attributes Beijing's removal of the barriers to the impending adverse decision. But why would the Chinese government be so reluctant for the panel report to be released? After all, China has lost WTO disputes in the past.

One possibility is that policy-makers were particularly sensitive about this case given it related to measures that had openly been characterised as coercive sanctions. Although China is alleged to have deployed economic coercion in multiple cases over the past two decades, none of the underlying measures have ever been formally ruled upon by the WTO. The only case to come close—one concerning Canadian canola—was also resolved via negotiation before a panel report was issued.[20]

The panel report would not have ruled on whether China's measures were 'coercive' or 'sanctions', but rather likely presented a detailed critique of the compatibility of China's approach with WTO anti-dumping rules. Nevertheless, Beijing might have wished to avoid a formal rebuke of its measures, which would give even more ammunition to critics arguing that the tariffs were 'blatant economic coercion',[21] rather than legitimate trade measures. In other words, it may have sought to avoid 'hypocrisy costs'.[22] Chinese officials have annually denounced the use of sanctions—so-called unilateral coercive measures—as a violation of international law at the United Nations General Assembly (UNGA) and other international forums since the 1990s.[23] Policy-makers may have had concerns that to be seen to be using sanctions might damage China's credibility and reputation in world politics (especially with states that sign onto its anti-sanction UNGA resolutions).[24]

According to this explanation, the draft WTO panel report created the space for a negotiated solution. It generated additional incentive for Beijing to find an alternative and avoid a formal and public ruling against it, thereby aligning with the goals of Australian industry and government to resume exports as soon as possible. Both sides preferred an outcome in which barriers were amicably removed.

One might think this explanation would generate optimism about wine, given that Beijing agreed to conduct a similar review in tandem with Australia suspending its WTO case.[25] However, it is possible that leverage from the WTO ruling alone was insufficient in achieving this outcome for barley, as we explain in the next section.

A third factor: Domestic drivers of China's barrier imposition and removal

One factor that is often overlooked in analyses of China's use of politically motivated trade barriers is the role of domestic interest groups and domestic policy objectives. As we have argued elsewhere,[26] these factors are important in understanding the logic of the sanctions imposed on Australia. Likewise, they may help explain their removal.

The imposition of barriers on barley

Policy-makers. Although China's barley tariffs could have been partly motivated by a coercive objective when they were imposed in 2020, the original 2018 anti-dumping investigation was driven by agricultural protectionism.[27] In particular, as revealed in legal case documents and other substantive reports on the issue,[28] Chinese policy-makers were acutely concerned with issues of food security or the 'choke point' 卡脖子 in China's barley supply.[29]

From a peak in the mid-1990s, China's domestic barley production has undergone a long-term decline. By the period of anti-dumping investigation (2017–18), domestic supply accounted for an exceptionally low 11 percent of total barley supply. At the same time, barley imports for brewing and livestock feed accelerated, especially after 2015, with Australian companies accounting for an exceptionally high 75 percent of all imports in some years (see figure 1). Chinese officials argued that the imports led to losses in farmers' incomes in the less developed areas of China where most barley is grown.

The barriers appear designed to arrest these trends, driven by a range of party and state units that have an interest in food security, including the Ministry of Agriculture and Rural Affairs (MARA 农业农村部), which assisted with the investigation.

Industry associations. Like other products, barley is grown both as an agricultural commodity and an industrial input (for brewing and livestock feed).[30] This brings into competition sectoral interests between agriculture and industry that need to be adjudicated at a higher level.

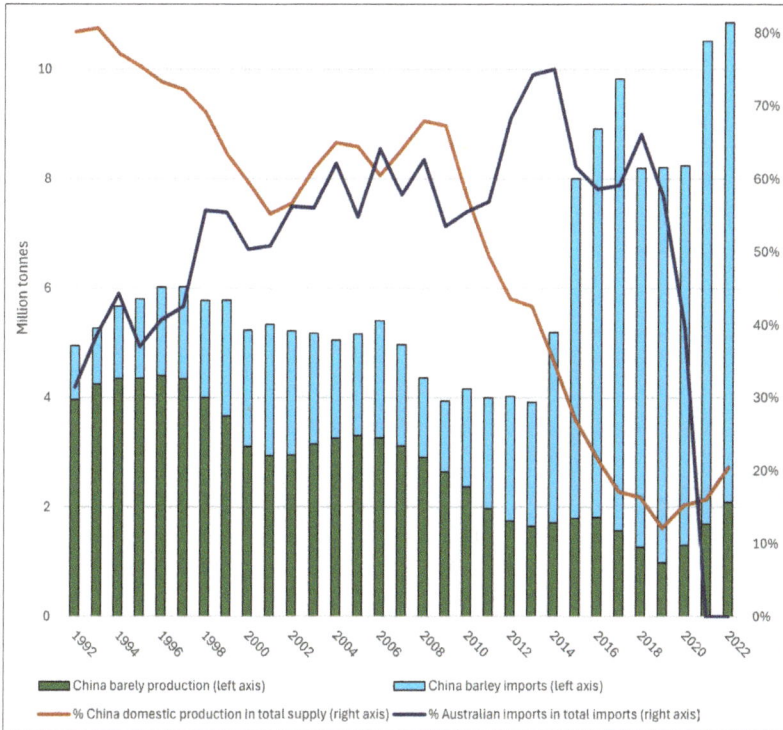

Figure 1: China's barley balance, 1992–2022
Source: *China Rural Statistical Yearbook*, UNComtrade

Industry associations and chambers of commerce are key players, both as representatives of their industries and as conduits for the interests of the party-state.

Although there is an array of industry organisations in China, the more established and influential organisations are a vestige of the central planning era, when government departments with specialised economic functions managed the operations of state-owned enterprises under their control. During administrative reforms in the 1990s, many specialised economic departments were devolved to become industry associations, comprising enterprise members that pay membership fees for representation and services. Reforms starting in 2016 and implemented through to 2019 aimed to further decouple associations and chambers of commerce from the party-state administratively, with caveats.[31] The key powers of party-building in associations were to be centralised and led by the Party Committee of the State-owned Assets Supervision and Administration Commission of the State Council (SASAC 国务院国有资产监督管理委员会), while foreign affairs were more clearly placed within the purview of the relevant (party-state) organs. A framework of state corporatism has been used to describe the ties that bind the party-state to associations and their enterprise members.[32]

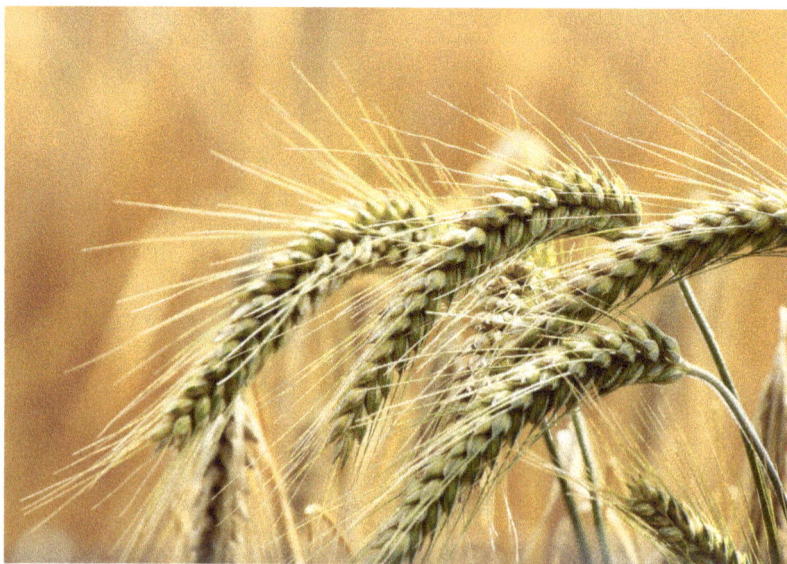

Barley was one of the most prominent export commodities targeted by China
Source: Marek Studzinski, Unsplash

Barley provides an interesting case study in industry representation. Barley is grown in China by a multitude of individual households not represented by any industry organisation and so, by default, by government. Jurisdiction over barley production and farmer incomes from agricultural activities like barley lies with MARA. The ministry has long been concerned about China's balance of production, consumption, and trade for barley.[33]

Government units rarely make anti-dumping applications.[34] The organisation chosen to apply for the dumping investigation on Australian barley was the China Chamber of International Commerce (CCOIC), which has a mandate to represent the interests of Chinese enterprises in international trade and investment. CCOIC falls under the umbrella of the China Council for the Promotion of International Trade (CCPIT 中国国际贸易促进委员会).[35] CCPIT has a vast network of branches within China, a legal affairs department and a network of overseas law firms used for dealing with anti-dumping, subsidy and safeguard issues.[36] It also runs the Economic and Trade Friction Early Warning System 中国国际贸易促进委员会经贸摩擦预警管理系统, which includes an international agricultural branch 中国国际商会农业行业经贸摩擦预警中心.

While the CCOIC notionally represents enterprises with foreign interests, the barriers on Australian barley are contrary to the interests of enterprises that use it for brewing and livestock feed. This is particularly the case for beer brewers that are members of the China Alcoholic Drinks Association (CADA 中国酒业协会). CADA has origins as a department within the former Ministry (and then Bureau) of Light Industry before being moved into SASAC. It gained greater administrative independence in the 2016–19 association reforms but retains links to the party-state.

CADA has been a participant in at least six international trade cases, either to support trade barriers (Australian wine, EU wine, US distillers' grains, EU brandy) or to oppose them (Australian barley, US sorghum). The differing positions reflect differences in the characteristics of alcoholic drinks, including the inputs and outputs used in manufacturing and the relationship with adjacent products (ethanol and various livestock feeds). Different interests are expressed through branches within CADA, representing at least eight types of alcohol including *baijiu*, beer and wine. Barley is of primary concern to the CADA Beer Sub-Association (CBSA 中国酒业协会啤酒分会) and the Beer Raw Material Expert Committee (中国酒业协会啤酒原料专业委员会).[37] With seventy-three members, CBSA is powerful and has a strong interest in maintaining supplies of Australia's malting barley. The attraction of Chinese brewers to Australian barley was not just access to consistent supplies of high-quality malting barley but also access to a lower-priced grade of barley ('Fair Average Quality') permitted under China's food laws for use in food (including beer) rather than being relegated to feed use.

CBSA made a forceful submission against the tariffs on Australian barley in the initial anti-dumping investigation in 2020, but to no avail. Policy-makers concerned with agriculture and food security and the foreign policy preferences of the central government held sway in the initial round leading to the imposition of barriers. There was no prospect for an early reversal in 2020–22, a period of high tensions from COVID-19, strained international relations, the dual circulation policy to promote self-reliance and heightened concerns about food security,[38] including for non-staple foods.[39]

The removal of barriers on barley

For Chinese policy-makers, the tariffs had generated mixed success by 2023. As shown for the period 2020–22 in figure 1, the tariffs successfully stopped Australian barley imports, forcing brewers and livestock companies to diversify inputs to other sources (Argentina, France, Canada, Ukraine). However, total imports in the period increased significantly, mainly for livestock feed. The trade barriers on Australian barley did not in themselves provide the protection that would generate an increase in Chinese barley production.[40] China did, however, use the period to pursue new domestic policy measures, including breeding, research and revised industry standards,[41] as well as the building of new barley production areas for breweries in China.[42]

Official statistics report a doubling of Chinese barley production over the period in which Australian barley was blocked (2019–22), but this is a statistical quirk. From 2020 onwards, reporting on Chinese barley production (*damai* 大麦) included a different variety, highland barley (*qingke* 青稞) grown in Tibet, Sichuan, Yunnan and Qinghai: this doubled the reported planted area and production of 'barley'. Nevertheless, with diversification away from Australian barley, policy-makers might have concluded that the barriers had served their purpose, or had abandoned the initial, unrealistic goal of a substantial increase in domestic supply. Accordingly, when discussion of relaxing the barriers occurred in 2023, less resistance from interests within the Chinese party-state could have been expected.

Simultaneously, domestic industry groups continued their opposition to the barriers. In fact, a submission made by CBSA earlier in 2023 became the centrepiece of the MOFCOM review.[43] The submission argued that China's domestic barley production programs were unsuccessful and that, with the barriers in place, international supplies were expensive and inconsistent and did not meet industry requirements, all of which hurt the viability of Chinese beer companies. It also argued that the tariffs were counter-productive to China's own policy objectives in three areas: industrial upgrading and international competitiveness; increasing consumer confidence and spending; and meeting national standards (*guobiao* 国标) on beer and malting barley. The MOFCOM ruling to drop the barriers also included consideration of submissions from the China Feed Industry Association and Australian industry organisations.[44] Chinese industry groups have similarly been active in government decisions to drop barriers on US sorghum and on lucerne, an item subject to China–US tariff escalations from 2018.[45]

To sum up, in 2020, opposition to the barriers on Australian barley from domestic industry groups was overridden by the preferences of the central government and parts of the Chinese bureaucracy that favoured the introduction of the tariffs—either to achieve domestic agricultural policy objectives or foreign policy objectives *vis-à-vis* Australia. By 2023, there was a realignment of interests in favour of the removal of the barriers, which helps to explain when and why the tariffs were dropped.

Implications for Australian wine

The three conditions that allowed for the lifting of barriers on Australian barley—improved bilateral relations, leverage from WTO proceedings, and an alignment of industry and policy interests in China—provide some guidance on prospects for a similar outcome for Australian wine, on which China applied similar anti-dumping tariffs.[46] Certainly, negotiations are occurring within a similarly conciliatory bilateral environment. Moreover, given that China's case for imposing tariffs on wine appears even more tenuous than barley, the confidential draft panel report might motivate Beijing to settle if it is deemed to raise the spectre of hypocrisy costs.

However, unlike barley, there is no alignment of domestic interests in China against the barriers on wine. To the contrary, both industry associations and industry-oriented policy-makers have vested interests in continuing the ban.

In the case of barley, the users of Australian product had close links to the state system and a strong stake in the resumption of the trade. But the buyers of Australian wine—importers, retailers and consumers—are not an organised group. Wine is also a luxury product that is not a priority for the party-state.

China's wine growers, meanwhile, are in an influential position. China has for many years sought to develop a large domestic wine sector as a pillar industry with high potential for value-adding, to raise farmer incomes, including in rural and undeveloped areas with grape-growing potential (Ningxia, Xinjiang and Gansu), and to promote 'ecological' land use and ecotourism.[47] Importantly, Chinese wineries are represented by an established industry organisation that falls under the same parent association that opposed the barriers on Australian barley: CADA, but a different branch, the CADA Wine Sub-Association (CWSA 中国酒业协会葡萄酒分会).[48] CWSA—which comprised 119 domestic wineries in 2022—was the applicant in the investigation into the dumping of Australian wine and compiled the information for the case. In the lead-up to the investigation, the association said that imports were 'robbing' Chinese wineries of the domestic market,[49] especially in the higher-value, cold-weather reds.[50] Thus, unlike the breweries of the CBSA that benefit from Australian barley imports, the wineries of the CWSA compete with Australian wine imports and have an interest in establishing and maintaining the barriers.

The barriers on Australian wine might not have fully allayed the concerns of Chinese industry and policy-makers. Chinese wine production and consumption continued to decline in 2022, and the proportion of domestic production in total supply decreased (to 56 percent; see figure 2). China's Minister of Commerce Wang Wentao 王文涛 relayed concerns about the production and profitability of the Chinese wine industry as a potential obstacle to his Australian counterpart in discussions about lifting the trade barriers on wine.[51] The potential for this to be a snag was also reflected in a cautious statement from the peak Australian industry group earlier in 2023.[52] As a way of addressing the concerns of Chinese industry and interest groups, the largest Australian exporter of wines to China entered into a joint venture in 2022 to produce Australian wine in China.[53] The venture involves an agreement with CWSA, which sees the venture as an opportunity to transfer expertise and build China's domestic industry.[54]

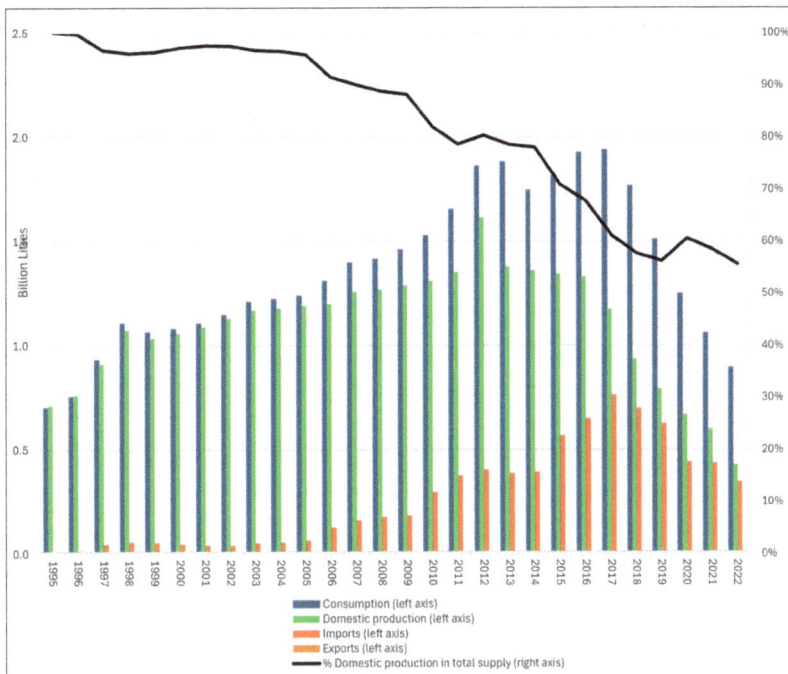

Figure 2: China's wine balance, 1995–2022
Source: International Organisation of Vine and Wine

Despite different industry dynamics within China, the process used to resolve the barriers on Australian barley appears under way for wine. Following the circulation of the WTO panel's draft report on the wine dispute in October, China and Australia reached an agreement to suspend the panel while Beijing conducts a five-month review of its barriers.[55] It is unclear where the review will land, although the expectation in Canberra on the eve of Prime Minister Albanese's visit to Beijing in early November was for a favourable outcome.[56] Chinese policy-makers might again wish to avoid a potentially adverse WTO ruling and signal their commitment to improving the bilateral relationship. However, it may also be possible that the relationship is sufficiently 'stabilised' and instead in a 'bargaining' phase, with Beijing therefore adopting a more transactional logic whereby it looks to extract concessions from Canberra as *quid pro quo*.

One possible concession is closing a separate WTO dispute with Australia. In September it was reported that Canberra had rejected a proposed 'package deal' in which the wine barriers would be removed if Australia dropped anti-dumping duties it had earlier imposed on Chinese wind towers.[57] A statement from China's Ministry of Commerce in October, however, linked the new wine review to progress on that exact issue.[58] Canberra denied this linkage, and anti-dumping duties are normally determined by an independent Anti-Dumping Commission that would not consider foreign policy interests in its decision. However, even if coincidental, the timing is hard to ignore: the commission released a preliminary report indicating a willingness to let the wind tower duties expire in the same week that Canberra decided not to cancel a lease held by a Chinese company over the port of Darwin,[59] just before the announcement of the deal on wine. Furthermore, the previous week Australian citizen Cheng Lei had been allowed to return to Australia following three years in detention.[60] Both sides pocketing 'wins' in the month before the first visit by an Australian prime minister in seven years speaks to a new phase in the relationship.

At the same time, unlike the barley case, the fact that there remains robust support for the wine barriers within China suggests the policy calculus is more complex. The fact that the wine review period is longer than that for barley might suggest Beijing anticipates a longer internal debate to reconcile unaligned interests, although it might also be designed to coincide with the expiration of the wind tower duties. It could be that domestic concerns are ultimately overruled, not merely by the shadow of a potentially adverse panel report but by a broader deal in an increasingly transactional relationship. In the end, if China does eventually remove the barriers, it will indicate the prioritisation of foreign policy goals and other equities over the preferences of the affected domestic industry and interest groups.

Broader implications

It is well recognised that domestic interest groups play an important role in trade formation, processes and the resolution of trade conflicts. While this is borne out in the case of China and Australian barley and wine, analysis of interest group representation has largely been absent from commentary both inside and outside China on Beijing's politically motivated trade barriers. Such analysis can be challenging, given the sprawling and opaque nature of party-state and societal linkages in the Chinese 'leviathan',[61] but is nevertheless crucial for informed public debate.

More generally, our analysis has implications both for policy and emerging research on the political economy of China's power in world politics. Concerned about China's apparent use of international trade as a 'weapon', several governments have recently announced plans to coordinate their responses to Beijing's behaviour.[62] If these coalitions are serious about influencing when and how China uses different international economic policies, they need to pay attention to the domestic micro-foundations that underpin them.

Since the Australia episode, China has continued to impose trade restrictions during political disputes. Notable instances have involved Lithuania, Taiwan, Japan and the European Union.[63] In each case, as with Australia, governments have looked to WTO dispute settlement as a mechanism to have the barriers removed. Brussels, Taipei and Tokyo should carefully study the domestic politics behind the when, how and why of China's removal of barriers in earlier cases—including those involving Australian barley and wine—and look for any parallels that could help them resolve their own disputes.

In terms of research, our findings illustrate the importance of exploring the mechanics and consequences of 'fragmented authoritarianism' in the trade domain.[64] It is well understood that the Chinese party-state is not unitary—even in the Xi era. But there remains considerable scope to further illuminate the mechanisms through and conditions under which domestic interest groups shape China's international economic policies.

One obvious avenue for future research is to conduct further comparisons within and across cases to look for patterns between the sequencing of barrier removal and other variables that are salient to interest group politics. In the Australia case, it is notable that the first barriers to be removed were those on six intermediate products that serve as inputs to large Chinese industries represented by well-organised, formal bodies. By contrast, the three commodities that continued to face barriers at the time of writing—wine, lobsters and beef—are all consumer goods that are distributed and retailed by large numbers of 'scattered' and unorganised actors that struggle to speak with one voice to policy-makers,[65] compounding the fact that their products are often already seen as luxury items of little strategic relevance to the state. This apparent pattern between product characteristics and the timing of sanctions being wound back should be investigated across a wider range of cases as it provides a potentially useful proxy for evaluating the potential influence of interest groups on China's sanctioning behaviour.

| NOTES

INTRODUCTION

China's New Era

1. Jane Golley, Linda Jaivin, Ben Hillman and Sharon Strange (eds), *China Dreams: China Story Yearbook 2019*, Canberra: ANU Press, 2020.

2. Ben Hillman, 'Ghosts of Mao and Deng', *Chains: China Story Yearbook 2022*, Canberra: ANU Press, 2023, pp. 59–66.

3. 'China stops releasing youth unemployment rates amid economic gloom', *Guardian*, 15 August 2023, online at: https://www.theguardian.com/world/2023/aug/15/china-unemployment-rate-youth-economy

4. Reuters, 'Chinese professor says youth jobless rate might have hit 46.5%', 20 July 2023, online at: https://www.reuters.com/article/idUSL4N3960Z5/

5. Li Yuan, 'China's young people can't find jobs. Xi Jinping says to "eat bitterness"', *New York Times*, 30 May 2023, online at: https://www.nytimes.com/2023/05/30/business/china-youth-unemployment.html

6. Geremie R. Barmé, 'Xi Jinping's harvest—from reaping garlic chives to exploiting huminerals', China Heritage, 6 January 2023, online at: https://chinaheritage.net/journal/xi-jinpings-harvest-from-reaping-garlic-chives-to-exploiting-huminerals/

7. Cyrielle Cabot, '"Let it rot": Once-flourishing middle class faces end of "Chinese Dream"', France24, 16 October 2022, online at: https://www.france24.com/en/asia-pacific/20221016-let-it-rot-once-flourishing-middle-class-faces-end-of-chinese-dream

8. Manya Koetse and Miranda Barnes, 'The story of Li Jun and Liang Liang: How the challenges of an ordinary Chinese couple captivated China's internet', What's on Weibo, 28 November 2023, online at: https://www.whatsonweibo.com/the-story-of-li-jun-liang-liang-how-the-challenges-of-an-ordinary-chinese-couple-captivated-chinas-internet/

9. Samuel Yang, 'Chinese developer Sunac defaults as Beijing struggles to save the trillion-dollar sector', ABC, 20 May 2022, online at: https://www.abc.net.au/news/2022-05-20/chinese-developer-sunac-defaults-on-dollar-bond/101077934

10. Koetse and Barnes, 'The story of Li Jun and Liang Liang'.

11. 'The most hard-working, most law-abiding and most optimistic Chinese citizen don't deserve to live the Chinese dream' 最勤劳、最守法、最乐观的公民，不配得到中国梦, China Digital Times, 22 November 2023, online at: https://chinadigitaltimes.net/chinese/702466.html

12. Xie Yu, 'Sunac wins creditors' approval for offshore debt restructuring plan', Reuters, 19 September 2023, online at: https://www.reuters.com/world/china/sunac-wins-creditors-approval-its-offshore-debt-restructuring-plan-2023-09-18/

13. Adam Liu, Jean C. Oi and Yi Zhang, 'China's local government debt: the grand bargain', *China Journal*, vol. 87, no. 1 (2022): 40–71.

14. Victor Shih and Jonathan Elkobi, 'Local government debt dynamics in China', policy paper, UC San Diego School of Global Policy and Strategy, 27 November 2023, online at: https://china.ucsd.edu/_files/2023-report_shih_local-government-debt-dynamics-in-china.pdf

15. Ibid.

16. Gu Ting, 'Chinese local governments struggle to pay civil servants' wages', Radio Free Asia, 8 September 2023, online at: https://www.rfa.org/english/news/china/wages-09082023112323.html

17. Keith Bradsher, Daisuke Wakabayashi and Claire Fu, 'Thousands of Chinese retirees protest government cuts to benefits', New York Times, 15 February 2023, online at: https://www.nytimes.com/2023/02/15/business/wuhan-china-protests.html

18. 'Nowcast of extreme poverty, 2015–2022', World Bank, online at: https://www.worldbank.org/en/understanding-poverty

19. 'Xi Jinping amends the Chinese Dream', Economist, 10 November 2022, online at: https://www.economist.com/china/2022/11/10/xi-jinping-amends-the-chinese-dream

20. 'Keynote speech by H.E. Xi Jinping President of the People's Republic of China at the China–Central Asia Summit', Ministry of Foreign Affairs of the People's Republic of China, 19 May 2023, online at: https://www.fmprc.gov.cn/eng/gjhdq_665435/2675_665437/3180_664322/3182_664326/202305/t20230519_11079941.html

21. Nicole Hong, 'As the US attends the G7, China hosts a summit of its own', New York Times, 18 May 2023, online at: https://www.nytimes.com/2023/05/18/world/asia/china-central-asia-g7.html

22. Richard Rigby, 'Tianxia 天下', Civilizing China: China Story Yearbook 2013, Canberra: ANU Press, pp. 74–79.

23. See Geremie R. Barmé, Linda Jaivin and Jeremy Goldkorn (eds), Shared Destiny: China Story Yearbook 2014, Canberra: ANU Press, 2015.

24. James Kynge, 'China's blueprint for global governance', Financial Times, 23 August 2023, online at: https://www.ft.com/content/8ac52fe7-e9db-48a8-b2f0-7305ab53f4c3

25. David Crowe and Eryk Bagshaw, 'Xi says China and Australia have "worked out some problems"—but trust issues remain', Sydney Morning Herald, 6 November 2023, online at: https://www.smh.com.au/politics/federal/china-hails-new-starting-point-with-australia-as-albanese-meets-xi-20231106-p5ei1i.html

26. Didi Tang, 'Journalists confront China censors over editorial', New York Times, 6 January 2013, online at: https://cn.nytimes.com/china/20130106/c06media-ap/zh-hant/dual/

27. Jonathan Kaiman, 'China's censorship rules were tested. But will it be back to business as usual?', Guardian, 14 January 2013, online at: https://www.theguardian.com/world/2013/jan/14/china-censorship-southern-weekly-incident

28. 'Commemorating the ten-year anniversary of the "Southern Weekly Incident"' 記《南方周末》新年獻詞事件十週年, Initium 端媒体, 2 January 2023, online at: https://theinitium.com/article/20230102-mainland-southern-weekly-new-year-address-censorship-10thyear

29. Elizabeth C. Economy, 'The great firewall of China: Xi Jinping's internet shutdown', *Guardian*, 29 June 2018, online at: https://www.theguardian.com/news/2018/jun/29/the-great-firewall-of-china-xi-jinpings-internet-shutdown

30. Linda Jaivin, 'First kisses and invisible red lines', Inside Story, 3 September 2021, online at: https://insidestory.org.au/first-kisses-and-invisible-red-lines/

31. 'China wants to be a polar power', Economist, 14 April 2018, online at: https://www.economist.com/china/2018/04/14/china-wants-to-be-a-polar-power

32. Geremie Barmé, 'The other China', China Heritage, online at: https://chinaheritage.net/the-other-china

CHAPTER 1: Political leadership and economic headwinds

The Mystery of Xi's Disappearing Officials

1. On the significance of the Xi Jinping Faction, see for example Lee Jonghyuk, 'The future of factional politics in China under Xi Jinping', RSIS.edu.sg, 31 August 2023, online at: https://www.rsis.edu.sg/rsis-publication/idss/the-future-of-factional-politics-in-china-under-xi-jinping/

2. For a discussion of corruption in China's Rocket Force, see 'Rocket force clean-up may hint at corruption', *Washington Post*, 2 August 2023, online at: https://www.washingtonpost.com/world/2023/08/02/china-military-rocket-force-xi-jinping/

3. Cited in 'The Red Princelings open fire: Liu Yuan published essay criticizing dictatorial behavior', Creaders.net, 7 November 2023, online at: https://news.creaders.net/china/2023/11/07/2666742.html

4. See 'He Lifeng has become Xi Jinping's economic czar: How much can he achieve?', Voice of America, 4 November 2023, online at: https://www.voachinese.com/a/7340905.html

5. See 'China's former economic tsar Liu He still has a big seat at the table, quietly meets with Western delegations: Sources', *South China Morning Post*, 24 October 2023, online at: https://www.scmp.com/economy/china-economy/article/3238906/chinas-former-economic-tsar-still-has-big-seat-table-quietly-meets-western-delegations-sources

6. For a discussion of the expansion of power of the national security establishment, see for example 'The power of China's state security system grows exponentially', Voice of America, 16 November 2023, online at: https://www.voachinese.com/a/unlimited-expansion-of-china-s-national-security-system-harms-the-economy/7355996.html

7. For a discussion of the competition between Xi Jinping followers from Fujian versus those from Zhejiang, see for example Wu Guoguang, 'Li Qiang versus Cai Qi in the Xi Jinping leadership: Checks and balances with CCP characteristics?', Hoover Institution, 29 August 2023, online at: https://www.prcleader.org/post/li-qiang-versus-cai-qi-in-the-xi-jinping-leadership-checks-and-balances-with-ccp-characteristics

8. See 'Ministry of State Security: People shorting the stock market are unleashing instability in China's finance sector', *Hong Kong Economic Times*, 2 November 2023, online at: https://inews.hket.com/article/3644620

9. Evan Osnos, 'China's Age of Malaise', *New Yorker*, 23 October 2023, online at: https://www.newyorker.com/magazine/2023/10/30/chinas-age-of-malaise

10. For an analysis of the future of FDI flows into China, see for example Iori Kawate, 'Foreign direct investment turning negative for the first time', *Nikkei Asia*, 4 November 2023, online at: https://asia.nikkei.com/Economy/Foreign-investment-in-China-turns-negative-for-first-time

11. For a study of the potentials of China's Free Trade Zones, see for example Tetra Consultants, 'China Free Trade Zones', n.d., online at: https://www.tetraconsultants.com/jurisdictions/register-company-in-china/china-free-trade-zones/

12. Clare Jim, David Barbuscia and Karin Strohecker, 'China needs to pull "multiple levers" for property turnaround, say analysts', Reuters, 20 November 2023, online at: http://www.reuters.com/world/china/china-needs-pull-multiple-levers-property-turnaround-say-analysts-2023-11-17/#:~:text=Bloomberg%20News%20reported%20on%20

13. For a discussion of corruption among the real estate and other sectors, see for example Michelle Toh, 'Another top executive is being investigated by China's corruption watchdog', CNN, 21 November 2023, online at: https://www.cnn.com/2023/11/21/business/china-shanghai-industrial-group-ceo-investigation-intl-hnk/index.html

14. 'China approves guidelines to boost affordable housing amid property debt crisis', Reuters, 25 August 2023, online at: https://www.reuters.com/world/china/chinas-cabinet-approves-guidelines-boost-affordable-housing-amid-property-woes-2023-08-25/

15. For a discussion of the issue of youth joblessness, see for example Benn Steil and Elizaberth Harding, 'The root of China's growing youth unemployment crisis', Council for Foreign Affairs, 18 September 2023, online at: https://www.cfr.org/blog/root-chinas-growing-youth-unemployment-crisis

16. Reuters, 'Chinese professor says youth jobless rate might have hit 46.5%', 20 July 2023, online at: https://www.reuters.com/article/china-economy-youth-unemployment/chinese-professor-says-youth-jobless-rate-might-have-hit-46-5-idUSL4N3960Z5/

17. For a discussion of programs to raise birth rates, see for example Amy Hawkins, 'Free college and IVF help: China hunts for ways to raise its birthrate', *Guardian*, 10 March 2023, online at: https://www.theguardian.com/world/2023/mar/10/free-college-and-ivf-help-china-hunts-for-ways-to-raise-its-birthrate

18. Adam Y. Liu, 'Making markets: The untold story of Chinese banking and why it matters', 1 December 2022, China Story, online at: https://www.thechinastory.org/making-markets-the-untold-story-of-chinese-banking-and-why-it-matters/

19. Reuters, 'China orders local governments to cut exposure to public-private projects as debt risks rise', 14 November 2023, online at: https://www.reuters.com/markets/asia/china-orders-local-governments-cut-exposure-public-private-projects-debt-risks-2023-11-14/

20. For a study of militia or security forces within China's state-owned enterprises, see Natalie Liu, 'Why is China highlighting militias in state owned enterprises?', Voice of America, 7 November 2023, online at: https://www.voanews.com/a/why-is-china-highlighting-militias-in-state-owned-enterprises-/7346238.html

21. For a discussion of increased emigration from China, see for example 'Shanghai woman in focus as probe shows fear of capital exit', Bloomberg, 14 August 2023, online at: https://www.bloomberg.com/news/articles/2023-08-14/shanghai-woman-in-focus-as-probe-shows-fear-of-capital-flight#xj4y7vzkg

22. See Alicia Chen, 'Growing numbers of Chinese citizens set their sights on the US—via the deadly Darién Gap', *Guardian*, 9 March 2023, online at: https://www.theguardian.com/world/2023/mar/09/growing-numbers-of-chinese-citizens-set-their-sights-on-the-us-via-the-deadly-darien-gap

China's Macroeconomy in 2023: An Overview

1. State Council, 'The State Council News Office held a press conference on the operation of the national economy in 2023' ('国务院新闻办就2023年国民经济运行情况举行发布会'), 17 January 2024, online at: https://www.gov.cn/lianbo/fabu/202401/content_6926619.htm

2. Xinhua News, 'Explainer: What do China's eased mortgage policies mean for home buyers, property sector', 1 September 2023, online at: https://english.news.cn/20230901/abc5ca4dd9b8431ea990458d6da84d21/c.html

3. Chris Buckley, 'Xi's post-virus economic strategy for China looks inward', *New York Times*, 7 September 2020, online at: https://www.nytimes.com/2020/09/07/business/china-xi-economy.html

4. XinhuaNet, 'How to understand dual circulation from Xi Jinping's recent speeches' ('看习近平这几次重要讲话，弄懂"大循环""双循环"'), 5 September 2020, online at: http://www.xinhuanet.com/politics/xxjxs/2020-09/05/c_1126455277.htm

5. China Briefing, 'China's Central Economic Work Conference outlines key priorities for 2024', 21 December 2023, online at: https://www.china-briefing.com/news/chinas-central-economic-work-conference-outlines-key-priorities-for-2024/

China's Local Government Debt

1. The Rhodium Group cited in Iori Kawate, 'China's hidden local government debt soars to over $8tn', *Nikkei Asia*, 15 June 2023, online at: https://asia.nikkei.com/Business/Markets/China-debt-crunch/China-s-hidden-local-government-debt-soars-to-over-8tn

2. Yu Hairong, Cheng Siwei, Zhang Yuzhe and Han Wei, 'Cover story: China's effort to move mountain of "hidden debt" faces uphill climb', *Caixin Global*, 22 May 2023, online at: https://www.caixinglobal.com/2023-05-22/cover-story-china-ramps-up-efforts-to-tackle-hidden-debts-102057722.html

3. James Kynge, Sun Yu and Thomas Hale, 'China's property crash: "A slow-motion financial crisis"', *Financial Times*, 4 October 2022, online at: https://www.ft.com/content/e9e8c879-5536-4fbc-8ec2-f2a274b823b4

4. Yu Hairong et al., 'China's effort'.

5. Shuli Ren, 'How can China contain its $8.3 trillion fiscal crisis?', Bloomberg, 16 April 2023, online at: https://www.bloomberg.com/opinion/articles/2023-04-16/china-fiscal-crisis-can-it-contain-this-8-3-billion-one

6. For details see Adam Y. Liu, Jean C. Oi and Yi Zhang, 'China's local government debt: The grand bargain', *China Journal*, vol. 87 (2022): 40–71, online at: https://doi.org/10.1086/717256; and Adam Yao Liu, 'Building markets within authoritarian institutions: The political economy of banking development in China', doctoral dissertation, Stanford University, 2018.

7. Liu, Oi and Zhang, 'China's local government debt'.

8. 'Self-isolated: China's lonely zero-COVID battle in spotlight as Xi seeks third term', *Nikkei Asia*, 12 October 2022, online at: https://asia.nikkei.com/Spotlight/The-Big-Story/Self-isolated-China-s-lonely-zero-COVID-battle-in-spotlight-as-Xi-seeks-third-term

9. Cheng Siwei and Denise Jia, 'Local Chinese governments add billions to multitrillion-dollar hidden-debt problem', *Caixin Global*, 27 June 2023, online at: https://www.caixinglobal.com/2023-05-05/in-depth-local-governments-struggle-to-get-on-top-of-their-hidden-debt-102043012.html

10. Cheng Siwei and Zhang Yukun, 'In depth: Local governments struggle to get on top of their hidden debt', *Caixin Global*, 5 May 2023, online at: https://www.caixinglobal.com/2023-05-05/in-depth-local-governments-struggle-to-get-on-top-of-their-hidden-debt-102043012.html

11. Ibid.

12. 'China banks offer 25-year loans to LGFVs to avert credit crunch', Bloomberg, 3 July 2023, online at: https://www.bloomberg.com/news/articles/2023-07-04/china-banks-offer-25-year-loans-to-lgfvs-to-avert-credit-crunch

13. 'China regulator asked banks to respond to bearish Goldman report', Bloomberg News, 12 July 2023, online at: https://www.bloomberg.com/news/articles/2023-07-12/china-regulator-asked-banks-to-respond-to-bearish-goldman-report

14. 'China's $77 billion bank rout shows who pays price for rescues', Bloomberg News, 10 July 2023, online at: https://www.bloomberg.com/news/articles/2023-07-11/china-s-77-billion-bank-rout-shows-who-pays-price-for-rescues

CHAPTER 2: Party-state capitalism

The Dreary and the Dramatic: What Happened to China's Platform Economy?

1. Sam Peach, 'Why did Alibaba's Jack Ma disappear for three months?', BBC, 20 March 2021, online at: https://www.bbc.com/news/technology-56448688

2. Jing Yang and Lingling Wei, 'China's President Xi Jinping personally scuttled Jack Ma's Ant IPO', *Wall Street Journal*, 12 November 2020, online at: https://www.wsj.com/articles/china-president-xi-jinping-halted-jack-ma-ant-ipo-11605203556

3. Peter Hoskins, 'Bao Fan: Missing Chinese billionaire assisting authorities, firm says', BBC, 27 February 2023, online at: https://www.bbc.com/news/business-64781374

4. See, for instance, 'China's tech crackdown starts to ease', *Economist*, 19 January 2023, online at: https://www.economist.com/business/2023/01/19/chinas-tech-crackdown-starts-to-ease; Giulia Interesse, 'Is China's "tech crackdown" over? Our 2023 regulatory outlook for the sector', *China Briefing*, February 2023, online at: https://www.china-briefing.com/news/is-chinas-tech-crackdown-over-our-2023-regulatory-outlook-for-the-sector/; Coco Liu, Zheping Huang and Sarah Zheng, 'China's tech giants lost their swagger and may never get it back', Bloomberg, 23 June 2023, online at: https://www.bloomberg.com/news/articles/2022-06-23/china-tech-crackdown-eases-but-startups-worry-xi-may-up-regulatory-pressure

5. Jialun Deng, 'As Beijing takes control, Chinese tech companies lose jobs and hope', *New York Times*, 5 January 2022, online at: https://www.nytimes.com/2022/01/05/technology/ china-tech-internet-crackdown-layoffs.html; 'Xi's tech crackdown fuels another crisis: Out-of-work youth', Bloomberg, 30 August 2022, online at: https://www.bloomberg.com/ news/articles/2022-08-30/xi-s-tech-crackdown-fuels-another-crisis-out-of-work-youth

6. Tanner Brown, 'China promises a regulatory reprieve for its tech sector. Why analysts are skeptical', *Barron's*, 6 May 2022, online at: https://www.barrons.com/ articles/china-promises-a-regulatory-reprieve-for-its-tech-sector-why-analysts-are-skeptical-51651849564

7. Rogier Creemers, 'China's emerging data protection framework', *Journal of Cybersecurity*, vol. 8, no. 1 (2022), online at: https://academic.oup.com/cybersecurity/ article/8/1/tyac011/6674794

8. State Council General Office, 'Guiding opinions concerning stimulating the healthy and standardised development of the platform economy' 关于促进平台经济规范健康发展的指导意见, 1 August 2019, online at: http://www.gov.cn/zhengce/content/2019-08/08/ content_5419761.htm

9. Matt Sheehan and Sharon Du, 'How food delivery workers shaped Chinese algorithm regulations', Carnegie Endowment for International Peace, 2 November 2022, online at: https://carnegieendowment.org/2022/11/02/how-food-delivery-workers-shaped-chinese-algorithm-regulations-pub-88310; Elliott Zaagman, 'The future of China's work culture', *TechCrunch*, 9 October 2021, online at: https://techcrunch.com/2021/10/09/the-future-of-chinas-work-culture

10. Jane Li, '"Er xuan yi": The business tactic that led to Alibaba's $2.8 billion antitrust fine', *Quartz*, 12 April 2021, online at: https://qz.com/1994879/what-is-erxuanyi-which-led-to-alibabas-2-8-billion-fine

11. Nicolle Liu, 'The China scam calls just won't die', *Politico*, 25 August 2022, online at: https://www.politico.com/newsletters/politico-china-watcher/2022/08/25/the-china-scam-calls-just-wont-die-00052537

12. Jiefei Liu, 'The dramatic rise and fall of online P2P lending in China', *TechCrunch*, 2 August 2018, online at: https://techcrunch.com/2018/08/01/the-dramatic-rise-and-fall-of-online-p2p-lending-in-china/

13. Simon Leys, 'The art of interpreting nonexistent inscriptions written in invisible ink on a blank page', *New York Review of Books*, 11 October 1990, online at: https://www. chinafile.com/library/nyrb-china-archive/art-interpreting-nonexistent-inscriptions-written-invisible-ink-blank

14. Rogier Creemers, 'The great rectification: A new paradigm for China's online platform economy', working paper, 9 January 2023, online at: https://papers.ssrn.com/sol3/ papers.cfm?abstract_id=4320952

15. Xu Ke, Vicky Liu, Yan Luo and Zhijing Yu, 'Analyzing China's PIPL and how it compares to the EU's GDPR', IAPP, 24 August 2021, online at: https://iapp.org/news/a/analyzing-chinas-pipl-and-how-it-compares-to-the-eus-gdpr/

16. Zibo Liu and Stavroula Vyrna, 'New antitrust tools for the digital economy in China and the EU', Clifford Chance, 5 October 2022, online at: https://www.cliffordchance. com/briefings/2022/10/new-antitrust-tools-for-the-digital-economy-in-china-and-the-eu-.html

17. Central Commission for Cybersecurity and Informatization, '14th Five-Year Plan for National Informatization' "十四五" 国家信息化规划, December 2021, translation online at: https://digichina.stanford.edu/work/translation-14th-five-year-plan-for-national-informatization-dec-2021/

18. Aaron Mak, 'Why China finally decided to ban bitcoin', *Slate*, 24 September 2021, online at: https://slate.com/business/2021/09/china-bans-crypto-sec-regulations.html

19. Sofia Brooke, 'China sets up new anti-monopoly bureau', *China Briefing*, 30 November 2021, online at: https://www.china-briefing.com/news/china-sets-up-new-anti-monopoly-bureau-strengthens-antitrust-investigation-capacity/

20. Julie Zhu and Jane Xu, 'China ends Ant Group's regulatory revamp with nearly $1 billion fine', Reuters, 7 July 2023, online at: https://www.reuters.com/technology/china-end-ant-groups-regulatory-revamp-with-fine-least-11-bln-sources-2023-07-07/

21. Xinhua, 'Li Qiang chairs conference with platform enterprises' 李强主持召开平台企业座谈会, 12 July 2023, online at: https://www.gov.cn/yaowen/liebiao/202307/content_6891546.htm?mc_cid=93fcac5be1&mc_eid=ad7c94e0d8

22. Central Committee, State Council, 'Opinions concerning stimulating the development and expansion of the private economy' 关于促进民营经济发展壮大的意见, 14 July 2023, online at: http://www.news.cn/politics/2023-07/19/c_1129758014.htm?mc_cid=8a1889d98f&mc_eid=ad7c94e0d8

23. Beijing Municipal Administration of Market Supervision, 'some measures concerning enhancing regularized supervision levels and supporting the sustained and healthy development of platform enterprises (draft for comment)' 关于提升常态化监管水平支持平台企业持续健康发展的若干措施 (征求意见稿), 14 July 2023, online at: https://www.beijing.gov.cn/hudong/gfxwjzj/zjxx/202307/t20230714_3162297.html?mc_cid=dbfb657904&mc_eid=ad7c94e0d8

24. 'SAMR: Perfect regularized oversight mechanisms to stimulate the healthy development of the platform economy' 市场监管总局：完善促进平台经济健康发展的常态化监管机制, *Jiemian News*, 25 July 2023, online at: https://www.jiemian.com/article/9805808.html?mc_cid=e76d4a964c&mc_eid=ad7c94e0d8

How Multinational Corporations are Coopted into Becoming China's Agents of Repression

1. Song Lin, 'H&M, Nike, Adidas could lose out by politicizing cotton-picking: Expert', *Global Times*, 27 March 2021, online at: https://www.globaltimes.cn/page/202103/1219587.shtml

2. Associated Press, 'Silver defends NBA employees' right to free speech as China cancels broadcasts', *Guardian*, 9 October 2019, online at: https://www.theguardian.com/sport/2019/oct/08/adam-silver-nba-china-tv-broadcasts-hong-kong

3. Tiffany May and Zoe Mou, '"Insult to China": A model's freckles spark an online storm', *New York Times*, 19 February 2019, online at: https://www.nytimes.com/2019/02/19/world/asia/china-freckles-zara-jing-wen.html#

4. Global Times, 'Shares of Chinese food flavoring giant plunge following standards controversy', *Global Times*, 10 October 2022, online at: https://www.globaltimes.cn/page/202210/1276802.shtml

5. South China Morning Post, 'Cathay Pacific airline fires 3 cabin crew members accused of insulting non-English speakers', *South China Morning Post*, 24 May 2023, online at: https://www.scmp.com/yp/discover/news/hong-kong/article/3221627/cathay-pacific-airline-fires-3-cabin-crew-members-accused-insulting-non-english-speakers

6. Cathay Pacific, 'Statement from Cathay Pacific CEO Ronald Lam' 国泰航空行政总裁林绍波声明', 23 May 2023, online at: https://news.cathaypacific.com/国泰航空行政总裁林绍波声明; Mike Gu, 'Cathay Pacific scandal widely condemned', *China Daily*, 25 May 2025, online at: https://www.chinadaily.com.cn/a/202305/25/WS646ebf3ba310b6054fad500f.html

7. Twinnie Siu and Farah Master, 'Cathay Pacific to hire cabin attendants from mainland China from July', Reuters, 19 June 2023, online at: https://www.reuters.com/business/aerospace-defense/cathay-pacific-hire-cabin-attendants-mainland-china-july-2023-06-19/

8. Amy King explains the origin of the foreign policy phrase 'hurting the feelings of the Chinese people', which traditionally was often used when Chinese officials believed the country's status was demeaned on the world stage. See Amy King, 'Hurting the Feelings of the Chinese People', *Sources and Methods Blog*, Washington, DC: Wilson Center, 15 February 2017, online at: https://www.wilsoncenter.org/blog-post/hurting-the-feelings-the-chinese-people. Recently, the phrase has frequently been used not only by officials but also by any Chinese nationals who feel that China or the Chinese people are perceived in a negative way.

9. RTHK News, 'Cathay incident damages HK's reputation: CE', *RTHK News*, 24 May 2023, online at: https://news.rthk.hk/rthk/en/component/k2/1701908-20230524.htm

10. Li Jieqiong, 'Cathay Pacific Airways can't fly far without rectification of old problems 老毛病老不改, 国泰航空飞不远', Xinhua News, 23 May 2023, online at: http://www.news.cn/comments/20230523/2346cd84610a440a9e2189da0b63ab50/c.html

11. CCTV, 'Cathay Pacific Union's so-called "zero tolerance" is ridiculous 国泰空乘工会所谓的"零容忍", 歪得离谱', 25 May 2023, online at: https://finance.sina.cn/2023-05-25/detail-imyuyzsw2125514.d.html

12. People's Daily, 'Cathay Pacific can't simply apologise 国泰航空不能只是道歉了事', 23 May 2023, online at: https://weibo.com/5476386628/N1Ur3xo36; People's Daily, 'Discrimination against Mandarin in Hong Kong is destined to be a joke 在香港歧视普通话, 注定是个笑话', 24 May 2023 online at: https://weibo.com/2803301701/N23mwsAfO

13. He Liangliang, '"Cathay Pacific incident" is not an isolated phenomenon "国泰事件"不是孤立现象', huanqiu.com, 24 May 2023, online at: https://opinion.huanqiu.com/article/4D19r8jMdpO

14. Antony Dapiran, 'Hong Kong's National Security Law', in Jane Golley, Linda Jaivin, and Sharon Strange (eds), *China Story Yearbook 2020: Crisis*, Canberra: ANU Press, 2021, pp. 60–65.

15. Jessie Yeung, Joshua Berlinger, Steve George, and Ben Westcott, 'Flights canceled, major roads blocked as Hong Kong protests escalate', CNN, 11 November 2019, online at: https://edition.cnn.com/asia/live-news/hong-kong-strike-protest-intl-hnk/h_596bec60320c056c9af8449be4122ca9

16. Eva Dou, 'China warns Hong Kong it will intervene if situation deteriorates', *New York Times*, 7 August 2019, online at: https://www.nytimes.com/2019/08/07/world/asia/hong-kong-protests-china-violence.html

17. Kris Cheng, 'Beijing deems Hong Kong protests "colour revolution", will not rule out intervention', *Hong Kong Free Press*, 8 August 2019, online at: https://hongkongfp.com/2019/08/08/beijing-deems-hong-kong-protests-colour-revolution-will-not-rule-intervention

18. Sophie Hui, 'Property giants condemn violence at protests', *The Standard*, 9 August 2019, online at: https://www.thestandard.com.hk/section-news/section/4/210500/Property-giants-condemn-violence-at-protests

19. Josephine Ma, Danny Lee, Karen Zhangand, and Kanis Leung, 'China bans Cathay Pacific staff involved in Hong Kong "unlawful" protests from mainland routes', *South China Morning Post*, 9 August 2019, online at: https://www.scmp.com/news/china/politics/article/3022200/china-bans-cathay-pacific-staff-involved-hong-kong-protests

20. BBC, 'Cathay Pacific boss Rupert Hogg quits after protest row', 16 August 2019, online at: https://www.bbc.com/news/business-49367949

21. The Standard, 'Cathay Pacific draws online hostility fueled by state media', *The Standard*, 9 August 2019, online at: https://www.thestandard.com.hk/breaking-news/section/4/132822/Cathay-Pacific-draws-online-hostility-fueled-by-state-media

22. Dan Conifer, 'Cathay Pacific crew say fear of China is fuelling paranoia and sackings amid Hong Kong protests', ABC News, 2 November 2019, online at: https://www.abc.net.au/news/2019-11-02/hong-kong-cathay-pacific-staff-speak-out/11657254; Dan Conifer, 'Cathay Pacific staff report culture of "terror" after pro-democracy sackings', ABC News, 2 November 2019, online at: https://www.abc.net.au/radio/programs/am/cathay-staff-report-culture-of-terror-after-protest-sackings/11661758

23. Tiffany May and Ezra Cheung, '"Big brother" in the sky: Cathay is in China's vise', *New York Times*, 13 September 2019, online at: https://www.nytimes.com/2019/09/11/business/cathay-pacific-hong-kong-protests.html

24. Amnesty International, 'Yahoo's data contributes to arrests in China: Free Shi Tao from prison in China!', Web Action WA 04/06; AI Index: ASA 17/040/2006 Start date: 20/07/06, London: Amnesty International, 2006, online at: https://www.amnesty.org/es/wp-content/uploads/2021/08/asa170402006en.pdf; Human Rights Watch, 'Appendix III: Details of Shi Tao's case', in *Race to the Bottom: Exploitation of Migrant Workers Ahead of Russia's 2014 Winter Olympic Games in Sochi*, New York, NY: Human Rights Watch, 6 February 2013, online at: https://www.hrw.org/reports/2006/china0806/11.htm

25. Amie Tsang and Alan Wong, 'Lancôme provokes fury after canceling a concert in Hong Kong', *New York Times*, 7 June 2016, online at: https://www.nytimes.com/2016/06/08/business/international/lancome-hong-kong-denise-ho.html

26. Maev Kennedy and Tom Phillips, 'Cambridge University Press backs down over China censorship', *Guardian*, 22 August 2017, online at: https://www.theguardian.com/education/2017/aug/21/cambridge-university-press-to-back-down-over-china-censorship

27. Xinhua, 'Chinese diplomat condemns Houston Rockets manager for erroneous comments on Hong Kong', 7 October 2019, online at: http://www.xinhuanet.com/english/2019-10/07/c_138452633.htm

28. People's Daily, 'Rockets general manager's remarks on "Hong Kong independence" angered fans: Don't you want the Chinese market? 火箭队总经理"港独"言论惹怒球迷: 中国市场不想要了?', *People's Daily*, 6 October 2019, online at: http://society.people.com.cn/n1/2019/1006/c428181-31385120.html

29. William D. O'Connell, 'Silencing the Crowd: China, the NBA, and Leveraging Market Size to Export Censorship', *Review of International Political Economy*, vol. 29, no. 4 (2022): 1112–1134, doi.org/10.1080/09692290.2021.1905683.

30. Eduardo Baptista, 'China's CCTV shows NBA game, ending 18-month blackout', Reuters, 30 March 2022, online at: https://www.reuters.com/lifestyle/sports/chinas-cctv-shows-nba-game-ending-18-month-blackout-2022-03-30/

31. Alvin Lum and Chris Lau, 'Hong Kong lawyer quits BNP Paribas after Facebook post supporting anti-government protests and ridiculing pro-Beijing activists', *South China Morning Post*, 27 September 2019, online at: https://www.scmp.com/news/hong-kong/article/3030581/hong-kong-lawyer-quits-bnp-paribas-after-facebook-post-supporting

32. Lea Mok, 'HSBC terminates bank accounts of Hong Kong opposition party League of Social Democrats without giving reason', Hong Kong Free Press, 2 June 2023, online at: https://hongkongfp.com/2023/06/02/hsbc-terminates-bank-accounts-of-hong-kong-opposition-party-league-of-social-democrats-without-giving-reason/

33. Bang Xiao, 'Google pulled its service from China more than a decade ago—can Australia learn from that?', ABC News, 30 January 2021, online at: https://www.abc.net.au/news/2021-01-30/google-leave-australia-what-to-learn-from-china-legislation-law/13102112

34. BBC, 'Google's Project Dragonfly "terminated" in China', 17 July 2019, online at: https://www.bbc.com/news/technology-49015516

35. See Denghua Zhang and Graeme Smith, 'China's Foreign Aid System: Structure, Agencies, and Identities', *Third World Quarterly*, vol. 38, no. 10 (2017): 2330–2346, doi.org/10.1080/01436597.2017.1333419; J. Mohan Malik, 'Myanmar's Role in China's Maritime Silk Road Initiative', *Journal of Contemporary China*, vol. 27, no. 111 (2018): 362–378, doi.org/10.1080/10670564.2018.1410969; Suisheng Zhao, 'China's Belt-Road Initiative as the Signature of President Xi Jinping Diplomacy: Easier Said than Done', *Journal of Contemporary China*, vol. 29, no. 123 (2020): 319–335, doi.org/10.1080/10670564.2019.1645483.

36. For instance, Christina Lai, 'More than Carrots and Sticks: Economic Statecraft and Coercion in China–Taiwan Relations from 2000 to 2019', *Politics*, vol. 42, no. 3 (2022): 410–425, doi.org/10.1177/0263395720962654; Darren J. Lim, Victor A. Ferguson, and Rosa Bishop, 'Chinese Outbound Tourism as an Instrument of Economic Statecraft', *Journal of Contemporary China*, vol. 29, no. 126 (2020): 916–933, doi.org/10.1080/10670564.2020.1744390.

CHAPTER 3: The challenges of common prosperity

Inequality in China: The Challenge of Common Prosperity

1. Ivailo Izvorsky, 'The middle-income trap, again?', World Bank Blogs, 9 February 2011, online at: https://blogs.worldbank.org/eastasiapacific/the-middle-income-trap-again

2. Ibid.

3. Junsen Zhang, 'A survey on income inequality in China', *Journal of Economic Literature*, vol. 59, no. 4 (2021): 1191–239.

4. Scott Rozelle and Natalie Hell, *Invisible China: How the Urban–Rural Divide Threatens China's Rise*, Chicago: University of Chicago Press, 2020.

5. OECD, *Education at a Glance 2016: OECD Indicators*, Paris: OECD Publishing, 2016.

6. Niny Khor, Lihua Pang, Chengfang Liu, Fang Chang, Di Mo, Prashant Loyalka and Scott Rozelle, 'China's looming human capital crisis: Upper secondary educational attainment rates and the middle-income trap', *China Quarterly*, vol. 228 (2016): 905–26.

7. Scott Rozelle and Matthew Boswell, 'Complicating China's rise: Rural underemployment', *Washington Quarterly*, vol. 44, no. 2 (2021): 61–74.

8. Yu Bai, Siqi Zhang, Lei Wang, Ruirui Dang, Cody Abbey and Scott Rozelle, 'Past successes and future challenges in rural China's human capital', *Journal of Contemporary China*, vol. 28, no. 120 (2019): 883–98.

9. Rozelle and Hell, *Invisible China*.

10. Zhang, 'A survey on income inequality in China'.

11. Chengfang Liu, Renfu Luo, Hongmei Yi, Linxiu Zhang, Shaoping Li, Yunli Bai, Alexis Medina, Scott Rozelle, Scott Smith, Guofei Wang and Jujun Wang, 'Soil-transmitted helminths in southwestern China: A cross-sectional study of links to cognitive ability, nutrition, and school performance among children', *PLoS Neglected Tropical Diseases*, vol. 9, no. 6 (2015): e0003877.

12. James J. Heckman, *Giving Kids a Fair Chance*, Boston: MIT Press, 2017.

13. Susan P. Walker, Susan M. Chang, Amika S. Wright, Rodrigo Pinto, James J. Heckman and Sally M. Grantham-McGregor, 'Cognitive, psychosocial, and behaviour gains at age 31 years from the Jamaica early childhood stimulation trial', *Journal of Child Psychology and Psychiatry*, vol. 63, no. 6 (2022): 626–35.

14. Lei Wang, Wilson Liang, Siqi Zhang, Laura Jonsson, Mengjie Li, Cordelia Yu, Yonglei Sun, Qingrui Ma, Yu Bai, Cody Abbey, Renfu Luo, Ai Yue and Scott Rozelle, 'Are infant/toddler developmental delays a problem across rural China?', *Journal of Comparative Economics*, vol. 47, no. 2 (2019): 458–69.

15. Dorien Emmers, Qi Jiang, Hao Xue, Yue Zhang, Yunting Zhang, Yingxue Zhao, Bin Liu, Sarah-Eve Dill, Yiwei Qian, Nele Warrinnier, Hannah Johnstone, Jianhua Cai, Xiaoli Wang, Lei Wang, Renfu Luo, Guirong Li, Jiajia Xu, Ming Liu, Yaqing Huang, Wenjie Shan, Zhihui Li, Yu Zhang, Sean Sylvia, Yue Ma, Alexis Medina and Scott Rozelle, 'Early childhood development and parental training interventions in rural China: A systematic review and meta-analysis', *BMJ Global Health*, vol. 6, no. 8 (2021): e005578.

16. Ibid.

17. Ai Yue, Nianrui Zhang, Xueyang Liu, Lei Tang, Renfu Luo, Meredith Yang and Scott Rozelle, 'Do infant feeding practices differ between grandmothers and mothers in rural China? Evidence from rural Shaanxi Province', *Family and Community Health*, vol. 41, no. 4 (2018): 233–43.

18. Sean Sylvia, Nele Warrinnier, Renfu Luo, Ai Yue, Orazio Attanasio, Alexis Medina and Scott Rozelle, 'From quantity to quality: Delivering a home-based parenting intervention through China's family planning cadres', *Economic Journal*, vol. 131, no. 635 (2021): 1365–400.

19. Walker et al., 'Cognitive, psychosocial, and behaviour gains at age 31 years from the Jamaica early childhood stimulation trial'.

20. United Nations, 'The 17 Goals', *United Nations: Department of Economic and Social Affairs–Sustainable Development*, 2023, online at: https://sdgs.un.org/goals

21. Dorien Emmers, Juan C. Caro, Scott Rozelle and Sean Sylvia, 'Early parenting interventions to foster human capital in developing countries', *Annual Review of Resource Economics*, vol. 14 (2022): 169–92.

22. World Bank, 'Lifting 800 million people out of poverty – New report looks at lessons from China's experience', press release, 1 April 2022, online at: https://www.worldbank.org/en/news/press-release/2022/04/01/lifting-800-million-people-out-of-poverty-new-report-looks-at-lessons-from-china-s-experience

23. Qiaoyi Li, '600m with $140 monthly income worries top', *Global Times*, 29 May 2020, online at: https://www.globaltimes.cn/content/1189968.shtml

24. Zhang, 'A survey on income inequality in China'.

25. Andrew Batson, Manoj Kewalramani, Yuen Yuen Ang, Barry Naughton and Bert Hofman, 'Can Xi Jinping Achieve "Common Prosperity"', CSIS Interpret: China, 27 December 2021, online at: https://interpret.csis.org/common-prosperity/

26. Xinhua, 'Xi: Principal contradiction facing Chinese society has evolved in new era', 18 October 2017, online at: http://english.www.gov.cn/news/top_news/2017/10/18/content_281475912458156.htm

From Poverty Elimination to Rural Revitalisation: The Party Takes Charge

1. Jane Golley, Linda Jaivin, Ben Hillman and Sharon Strange (eds), *China Dreams: China Story Yearbook 2019*, Canberra: ANU Press, 2020.

2. In 2010 Chinese government statistics identified 98.99 million rural residents living below the official poverty line of 2,300 yuan per year (at 2010 prices). The State Council Information Office of the People's Republic of China, 2021, *Poverty Alleviation: China's Experience and Contribution* (April), online at: www.scio.gov.cn/gxzt/dtzt/2021/rljpdzgsjbps/

3. For a discussion of earlier approaches to poverty alleviation in China, see Ben Hillman, 'Opening up: The politics of poverty and development in Rural China', *Development Bulletin*, 61 (May) 2003: 47–50.

4. Xinhua, 2021, 'Xi declares "complete victory" in eradicating absolute poverty in China', online at: http://www.xinhuanet.com/english/2021-02/26/c_139767705.htm

5. World Bank, 'Understanding poverty', online at: https://www.worldbank.org/en/understanding-poverty

6. The premier, who died of a heart attack in October 2023, observed that about 600 million Chinese citizens have an income of only RMB 1,000 ($207) per month, which translates to approximately $6.85 per day. See "600m with $140 monthly income worries top", *Global Times*, 29 May 2020, online at: https://www.globaltimes.cn/content/1189968.shtml. On the challenge of underdevelopment in rural China, see also Scott Rozelle in this volume.

7. State Council, People's Republic of China, 'China's No. 1 central document highlights rural vitalization tasks', Xinhua, 23 February 2023, online at: https://english.www.gov.cn/policies/policywatch/202302/14/content_WS63eb0acbc6d0a757729e6bbc.html

8. Ibid.

9.   Zhao Tan, 'First democracy, then centralism: The new shape of village elections under the "One-Shoulder Pole" Policy', paper presented at the Australian Centre on China in the World, 9 August 2023.

10.   Ben Hillman, 'Law, order and social control in Xi's China', *Issues and Studies*, vol. 57, no. 2 (2021): 1–21.

11.   Xinhua Daily Telegraph, 'Strive to be a "leader" in rural revitalization', 15 May 2023, online at: http://www.xinhuanet.com/mrdx/2023-05/16/c_1310719123.htm

12.   Elizabeth Perry, 'Missionaries of the Party: Work-team participation and intellectual incorporation', *China Quarterly*, vol. 248, no. 1 (2021): 73–94.

13.   National Rural Revitalization Administration, 'Key tasks', 16 June 2023, online at: https://nrra.gov.cn/2023/06/16/ARTI5kxZZLI2oNMAZZLLvM1I230616.shtml

14.   Ben Hillman, 'The end of village democracy in China', *Journal of Democracy*, vol. 34, no. 3 (2023): 62–76.

15.   On informal power and the limits of formal institutions in the countryside, see Ben Hillman, 'Factions and spoils: Examining political behavior within the local state in China', *China Journal*, 64 (2010): 1–18.

16.   This estimate is based on the assumption that each first party secretary and work team member earns a salary of 5,000 yuan per month. Salaries are likely to be higher in many cases.

17.   Adam Liu, Jean C. Oi and Yi Zhang, 'China's local government debt: The grand bargain', *China Journal*, vol. 87, January (2020): 40–71.

18.   Jean C. Oi, *Rural China Takes Off: Institutional Foundations of Economic Reform*, Berkeley: University of California Press, 1999.

19.   Lior Rosenberg, 2015, 'Why do local officials bet on the strong? Drawing lessons from China's Village Redevelopment Program', *China Journal*, vol. 74, July (2015), 18–42.

Are the *Nongguan* Coming? The Evolution of the Rural Comprehensive Administrative Enforcement Team in China's Rural Governance

1.   National Business Daily, 'The *nongguan* is coming, the peasants are panicking?' 农管来了，农民慌了?, 21 April 2023, online at: https://mp.weixin.qq.com/s/Pqahd5CqRPWvLgeVh9q7fA.

2.   William Zheng, 'China's new rural law force accused of bullying farmers after videos of overreach raise concern about tactics', *South China Morning Post*, 16 May 2023, online at: https://www.scmp.com/news/china/politics/article/3220690/chinas-new-rural-law-force-accused-bullying-farmers-after-videos-overreach-raise-concern-about

3.   Article 87, Agriculture Law of the People's Republic of China (2002).

4.   Ministry of Agriculture and Rural Affairs, 'Build and manage law enforcement teams, protect the interest of farmers' 建好管好执法队伍，保护农民群众利益, moa.gov.cn, 15 April 2023, online at: https://www.gov.cn/zhengce/2023-04/15/content_5751641.htm

5.   Caixin, 'Organization reform: The establishment of the Ministry of Agriculture and Rural Affairs and the fulfilment of big agriculture' 机构改革：组建农业农村部' 大农业' 成真, Caixin.com, 3 March 2018, online at: https://topics.caixin.com/2018-03-13/101220429.html

6. Ministry of Agriculture and Rural Affairs, 'Catalogue of Tasks for Rural Comprehensive Administrative Enforcement' 农业农村部印发《农业综合行政执法事项指导目录》（2020年版）的通知, moa.gov.cn, 14 July 2020, online at: http://www.moa.gov.cn/nybgb/2020/202006/202007/t20200714_6348621.htm

7. Hunan Daily, 'The recent response from the Ministry of Agriculture and Rural Affairs' 为什么，管什么，怎么管？农业农村部最新回应来了, 17 April 2023, online at: https://baijiahao.baidu.com/s?id=1763389916725290641&wfr=spider&for=pc

8. Ministry of Agriculture and Rural Affairs, 'The Regulation on the Process of Rural Administration Sanction' 农业行政处罚程序规定, moa.gov.cn, 4 January 2020, online at: https://www.gov.cn/zhengce/zhengceku/2020-01/19/content_5470721.htm

9. Ministry of Agriculture and Rural Affairs, 'Guidelines for the Basic Equipment of Rural Administrative Enforcement' 农业农村部关于印发《全国农业综合行政执法基本装备配备标准》（2022年版）的通知, moa.gov.cn, 27 May 2022, online at: http://www.moa.gov.cn/govpublic/CYZCFGS/202206/t20220602_6401402.htm

10. Ministry of Agriculture and Rural Affairs, 'Management Measures on Rural Comprehensive Administrative Enforcement', 农业综合行政执法管理办法, moa.gov.cn, 1 January 2023, online at: https://www.gov.cn/zhengce/2022-12/23/content_5733210.htm

11. Hunan Daily, 'The recent response from the Ministry of Agriculture and Rural Affairs' 为什么，管什么，怎么管？农业农村部最新回应来了, 17 April 2023, online at: https://baijiahao.baidu.com/s?id=1763389916725290641&wfr=spider&for=pc

12. Xinhua Agency, 'The initiation of the national agricultural comprehensive administrative enforcement of "Guaranteeing Food Supply" campaign' 全国农业综合行政执法' 稳粮保供' 专项行动启动, 31 March 2023, online at: https://news.cctv.com/2023/03/31/ARTIpSktxiYdXsBiQbcFQI9K230331.shtml

13. Ministry of Agriculture and Rural Affairs, Successful Cases of 'Guaranteeing Food Supply' Conducted by Rural Enforcement Teams 农业农村部公布2023年全国农业行政执法' 稳粮保供' 典型案例, moa.gov.cn, 14 September 2023, online at: http://www.moa.gov.cn/xw/zwdt/202309/t20230914_6436536.htm

14. Ministry of Agriculture and Rural Affairs, 'The Ministry of Agriculture and Rural Affairs Convenes the Rural Comprehensive Administrative Enforcement Team Working Style Meeting' 农业农村部召开农业综合行政执法队伍作风建设座谈会, moa.gov.cn, 13 September 2023, online at: http://www.moa.gov.cn/jg/leaders/zyd/hd/202309/t20230913_6436452.htm

CHAPTER 4: Disgruntled communities

Disturbing but Not Politically Threatening: Veterans' Activism in the Xi Era

1. Bo Xu, 'Veterans petitioned Beijing again, their activism poses potential hidden danger 退伍军人再度进京请愿, 老兵维权成中共隐患', Voice of America, 27 February 2017, online at: https://www.voachinese.com/a/VOAWeishi-20170227-VOAIO/3741843.html

2. James Mulvenon, 'Like Donkeys Slaughtered After They Are Too Old to Work a Grindstone: PLA Veterans' Protests and Party–Military Relations under Xi Jinping', *China Leadership Monitor*, no. 57 (2017): 1–7.

3. Kevin J. O'Brien, 'China's Disaffected Insiders', *Journal of Democracy*, vol. 28, no. 3 (2017): 5–13.

4. *Ministry of Interior Bulletin* 內務部通訊, vol. 5 (1956): 1–5. Accessed from the University Service Centre for China Studies, Chinese University of Hong Kong.

5. Gordon White, 'The Politics of Demobilized Soldiers from Liberation to Cultural Revolution', *China Quarterly*, no. 82 (1980): 203.

6. Neil J. Diamant and Kevin J. O'Brien, 'Veterans' Political Activism in China', *Modern China*, vol. 41, no. 3 (2015): 281.

7. Chunni Zhang, 'Military Service and Life Chances in Contemporary China', *Chinese Sociological Review*, vol. 47, no. 3 (2015): 230–54.

8. Xinhua, 'A civil affairs cadre in Jiangxi was sentenced for embezzling more than 2 million yuan in preferential treatment funds' 江西一民政干部侵吞优抚金200多万获刑, *People's Daily*, 28 November 2013, online at: http://politics.people.com.cn/n/2013/1128/c70731-23684018.html

9. Tangbiao Xiao and Da Chen, 'The Evolution of Public Expressive Actions and Its Policy Implications: Case Study of Enterprise Military-Transfer Cadres in County G (2000–2007) 民众表达行动的转型及其政策含义: 以G县企业军转干部为例 (2000–2007)', *Journal of Beijing Academy of Administration* 北京行政学院学报, no. 5 (2012): 42.

10. Ministry of Veterans Affairs, *2019 Annual Report on Government Information Disclosure Work* 2019 年政府信息公开工作年度报告, Beijing: Ministry of Veterans Affairs of the People's Republic of China, 6 February 2020, online at: http://www.mva.gov.cn/gongkai/zfxxgkpt/zfxxgknb/202001/t20200121_34751.html

Why are China's Unemployed Graduates Comparing Themselves to Lu Xun's Character?

1. Andrew Methven, 'Kong Yiji literature', The China Project, 31 March 2023, online at: https://thechinaproject.com/2023/03/31/kong-yiji-literature-phrase-of-the-week/

2. 'Monthly surveyed urban unemployment rate of people aged 16 to 24 in China from June 2021 to June 2023', Statista, online at: https://www.statista.com/statistics/1244339/surveyed-monthly-youth-unemployment-rate-in-china/

3. 'China stops releasing youth unemployment rates amid economic gloom', *Guardian*, 15 August 2023, online at: https://www.theguardian.com/world/2023/aug/15/china-unemployment-rate-youth-economy

4. Ibid.

5. Claire Fu and Daisuke Wakabayashi, 'Don't be so picky about a job, China's college graduates are told', *New York Times*, 8 August 2023, online at: https://www.nytimes.com/2023/08/08/business/china-youth-unemployment.html

6. Izzah Imran, 'After 800 job applications and 30 failed interviews, woman in China questions point of having a university degree', *Today*, 10 March 2023, online at: https://www.todayonline.com/world/job-interviews-graduate-unemployed-university-degree-2126761

7. 'What is "Kong Yiji literature"' "孔乙己文学"是什么梗, *China Digital Times*, 21 March 2023, online at: https://chinadigitaltimes.net/chinese/694043.html

8. Ibid.

9. 'Kong Yiji literature', *China Digital Times*, online at: https://chinadigitaltimes.net/chinese/tag/%E5%AD%94%E4%B9%99%E5%B7%B1%E6%96%87%E5%AD%A6/page/3

10. 'CCTV: We must look seriously at the anxiety behind "Kong Yiji Literature"' 央视网：正视孔乙己文学背后的焦虑, Sina, 16 March 2023, online at: https://finance.sina.com.cn/jjxw/2023-03-16/doc-imykzwvx4559491.shtml

11. Ibid.

12. 'Netizens question young couple earning 9000 yuan a day: did they pay tax' "95后" 夫妻摆摊日入9000元被质疑，网友建议查一下税, Sina, 27 March 2023, online at: https://finance.sina.com.cn/jjxw/2023-03-27/doc-imynfpit8836804.shtml

13. 'So Lu Xun wrote the story to criticise Kong Yiji? I thought it was to criticise old China' 原来鲁迅写《孔乙己》是批判孔乙己？我还以为批判旧社会呢, China Digital Times, 17 March 2023, online at: https://chinadigitaltimes.net/chinese/693937.html

14. 'Why are young people refusing to take off their "Kong Yiji's gown?' 年轻人为何脱不下孔乙己的长衫, Zhihu, 5 May 2023, online at: https://zhuanlan.zhihu.com/p/627031081

15. Translation modified based on Alexander Boyd, 'Censors delete viral "Kong Yiji Literature" anthem', China Digital Times, 30 March 2023, online at: https://chinadigitaltimes.net/2023/03/censors-delete-viral-kong-yiji-literature-anthem/?ref=neican.org

16. Ibid.

17. Simon Leys, The Burning Forest, London: Paladin, 1988, p. 101.

18. Simon Leys, The Hall of Uselessness: Collected Essays, Collingwood: Black Inc., 2011, p. 258.

19. W.J.F. Jenner, 'Lu Xun's last days and after', China Quarterly, no. 91 (1982): 440.

20. Yu Hua 余华, China in Ten Words 十個詞彙裡的中國, Taipei: Rye Field Publishing Co., 2010, p. 100.

21. He Huifeng, 'Parents angry at removal of Lu Xun's works from China's school textbooks', 8 September 2013, South China Morning Post, online at: https://www.scmp.com/news/china/article/1305905/parents-angry-removal-lu-xuns-works-chinas-school-textbooks

22. Kiki Zhao, 'Leveling criticism at China's elite, some borrow words from the past', New York Times, 4 January 2016, online at: https://www.nytimes.com/2016/01/05/world/asia/china-lu-xun-zhao-family.html

23. 'Millions in the capital march to show their support for college students on a hunger strike' 首都各界百余万人游行声援绝食请愿的大学生, People's Daily, 17 May 1989, online at: https://cn.govopendata.com/renminribao/1989/5/17/1/

24. 'Millennial volunteers: Rumours stop with us now' 90后志愿者团队：我們要當謠言粉碎機, People.cn, 18 February 2020, online at: http://media.people.com.cn/BIG5/n1/2020/0218/c40606-31591414.html; Li Chengpeng 李承鹏, 'Could you preserve some dignity for this country', 我想，你给这个国家留点碧莲，也是应该的, Yibao, 5 December 2022, online at: https://yibaochina.com/?p=248635

25. Thomas S. Mullaney, 'To abolish the Chinese language: On a century of reformist rhetoric', Literary Hub, 15 September 2017, online at: https://lithub.com/to-abolish-the-chinese-language-on-a-century-of-reformist-rhetoric/

26. Tsi-an Hsia, The Gate of Darkness: Studies on the Leftist Literary Movement in China, Seattle and London: University of Washington Press, 1968, pp. 146–47.

27. Ibid.

28. Lu Hsun, Wild Grass, trans. Yang Hsien-yi and Gladys Yang, Beijing: Foreign Language Press, 1974, p. 3.

29. Ibid., p. 44.

30. Julia Lovell, 'The afterlife of Lu Xun', China Channel, 28 September 2017, online at: https://chinachannel.lareviewofbooks.org/2017/09/28/lu-xun-afterlife/

31. Geremie R. Barmé, 'The true story of Lu Xun', China File, 23 November 2017, online at: https://www.chinafile.com/library/nyrb-china-archive/true-story-of-lu-xun

32. Ibid.

33. Nicolas D. Kristof, 'China's greatest dissident writer: Dead but still dangerous', *New York Times*, 19 August 1990, online at: https://www.nytimes.com/1990/08/19/books/china-s-greatest-dissident-writer-dead-but-still-dangerous.html?pagewanted=all

Chinese 'Incels'? Misogynist Men on Chinese Social Media

1. Xuejiao Cai, 'Quick-to-quip comedy queen called out for comments on men', Sixth Tone.com, 28 December 2020, online at: https://www.sixthtone.com/news/1006636

2. Chong Han, 'Yang Li faces physical threat, Xiaoguo Culture Media response: We will increase security measures' 杨笠遭人身威胁 笑果文化回应：会加强安全防范, NetEase Entertainment, 16 April 2022, online at: https://www.163.com/ent/article/H52E8LOA00038FO9.html

3. Xinyu Du and Qi'an Chen, 'After male backlash, Intel China cuts ties with comedy queen', Sixth Tone.com, 22 March 2021, online at: https://www.sixthtone.com/news/1007019

4. Debbie Ging, 'Alphas, betas and incels: Theorizing the masculinities of the manosphere', *Men and Masculinities*, vol. 22, no. 4 (2019): 638–57.

5. Donna Zuckerberg, *Not All Dead White Men: Classics and Misogyny in the Digital Age*, Cambridge, MA: Harvard University Press, 2018.

6. Rebecca Jennings, 'Incels categorize women by personal style and attractiveness', Vox.com, 28 April 2018, online at: https://www.vox.com/2018/4/28/17290256/incel-chad-stacy-becky

7. Alexandra Stevenson, 'China's male leaders signal to women that their place is in the home', *New York Times*, 2 November 2023, online at: https://www.nytimes.com/2023/11/02/world/asia/china-communist-party-xi-women.html

8. National Bureau of Statistics of China, *Communiqué of the Seventh National Population Census (No. 4)*, 11 May 2021, online at: http://www.stats.gov.cn/english/PressRelease/202105/t20210510_1817189.html

9. Lisa Cameron, Xin Meng and Dandan Zhang, 'China's sex ratio and crime: Behavioural change or financial necessity?', *Economic Journal*, vol. 129, no. 618 (2019), 790–820.

10. Altman Yuzhu Peng, 'Digital nationalism versus gender politics in post-reform China: Gender-issue debates on Zhihu', *Global Media and Communication*, vol. 18, no. 3 (2022): 281–99.

11. Teacher Precious 宝宝老师, Sina Weibo, online at: https://weibo.com/p/1005051918628847

12. China Team, 'Weibo is "treating the incels like the royal family"', Protocol.com, 15 April 2021, online at: https://www.protocol.com/china/weibo-incels

13. Wanqing Zhang, 'Heavily persecuted, highly influential: China's online feminist revolution. On Chinese social media, women are censored and harassed, but undeterred', Rest of World, 26 September 2023, online at: https://restofworld.org/2023/china-online-feminist-movement/

14. Suzhi Jia, 'Two types of misogyny as "the state's will": What does "radical feminists" battling the Communist Youth League of China reveal? 作为'国家意志'的两种厌女观：'极端女权'大战共青团中央揭示了什么问题？', Initium Media, 24 April 2022, online at: https://theinitium.com/zh-Hans/article/20220425-opinion-china-feminism-nationalism-incel

15. Mumianshuo 木棉说, '3 female university students were attacked with sulphuric acid 3名女大学生被泼硫酸', Paper, 30 December 2020, online at: https://www.163.com/dy/article/FV8FGMMU0548LAJN.html

16. Yating Yang, 'Assault on women by drunk man in China after refusing to share contact details sparks outrage, echoing infamous 2022 Tangshan vicious attack', South China Morning Post, 9 October 2023, online at: https://sc.mp/5p09?utm_source=copy-link&utm_campaign=3237116&utm_medium=share_widget

17. James Palmer, 'A brutal attack stirs anger and shame in China', Foreign Policy, 15 June 2022, online at: https://foreignpolicy.com/2022/06/15/china-tangshan-attack-gender-violence-anger/

18. Xiaoai Yi, Shuyue Chen, Wenxiao Zhou, Li Xie, Ji Yu and Shituo Hu, 'Their fear and anger after Tangshan incident 唐山事件后，她们的恐惧与愤怒', Initium Media, 16 June 2022, online at: https://theinitium.com/zh-Hans/article/20220616-mainland-tangshan-gender-violence-girls

CHAPTER 5: Voices of the ordinary people

Loneliness, Death and Desolation: Why I Return to Antarctica Time and Again

1. 越冬 yuedong or 'winter-over' is a specific term used to denote the process by which researchers in the Antarctic steel themselves to pass through the long and often difficult winters. It implies a degree of tenacity on the part of the researchers to adjust their way of living in the research centre to wait out the winter season.

2. Note from translator: Many research stations in the Antarctic have, however, set up hydroponic gardens in greenhouses for research purposes as early as 1902. By 2015 there were at least forty-six different facilities in Antarctica where researchers had grown plants at some time or another as scientific experiments. Matthew Bamsey, Paul Zabel, Conrad Zeidler David Gyimesi, Daniel Schubert, Eberhard Kohlberg, Dirk Mengedoht, Joanna Rae and Thomas Graham, 'Review of Antarctic greenhouses and plant production facilities: A historical account of food plants on the ice', Paper presented at the 45th International Conference on Environment Systems, Bellevue, WA, USA, 12–16 July 2015: 1–37, online at: https://www.researchgate.net/publication/280738927_Review_of_Antarctic_Greenhouses_and_Plant_Production_Facilities_A_Historical_Account_of_Food_Plants_on_the_Ice

CHAPTER 6: China's global ambitions

From Riyadh and Tehran to Beijing: China's Diplomatic Role in a Changing World

1. 'China's Xi tells Putin of "changes not seen for 100 years"', Al Jazeera, 22 March 2023, online at: https://www.aljazeera.com/news/2023/3/22/xi-tells-putin-of-changes-not-seen-for-100

2. 'Xi offers no help on Ukraine after meeting with Macron and von der Leyen', China Project, 6 April 2023, online at: https://thechinaproject.com/2023/04/06/xi-offers-no-help-on-ukraine-after-meeting-with-macron-and-von-der-leyen/

3. Maria Siow, 'Will India end up alienated from Brics over US tilt, attempts to dilute China's influence?', South China Morning Post, 3 September 2023, online at: https://www.scmp.com/week-asia/politics/article/3233159/will-india-end-alienated-brics-over-us-tilt-attempts-dilute-chinas-influence

4. Felix Richter, 'The rise of the BRICS', Statista, 22 August 2023, online at: https://www.statista.com/chart/amp/30638/brics-and-g7-share-of-global-gdp/

5. Wandiswa Ntengento, 'BRICS GDP to grow to 36% following expansion', Africanews, 25 August 2023, online at: https://www.africanews.com/amp/2023/08/25/brics-gdp-to-grow-by-36-following-expansion/

6. Alex Lo, 'Why so many nations suddenly want to become part of Brics', South China Morning Post, 27 August 2023, online at: https://www.scmp.com/comment/opinion/article/3232465/why-so-many-nations-suddenly-want-become-part-brics

7. Lo Kinling, 'Will China's belt and road plan, ASEAN provide silver lining as US step ups de-risking and trade prospects dim?', South China Morning Post, 5 September 2023, online at: https://www.scmp.com/economy/global-economy/article/3233363/will-chinas-belt-and-road-plan-asean-provide-silver-lining-us-step-ups-de-risking-and-trade

8. David Sacks, 'China's Belt and Road Initiative enters its second decade: Which leaders went to celebrate with Xi Jinping?', Council on Foreign Relations blog, 17 October 2023, online at: https://www.cfr.org/blog

9. Sheena Chestnut Greiters, 'Xi Jinping's quest for order', Foreign Affairs, 3 October 2022, online at: https://www.foreignaffairs.com/china/xi-jingping-quest-order; Gabriel Wildau, 'China: What is the Global Security Initiative?', Teneo, online at: https://www.teneo.com/china-what-is-the-global-security-initiative/

10. Shanghai Cooperation Organisation members are: China, India, Iran, Kazakhstan, Kyrgyzstan, Pakistan, Russia, Tajikistan and Uzbekistan.

11. Asian Infrastructure Investment Bank website, online at: https://www.aiib.org/en/index.html

12. Ehsan Soltani, 'How China became Saudi Arabia's largest trading partner', Visual Capitalist, 19 February 2023, online at: https://www.visualcapitalist.com/cp/how-china-became-saudi-arabias-largest-trading-partner/

13. 'What Xi Jinping's Saudi Arabia visit means for the Middle East', Atlantic Council, 9 December 2022, online at: https://atlanticcouncil.org/blogs/new-atlanticist/whatxi-jinpings-saudi-arabia-visit-means-for-the-middle-east

14. Shannon Tiezzi, 'Iran's President visits China, hoping to revitalize ties', The Diplomat, 15 February 2023, online at: https://thediplomat.com/2023/02/irans-president-visits-china-hoping-to-revitalize-ties/

15. Eugene Tang, 'Global impact: Banking, investments, food security, health sciences and future mobility on the table as China seeks to boost Saudi Arabia ties', South China Morning Post, 26 June 2023, online at: https://www.scmp.com/economy/global-economy/article/3225324/global-impact-banking-investments-food-security-health-sciences-and-future-mobility-table-china

16. Lo Kinling, 'China, Saudi Arabia enter "new stage" of financial cooperation as state-owned bank opens Riyadh Branch', *South China Morning Post*, 6 September 2023, online at: https://www.scmp.com/economy/global-economy/article/3233565/china-saudi-arabia-enter-new-stage-financial-cooperation-state-owned-bank-opens-riyadh-branch

17. Yasmine Farouk, 'Riyadh's motivations behind the Saudi–Iran deal', Carnegie Endowment for International Peace, 30 March 2023, online at: https://carnegieendowment.org/2023/03/30/riyadh-s-motivations-behind-saudi-iran-deal-pub-89421

18. David E. Sanger, 'Candidate Biden called Saudi Arabia a "pariah". He now has to deal with it', New York Times, 24 February 2021, online at: https://www.nytimes.com/2021/02/24/us/politics/biden-jamal-khashoggi-saudi-arabia.html

19. 'Top Chinese envoy heads to Ukraine, Russia in Europe "peace" tour', Al Jazeera, 15 May 2023, online at: https://www.aljazeera.com/amp/news/2023/5/15/top-chinese-envoy-heads-to-ukraine-russia-in-europe-peace-tour

20. Kawala Xie, 'China's Ukraine peace plan: What does it say and what are its chances of success?', *South China Morning Post*, 27 April 2023, online at: https://www.scmp.com/news/china/diplomacy/article/3218610/chinas-ukraine-peace-plan-what-does-it-say-and-what-are-its-chances-success

21. Agence France-Presse, 'China ready to broker Israel–Palestine peace talks, says foreign minister', *Guardian*, 18 April 2023, online at: https://amp.theguardian.com/world/2023/apr/18/china-ready-to-broker-israel-palestine-peace-talks-says-foreign-minister

22. Vivian Wang, 'Hosting Palestinian leader, Xi pushes China as a peacemaker for Israel', *New York Times*, 14 June 2023, online at: https://www.nytimes.com/2023/06/14/world/asia/china-mahmoud-abbas-xi-jinping.html

23. Brian Peach, 'China's response to the Israel–Gaza war shows how Beijing is firmly aligned with the Global South', *South China Morning Post*, 29 October 2023, online at: https://scmp.com/news/china/diplomacy/article/3237357/conflict-between-israel-and-hamas-puts-chinas-approach-middle-east-test

24. Kinling, 'Will China's Belt and Road plan, ASEAN provide silver lining'.

25. Alexander Gabuev, 'China's new vassal', *Foreign Affairs*, 9 August 2022, online at: https://www.foreignaffairs.com/china/chinas-new-vassal

26. Howard French, 'Why Lula's visit to Beijing matters more than Macron's', *Foreign Policy*, 24 April 2023, online at: https://foreignpolicy.com/2023/04/24/lula-brazil-china-xi-jinping-meeting-ukraine-france-macron-vassal

27. Jarrett Renshaw, Andrea Shalal and Michael Martina, 'Biden says China won't surpass the US as global leader on his watch', Reuters, 26 March 2021, online at: https://www.reuters.com/article/idUSKBN2BH32Z/

The Belt and Road's Midlife Crisis: Perspectives from Latin America and the Caribbean

1. Michael Clarke, 'The Belt and Road Initiative: China's new grand strategy?', *Asia Policy*, vol. 24 (2017): 71–79.

2. Lee Jones and Zeng Jinghan, 'Understanding China's "Belt and Road Initative": Beyond "grand strategy" to a state transformation analysis', *Third World Quarterly*, vol. 40, no. 8 (2019): 1415–39.

3. Ana Swanson, 'How China used more cement in 3 years than the US did in the entire 20th century', *Washington Post*, 24 March 2015, online at: https://www.washingtonpost. com/news/wonk/wp/2015/03/24/how-china-used-more-cement-in-3-years-than-the-u-s-did-in-the-entire-20th-century/

4. Rebecca Ray and Blake Alexander Simmons, 'Tracking china's overseas development finance', Global Development Policy Center, online at: https://www.bu.edu/ gdp/2020/12/07/tracking-chinas-overseas-development-finance/

5. 'China–Latin America finance database', Dialogue, online at: https://www.thedialogue. org/blogs/2013/07/china-latin-america-finance-database/

6. Rhys Jenkins, 'China's Belt and Road Initiative in Latin America: What has changed?', *Journal of Current Chinese Affairs*, vol. 51, no. 1 (2022): 13–39.

7. Nancy Birdsall, Augusto de la Torre and Felipe Valencia Caicedo, 'The Washington consensus: Assessing a damaged brand', World Bank, Policy Research Working Paper 5316 (2010).

8. Anna Gelpern, Sebastian Horn, Scott Morris, Brad Parks and Christoph Trebesch, 'How China lends: A rare look into 100 debt contracts with foreign governments', *Economic Policy*, vol. 38, no. 114, (April 2023): 345–416.

9. Maria Haro Sly, 'Anarcho-capitalism: Argentina between the IMF and China', Phenomenal World, 21 December 2023, online at: https://www.phenomenalworld.org/ analysis/anarcho-capitalism/

10. Jeannette Larde and Ricardo J. Sánchez, 'The economics infrastructure gap and investment in Latin America', CEPAL Bulletin, FAL 332, no. 4 (2014).

11. Ruben Gonzalez-Vicente, 'In the name of the nation: Authoritarian practices, capital accumulation and the radical simplification of development in China's global vision', *Globalizations*, online first (2022); Anthony J. Bebbington, Denise Humphreys Bebbington, Laura Aileen Sauls, John Rogan, Sumali Agrawal, César Gamboa, Aviva Imhof, Kimberly Johnson, Herman Rosa, Antoinette Royo, Tessa Toubourou and Ricardo Verdum, 'Resource extraction and infrastructure threaten forest cover and community rights', *Proceedings of the National Academy of Sciences of the United States of America*, vol. 115, no. 52 (2018): 13164–73.

12. Mauro Nogarin, 'El Sillar—Bolivia's challenging road project', World Highways, 6 February 2020, online at: https://www.worldhighways.com/wh10/feature/el-sillar-bolivias-challenging-road-project

13. Ruben Gonzalez-Vicente, 'Over hills and valleys too: China's Belt and Road Initiative in the Caribbean', in Florian Schneider (ed.), *Global Perspectives on China's Belt and Road Initiative: Asserting Agency through Regional Connectivity*, Amsterdam: Amsterdam University Press, p. 171.

14. Benjamin Russell, 'What a controversial deal in El Salvador says about China's bigger plans', *Americas Quarterly*, 12 April 2019, online at: https://www.americasquarterly. org/article/what-a-controversial-deal-in-el-salvador-says-about-chinas-bigger-plans/

15. Ruben Gonzalez-Vicente and Annita Montoute, 'A Caribbean perspective on China–Caribbean relations: Global IR, dependency and the postcolonial condition', *Third World Quarterly*, vol. 42, no. 2 (2021): 219–38.

16. Antonio M. Vélez, 'España, el país de la OCDE con más empresas en la "Lista Negra" de Sanciones del Banco Mundial', *ElDiario.es*, 24 March 2021, online at: https://www.eldiario.es/economia/espana-lidera-sanciones-empresas-ricos-lista-negra-banco-mundial_1_7343009.html; Ben Miller and Fernanda Uriegas, 'Latin America's biggest corruption cases: A retrospective', *Americas Quarterly*, 11 July 2019, online at: https://www.americasquarterly.org/article/latin-americas-biggest-corruption-cases-a-retrospective/

17. 'Undercover in Guyana: Exposing Chinese business in South America', Vice News, 7 July 2022, online at: https://www.youtube.com/watch?v=sOOFSJqBYTY. Lorena Baires, 'Peru freezes contracts with Chinese companies', Diálogo Américas, 1 August 2023, online at: https://dialogo-americas.com/articles/peru-freezes-contracts-with-chinese-companies/

18. Wanjing (Kelly) Chen, 'Sovereign debt in the making: Financial entanglements and labor politics along the Belt and Road in Laos', *Economic Geography*, vol. 96, no. 4 (2020): 295–314.

19. Diana Castro, 'Coca Codo Sinclair Hydroelectric Project', People's Map of Global China (2022), online at: https://thepeoplesmap.net/project/coca-codo-sinclair-hydroelectric-project/

20. LatinoAmérica, 'Santa Cruz River Hydroelectric Complex', People's Map of Global China (2022), online at: https://thepeoplesmap.net/project/santa-cruz-river-hydroelectric-complex/

21. Margaret Myers and Kevin Gallagher, 'Scaling back: Chinese development finance in LAC, 2019', Dialogue and BU Global Development Center, China–Latin America Report (2020).

22. Margaret Myers and Rebecca Ray, 'At a crossroads: Chinese development finance to Latin America and the Caribbean, 2022', Dialogue and BU Global Development Center, China–Latin America Report (2023).

23. 'No new loans from China, says PM', *Jamaica Gleaner*, 10 November 2019, online at: https://jamaica-gleaner.com/article/news/20191110/no-new-loans-china-says-pm

24. Andreea Brînză (2022) 'What happened to the Belt and Road Initiative?', *Diplomat*, 6 September 2022, online at: https://thediplomat.com/2022/09/what-happened-to-the-belt-and-road-initiative/

25. 'China reckons with its first overseas debt crisis', *Financial Times*, 21 July 2022, online at: https://www.ft.com/content/ccbe2b80-0c3e-4d58-a182-8728b443df9a

26. Kjeld van Wieringen and Tim Zajontz, 'From loan-financed to privatised infrastructure? Tracing China's turn towards public–private partnerships in Africa', *Journal of Current Chinese Affairs*, vol. 42, no. 3 (2023): 434–63.

27. Hong Zhang, 'Is China's Belt and Road Initiative slowing down?', *The People's Map of Global China*, 21 June 2021, online at: https://thepeoplesmap.net/2021/06/21/is-chinas-belt-and-road-initiative-slowing-down/

28. Ralph Jennings, '5 trade moves China has made in 2023 in Latin America—the traditional backyard of the US', *South China Morning Post*, 20 May 2023, online at: https://www.scmp.com/economy/global-economy/article/3221178/5-trade-moves-china-has-made-2023-latin-america-traditional-backyard-us

CHAPTER 7: New frontiers

China: The New No. 2 Space Power

1. Sun Ye, 'In pictures: China's manned space program marks 30 years with grand exhibition in Beijing', China Global Television Network, 25 February 2023, online at: https://news.cgtn.com/news/2023-02-24/China-s-manned-space-program-marks-30-years-with-grand-exhibition-1hGTuxSHQCk/index.html

2. Rocket Lab Official Website, online at: https://www.rocketlabusa.com/

3. 'New mineral found by Chinese scientists', China National Space Administration, 9 September 2022, online at: https://www.cnsa.gov.cn/english/n6465652/n6465653/c6840851/content.html

4. 'Asteroid Explorer Hayabusa2 Initial Analysis: Soluble Organic Matter (SOM) Team reveals organic molecule compositions in samples of asteroid Ryugu', press release, Japan Aerospace Exploration Agency, 24 February 2023, online at: https://global.jaxa.jp/press/2023/02/20230224-1_e.html

5. Mike Wall, 'X-37B: The air force's mysterious space plane', Space.com, 31 August 2021, online at: https://www.space.com/25275-x37b-space-plane.html

6. Fan Anqi, 'China's reusable suborbital spacecraft makes successful maiden flight', *Global Times*, 18 July 2021, online at: https://www.globaltimes.cn/page/202107/1228956.shtml

7. CAS Space website, online at: https://en.cas-space.com/

8. 'Все компоненты стыковочного механизма были разработаны и произведены собственными силами Китая' [All components of the docking mechanism were designed and manufactured by China in-house], Russian.News.Cn, 3 November 2011, online at: https://web.archive.org/web/20120426010439/http:/russian.news.cn/dossiers/2011-11/03/c_131228371.htm

9. 'China hopes to expand cooperation with Russia in space', TASS, 16 October 2016, online at: https://tass.com/science/906725

10. 'Government expenditure on space programs in 2020 and 2022, by major country', Statista, online at: https://www.statista.com/statistics/745717/global-governmental-spending-on-space-programs-leading-countries/

11. Elizabeth Howell, 'No, Russia hasn't claimed it will abandon an American astronaut on the space station', Space.com, 12 March 2022, online at: https://www.space.com/russia-will-not-abandon-nasa-astronaut-on-iss

12. Thomas Seal, 'OneWeb takes $230 million hit after Russia seized its satellites', Bloomberg, 3 September 2022, online at: https://www.bloomberg.com/news/articles/2022-09-02/oneweb-takes-230-million-hit-after-russia-seized-its-satellites#xj4y7vzkg

The Frontiers of History: China Discovers the Pacific's Dark Colonial Legacy

1. CGTN Global Watch, 9 July 2023, online at: https://twitter.com/GlobalWatchCGTN/status/1677950717695254531

2. CGTN, Exclusive with Solomon Islands PM Manasseh Sogavare, 15 July 2023, online at: https://www.youtube.com/watch?v=w4i4xABX-x4

3. Xinhua, 'Xi Jinping: China's policy on Pacific Island countries adheres to the "Four Fully Respects"' 习近平：中国的太平洋岛国政策秉持'四个充分尊重', Gov.cn, 10 July 2023, online at: https://www.gov.cn/yaowen/liebiao/202307/content_6890928.htm

4. Ibid.

5. Susannah Luthi, 'Meth, vanilla and "gulags": How China has overtaken the South Pacific one island at a time', Politico, 29 August 2021, online at: https://www.politico.com/news/magazine/2021/08/29/tonga-china-south-pacific-influence-506370; Taina Kami Enoka, 'China insists Tonga loans come with "no political strings attached"', Guardian, 29 June 2022, online at: https://www.theguardian.com/world/2022/jun/29/china-tonga-loans-no-political-strings-attached-pacific

6. Most Pacific nations refer to their strategies of engaging with China – and Asia more broadly – as the 'Look North' policy.

7. Graeme Smith, George Carter, Mao Xiaojing, Almah Tararia, Elisi Tupou and Xu Weitao, The Development Needs of Pacific Island Countries, Beijing: UNDP China, 2014.

8. Denghua Zhang, 'Pacific studies in China: Policies, structure and research', Journal of Pacific History, vol. 55, no. 1 (2020), 80–96.

9. Shandong is one of three provinces heavily involved in distant-water fishing. Graeme Smith, 'Fishy business: China's mixed signals on sustainable fisheries', in Linda Jaivin and Esther Sunkyung Klein with Sharon Strange (eds), China Story Yearbook: Contradiction, Canberra: ANU Press, 2022, p. 220.

10. See for example Shuo Luan, 'Chinese pacificism: Exploring Chinese news media representation of Pacific island countries', Pacific Studies, vol. 45, no. 2 (2022), 157–86.

11. Australian Department of Foreign Affairs and Trade, Australia–Tuvalu Falepili Union treaty, November 2023, online at: https://www.dfat.gov.au/geo/tuvalu/australia-tuvalu-falepili-union-treaty

12. Jessica Marinaccio, 'The Australia–Tuvalu Falepili Union: Tuvaluan values or Australian interests?', DevPolicy blog, 15 November 2023, online at: https://devpolicy.org/the-australia-tuvalu-falepili-union-tuvaluan-values-or-australian-interests-20231115/

13. Editor, 'Do not make the resettlement offer to Pacific a geopolitical chess move', Global Times, 14 November 2023, online at: https://www.globaltimes.cn/page/202311/1301824.shtml

14. Sean Rubinsztein-Dunlop and Echo Hui, 'Australia revokes Chinese scholar visas and targets media officials, prompting furious China response', ABC News, 9 September 2020, online at: https://www.abc.net.au/news/2020-09-09/chinese-scholars-have-visas-revoked-as-diplomatic-crisis-grows/12644022

15. Kyle Hill, 'The Castle Bravo disaster', youtube.com, 23 January 2021, online at: https://www.youtube.com/watch?v=ew064gt2thY

16. Nic Maclellan, Prohibiting Nuclear Weapons: A Pacific Priority, Melbourne: ICANW, online at: https://icanw.org.au/wp-content/uploads/Pacific-Report-2017.pdf

17. Stephen Howes, 'The Opposition's opposition to the Pacific Engagement Visa', DevPolicy blog, 8 March 2023, online at: https://devpolicy.org/the-oppositions-opposition-to-the-pacific-engagement-visa-20230308/

18. Stephen Dziedzic and Dubravka Voloder, 'Parliament clears path for Pacific visa and opens the door to 3,000 annual immigrants', ABC News, 19 October 2023, online at: https://www.abc.net.au/news/2023-10-19/labor-expands-pacific-immigration-with-new-visa/102997646

19. Bruce Hunt, *Australia's Northern Shield? Papua New Guinea and the Defence of Australia since 1880*, Melbourne: Monash University Press, 2017.

20. Frank Sade Bilaupaine, 'US geopolitical point-scoring means little to Pacific Island countries', *Global Times*, 4 August 2022, https://www.globaltimes.cn/page/202208/1272183.shtml

21. Renju Jose, 'Australia's Telstra completes Digicel Pacific buyout', Reuters, 14 July 2022, online at: https://www.reuters.com/markets/deals/australias-telstra-completes-digicel-pacific-buyout-2022-07-14/

22. Alexandre Dayant, Meg Keen and Roland Rajah, 'Chinese aid to the Pacific: Decreasing, but not disappearing', Lowy Interpreter, 23 January 2023, online at: https://www.lowyinstitute.org/the-interpreter/chinese-aid-pacific-decreasing-not-disappearing

23. Ibid.

24. 'Canberra's arrogance won't block planned fishery project', *Global Times*, 27 January 2021, https://www.globaltimes.cn/page/202101/1214169.shtml

CHAPTER 8: The pointy end of Australia–China relations

How Fearful is China's Military Rise?

1. 'China's "two sessions" 2023: Xi Jinping tells defence delegation new policy crucial for stronger army and nation', *South China Morning Post*, 9 March 2023, online at: https://www.scmp.com/news/china/politics/article/3212893/chinas-two-sessions-2023-xi-jinping-tells-defence-delegation-new-policy-crucial-stronger-army-and-nation

2. 'What does China really spend on its military?', China Power, 2023, online at: https://chinapower.csis.org/military-spending/

3. Australian Department of Defence, *Defence Strategic Review, 2023*.

4. 'China', Lowy Institute, 2023, online at: https://poll.lowyinstitute.org/themes/china/

5. Ibid.

6. 'Quad', 2023, online at: https://www.dfat.gov.au/international-relations/regional-architecture/quad

7. Collin Koh, 'FONOP table', X, 10 April 2023, available at: https://twitter.com/CollinSLKoh/status/1645259606673993730. See also Eleanor Freund, *Freedom of Navigation in the South China Sea: A Practical Guide*, Belfer Center for Science and International Affairs, Cambridge, MA: Harvard Kennedy School, 2017.

8. 'Joint leaders statement on AUKUS', 2023, online at: https://www.whitehouse.gov/briefing-room/statements-releases/2023/03/13/joint-leaders-statement-on-aukus-2/

9. Richard Wood, 'Australia "facing threat of war with China within three years"', 9News, 7 March 2023, online at: https://www.9news.com.au/national/australia-faces-threat-of-war-with-china-within-three-years-experts-warn/9c757e9c-d0e7-4b33-9a0f-

70546858c736; 'Military confrontation in the South China Sea', Council on Foreign Relations, 2020, online at: https://www.cfr.org/report/military-confrontation-south-china-sea

10. Yun Jiang, 'Media hype of war with China forgets the impact on Australian society', *Guardian*, 9 March 2023, online at: https://www.theguardian.com/australia-news/commentisfree/2023/mar/09/media-hype-of-war-with-china-forgets-the-impact-on-australian-society-yun-jiang

11. See SIPRI Military Expenditure Database, consulted August 2023, online at: https://milex.sipri.org/sipri. However, the official defence budget in China can sometimes be misleading, as some research and development may fall under the category of science and technology. See 'Making sense of China's government budget', China Power, 2023, online at: https://chinapower.csis.org/making-sense-of-chinas-government-budget/

12. For China's naval capability building, see: Edward Sing Yue Chan, *China's Maritime Security Strategy: The Evolution of a Growing Sea Power*, Abingdon, Oxon, and New York: Routledge, 2022; *China Naval Modernization: Implications for US Navy Capability – Background and Issues for Congress*, Congressional Research Service, Washington, DC, 2022.

13. For example: Ni Guanghui, 'Strong military dream supports the China dream' 强军梦支撑中国梦, People.cn, 15 October 2017, online at: http://cpc.people.com.cn/n1/2017/1015/c412690-29587718.html. 'Strong military dream: The strong guarantee for achieving the China Dream' 强军梦：实现中国梦的坚强力量保证, People.cn, 31 July 2013, online at: http://theory.people.com.cn/n/2013/0731/c40531-22386933.html

14. 'Xi Jinping: Strive to build a people's army that obeys the party's command and can win battles with a good style of work' 习近平：努力建设一支听党指挥能打胜仗作风优良的人民军队, People.cn, 12 March 2013, online at: http://cpc.people.com.cn/n/2013/0312/c64094-20755159.html. 'Carry out the goal of strengthening the army and strengthen the consciousness of war fighting' 贯彻强军目标 强化打仗意识, People.cn, 14 March 2013, online at: http://theory.people.com.cn/n/2013/0314/c40531-20787798.html

15. 'Xi Jinping: Strive to achieve the party's goal of strengthening the military in the new era and build the people's army into a world-class army in an all-round way' 习近平：为实现党在新时代的强军目标 把人民军队全面建成世界一流军队而奋斗, News.cn, 26 October 2017, online at: http://www.news.cn/politics/19cpcnc/2017-10/26/c_1121862632.htm

16. Chu Dangyang, Shen Hongxin and Gao Liping, 'How should we see the new "three-step" strategic arrangement for national defence and military modernisation' 怎么看国防和军队现代化新'三步走'战略安排, 81.cn, 2 September 2022, online at: http://www.81.cn/yw_208727/10182296.html

17. 'Build the People's Army into a world-class military in an all-round way' 把人民军队全面建成世界一流军队, Qiushi, 29 June 2018, online at: http://www.qstheory.cn/dukan/qs/2018-06/29/c_1123054429.htm; 'Holding the scientific implications of building a world-class military' 把握建设世界一流军队科学内涵, People.cn, 16 January 2018, online at: http://military.people.com.cn/n1/2018/0116/c1011-29767236.html; Xiao Tiefeng, 'Explore the characteristics and laws of building a world-class military' 探索建设世界一流军队的特点规律, *Jiefangjun Bao*, 27 February 2018: 7.

18. Jun Zheng, 'A comprehensive plan to speed up national defene and military modernisation' 加快国防和军队现代化的全面擘画, Jiefangjun Bao, 29 August 2022, online at: http://www.mod.gov.cn/gfbw/sy/tt_214026/4919717.html; Chu, Shen and Gao, 'How should we see the new "three-step" strategic arrangement'.

19. State Council, China's National Defence in the New Era 新时代的中国国防, Beijing, 2019.

20. US Department of Defense, 'Military and security developments involving the People's Republic of China', 2023, online at: https://media.defense.gov/2023/Oct/19/2003323409/-1/-1/1/2023-military-and-security-developments-involving-the-peoples-republic-of-china.pdf

21. Joel Wuthnow and Taylor M. Fravel, 'China's military strategy for a "new era": Some change, more continuity, and tantalizing hints', Journal of Strategic Studies, 2022, vol. 46, no. 6–7: 1149–84.

22. Jun Zheng, 'Strategic guidance for military struggles in the new era' 进行新时代军事斗争的战略指导, People.cn, 2 September 2022, online at: http://dangjian.people.com.cn/n1/2022/0902/c117092-32517942.html; State Council, China's National Defence in the New Era.

23. 'China ramps up sci-tech self-reliance drive with establishment of new central commission', Global Times, 17 March 2023, online at: https://www.globaltimes.cn/page/202303/1287490.shtml

24. 'China releases plan on reforming Party and state institutions', Xinhua, 16 March 2023, online at: http://english.www.gov.cn/policies/latestreleases/202303/16/content_WS6413be82c6d0f528699db58e.html

25. Eduardo Baptista, 'China to restructure sci-tech ministry to achieve self-reliance faster', Reuters, 7 March 2023, online at: https://www.reuters.com/world/china/china-restructure-sci-tech-ministry-reach-self-reliance-faster-state-media-2023-03-07/; Arthur Ding and K. Tristan Tang, 'At a dead end? China's drive to reform defense science and technology institutes stalls', China Brief, 19 January 2023, online at: https://jamestown.org/program/at-a-dead-end-chinas-drive-to-reform-defense-science-and-technology-institutes-stalls/; Jiang Jiang, Jia Yuxuan and Yu Liaojie, 'China's plan on reforming Party and state institutions—Near-full translation of official document', Ginger River Review, 17 March 2023, online at: https://www.gingerriver.com/p/chinas-plan-on-reforming-party-and; Scott Kennedy, Claire Reade, Paul Triolo Jeannette Chu, John L. Holden and Ilaria Mazzocco, 'The completed construction of the Xi Jinping system of governance', Center for Strategic and International Studies, 15 March 2023, online at: https://www.csis.org/blogs/trustee-china-hand/completed-construction-xi-jinping-system-governance

26. 'We must seek motivation from reform and innovation' 必须向改革创新要动力, 81.cn, 14 March 2023, online at: http://www.81.cn/xxqj_207719/tsysb_207739/qjxjc/16209241.html

27. 'Tracking the fourth Taiwan Strait crisis', Centre of Strategic and International Studies, 2022, online at: https://chinapower.csis.org/tracking-the-fourth-taiwan-strait-crisis

28. Ryan D. Martinson, Incubators of Sea Power: Vessel Training Centers and the Modernization of the PLAN Surface Fleet, China Maritime Studies Institute, Newport, RI, 2023.

29. Minnie Chan, 'Chinese navy struggles to find enough pilots for 3 aircraft carriers', *South China Morning Post*, 1 October 2022, online at: https://www.scmp.com/news/china/military/article/3194213/chinese-navy-struggles-find-enough-pilots-3-aircraft-carriers

30. Edward Sing Yue Chan, 'The emerging world-class navy: How China acquired its first aircraft carrier', China Story, 11 July 2022, online at: https://www.thechinastory.org/the-emerging-world-class-navy-how-china-acquired-its-first-aircraft-carrier

31. Valerie Insinna, 'A US Air Force war game shows what the service needs to hold off – or win against—China in 2030', *Defense News*, 12 April 2021, online at: https://www.defensenews.com/training-sim/2021/04/12/a-us-air-force-war-game-shows-what-the-service-needs-to-hold-off-or-win-against-china-in-2030/; Stacie Pettyjohn, Becca Wasser and Chris Dougherty, 'Dangerous straits: Wargaming a future conflict over Taiwan', Center for a New American Security, 15 June 2022, online at: https://www.cnas.org/publications/reports/dangerous-straits-wargaming-a-future-conflict-over-taiwans

32. David Flatley, 'China doesn't want a war over Taiwan, US spy chief says', *Sydney Morning Herald*, 10 March 2023, online at: https://www.smh.com.au/world/asia/china-doesn-t-want-a-war-over-taiwan-us-spy-chief-says-20230310-p5cqy8.html

33. Taylor M. Fravel, 'China's "world-class military" ambitions: Origins and implications', *Washington Quarterly* vol. 43, no. 1 (2020): 85–99.

34. Benjamin Herscovitch, 'China's sound and fury over AUKUS will mean little for ties with Australia', *Guardian*, 16 March 2023, online at: https://www.theguardian.com/commentisfree/2023/mar/16/chinas-sound-and-fury-over-aukus-will-mean-little-for-ties-with-australia

35. Michael J. Green and Peter Dean, 'AUKUS' strategic deterrence good for the nation and region', United States Studies Centre, University of Sydney, 10 March 2023, online at: https://www.ussc.edu.au/analysis/aukus-strategic-deterrence-good-for-the-nation-and-region

36. Bec Strating, 'Those worried about Australia's sovereign capability under AUKUS miss the point. That ship has sailed', *Guardian*, 15 March 2023, online at: https://www.theguardian.com/commentisfree/2023/mar/15/those-worried-about-australias-sovereignty-under-aukus-miss-the-point-that-ship-has-sailed

37. Herscovitch, 'China's sound and fury'.

38. *China Naval Modernization: Implications for US Navy Capability*.

39. Chan, 'The emerging world-class navy'; Chan, *China's Maritime Security Strategy*.

40. Jonathan D. Caverley, 'AUKUS: When naval procurement sets grand strategy', *International Journal of China Studies*, vol. 74, no. 3 (2023), 327–34.

41. Lesley Seebeck, 'AUKUS and Australian grand strategy', Strategist, 9 November 2021, online at: https://www.aspistrategist.org.au/aukus-and-australian-grand-strategy/

42. Caverley, 'AUKUS'.

43. Daniel Hurst, 'Supporting US military against China could draw Australia into nuclear war, expert warns', *Guardian*, 17 July 2023, online at: https://www.theguardian.com/australia-news/2023/jul/17/supporting-us-military-against-china-could-draw-australia-into-nuclear-war-expert-warns

44. Rory Medcalf, 'The AUKUS debate needs clear reasoning, not hot air', *Financial Review*, 24 March 2023, online at: https://www.afr.com/policy/foreign-affairs/the-aukus-debate-needs-clear-reasoning-not-hot-air-20230322-p5cugo; Stephen Nagy and Jonathan Ping, 'The end of the normative middle power ship', *Australian Institute of International Affairs*, 14 March 2023, online at: https://www.internationalaffairs.org.au/australianoutlook/the-end-of-the-normative-middle-power-ship/; Matthew Sussex, 'Time to grow up: Australia's national security dilemma demands a mature debate', Conversation, 24 March 2023, online at: https://theconversation.com/time-to-grow-up-australias-national-security-dilemma-demands-a-mature-debate-202040; Sam Roggeveen, 'What "Utopia" got wrong about China and defence policy', *Interpreter*, 6 April 2023, online at: https://www.lowyinstitute.org/the-interpreter/what-utopia-got-wrong-about-china-defence-policy

45. Sam Roggeveen, 'The big AUKUS question that Albanese has yet to answer', *Australian Financial Review*, 17 March 2023, online at: https://www.afr.com/policy/foreign-affairs/the-big-aukus-question-that-albanese-has-yet-to-answer-20230316-p5csl5

Caution and Compromise in Australia's China Strategy

1. Benjamin Herscovitch, 'US military action', Beijing to Canberra and Back, 17 November 2021, online at: https://beijing2canberra.substack.com/i/44148008/us-military-action

2. Benjamin Herscovitch, '1930s redux?', Beijing to Canberra and Back, 16 May 2022, online at: https://beijing2canberra.substack.com/i/54754841/s-redux

3. Anthony Albanese, 'Press conference – Sydney, NSW', Prime Minister of Australia, 23 December 2022, online at: https://www.pm.gov.au/media/press-conference-sydney-nsw-2; Richard Marles, 'Doorstop interview, Parliament House, ACT', Defence Ministers, 23 May 2023, online at: https://www.minister.defence.gov.au/transcripts/2023-05-23/doorstop-interview-parliament-house-act

4. Ben Packham, 'ALP turns up heat on foreign agents', *Australian*, 14 February 2023, online at: https://www.theaustralian.com.au/nation/politics/alp-turns-up-heat-on-foreign-agents/news-story/3bfebd4fcb5b1f404637679bed502f9a

5. Darren J. Lim, Benjamin Herscovitch and Victor A. Ferguson, 'Australia's reassessment of economic interdependence with China', in Ashley J. Tellis, Alison Szalwinski and Michael Wills (eds), *Strategic Asia: Reshaping Economic Interdependence in the Indo-Pacific*, Washington, DC: National Bureau of Asian Research, 2023, pp. 236–75.

6. Benjamin Herscovitch, 'Tactically timed investment rejections, a leader-level visit to China, and barley exports', Beijing to Canberra and Back, 27 July 2023, online at: https://beijing2canberra.substack.com/p/tactically-timed-investment-rejections

7. Ibid.

8. Anthony Galloway and Eryk Bagshaw, 'Victoria's Belt and Road deal with China torn up', *Sydney Morning Herald*, 22 April 2021, online at: https://www.smh.com.au/politics/federal/victoria-s-belt-and-road-deal-with-china-torn-up-20210421-p57l9q.html; Matthew Killoran, 'Govt cracks down on Chinese interference', *Courier Mail*, 15 February 2023, online at: https://www.senatorpaterson.com.au/news/govt-cracks-down-on-chinese-interference

9. United Nations Office of the High Commissioner for Human Rights, 'OHCHR assessment of human rights concerns in the Xinjiang Uyghur Autonomous Region, People's Republic of China', 31 August 2022, online at: https://www.ohchr.org/sites/default/files/documents/countries/2022-08-31/22-08-31-final-assesment.pdf; Human Rights Watch, 'China: Mosques shuttered, razed, altered in Muslim areas', 22 November 2023, online at: https://www.hrw.org/news/2023/11/22/china-mosques-shuttered-razed-altered-muslim-areas

10. Elena Collinson and Paul Burke, 'UTS:ACRI/BIDA Poll 2023 The Australia–China relationship: What do Australians think?', Broadway: Australia–China Relations Institute, 2023, p. 100, online at: https://www.australiachinarelations.org/content/utsacribida-poll-2023; Lowy Institute, 'Australian government policies towards China', Lowy Poll, 2020, online at: https://poll.lowyinstitute.org/charts/australian-government-policies-towards-china; United Nations Office of the High Commissioner for Human Rights, 'OHCHR assessment of human rights concerns in the Xinjiang Uyghur Autonomous Region, People's Republic of China'; Human Rights Watch, 'China: Mosques shuttered, razed, altered in Muslim areas'.

11. Benjamin Herscovitch, 'Did Canberra compromise on targeted sanctions?', Beijing to Canberra and Back, 16 December 2022, online at: https://beijing2canberra.substack.com/i/90969545/did-canberra-compromise-on-targeted-sanctions

12. Benjamin Herscovitch, 'A revised list of Canberra's contentious China policy choices', Beijing to Canberra and Back, 23 March 2023, online at: https://beijing2canberra.substack.com/i/110113968/a-revised-list-of-canberras-contentious-china-policy-choices; Penny Wong, 'Ambassador for Human Rights', Minister for Foreign Affairs, 20 December 2022, online at: https://www.foreignminister.gov.au/minister/penny-wong/media-release/ambassador-human-rights

13. Herscovitch, 'A revised list of Canberra's contentious China policy choices'.

14. Don Farrell, 'Resolution of barley dispute with China', Minister for Trade and Tourism, 4 August 2023, online at: https://www.trademinister.gov.au/minister/don-farrell/media-release/resolution-barley-dispute-china

15. Benjamin Herscovitch, 'How transactional was recent relationship repair?', Beijing to Canberra and Back, 1 November 2023, online at: https://beijing2canberra.substack.com/i/138475543/how-transactional-was-recent-relationship-repair

16. Ibid.

17. Ministry of Foreign Affairs of the People's Republic of China, 'Foreign Ministry spokesperson Mao Ning's regular press conference', 24 October 2023, online at: https://www.fmprc.gov.cn/eng/xwfw_665399/s2510_665401/2511_665403/202310/t20231024_11167118.html

18. Prime Minster Anthony Albanese, 'Press conference—Melbourne', 11 October 2023, online at: https://www.pm.gov.au/media/press-conference-melbourne-3

19. Herscovitch, 'How transactional was recent relationship repair?'

20. Department of the Prime Minister and Cabinet, 'Review—Port of Darwin lease', 20 October 2023, online at: https://www.pmc.gov.au/news/review-port-darwin-lease

21. US Department of Commerce's Bureau of Industry and Security, 'Commerce implements new export controls on advanced computing and semiconductor manufacturing items to the People's Republic of China (PRC)', 7 October 2022, online at: https://www.bis.doc. gov/index.php/about-bis/newsroom/2082; White House, 'Executive Order on addressing United States investments in certain national security technologies and products in countries of concern', 9 August 2023, online at: https://www.whitehouse.gov/briefing-room/presidential-actions/2023/08/09/executive-order-on-addressing-united-states-investments-in-certain-national-security-technologies-and-products-in-countries-of-concern/

22. Andrew Tillett, 'Labor considers following US on China tech ban', *Australian Financial Review*, 14 August 2023, online at: https://www.afr.com/politics/federal/labor-considers-following-us-on-china-tech-ban-20230811-p5dvwx

23. Benjamin Herscovitch, 'Backing Taipei's trade block bid', Beijing to Canberra and Back, 23 March 2023, online at: https://beijing2canberra.substack.com/i/138089045/backing-taipeis-trade-block-bid

24. Government of Canada, 'Read the agreement', online at: https://www.international. gc.ca/trade-commerce/trade-agreements-accords-commerciaux/agr-acc/cptpp-ptpgp/ agreement-entente.aspx?lang=eng

25. Author's interviews with officials, and Michael Smith, '"Not tolerated": Japan opposes China joining regional trade pact', *Australian Financial Review*, 7 November 2023, online at: https://www.afr.com/world/asia/not-tolerated-japan-opposes-china-joining-regional-trade-pact-20231107-p5ei6h

26. Office of the Director of National Intelligence, 'Support provided by the People's Republic of China to Russia', July 2023, online at: https://democrats-intelligence.house. gov/uploadedfiles/odni_report_on_chinese_support_to_russia.pdf

Ending Economic Sanctions: The Role of Chinese Industry Associations in the Removal of Barriers on Australian Barley and Wine

1. Victor A. Ferguson, Scott Waldron and Darren J. Lim, 'Market adjustments to import sanctions: Lessons from Chinese restrictions on Australian trade, 2020–21', *Review of International Political Economy*, vol. 30, no. 4 (2023): 7 July 2022: 1255–81.

2. See 'China – Anti-dumping and countervailing duty measures on barley from Australia' (DS598), online at: https://www.wto.org/english/tratop_e/dispu_e/cases_e/ds598_e.htm

3. See for example Hana Attia and Julia Grauvogel, 'International sanctions termination, 1990–2018: Introducing the IST dataset', *Journal of Peace Research*, vol. 60, no. 4 (2022): 709–19; Valentin L. Krustev and T. Clifton Morgan, 'Ending economic coercion: Domestic politics and international bargaining', *Conflict Management and Peace Science*, vol. 28, no. 4 (2011): 351–76.

4. Don Farrell, 'Resolution of barley dispute with China', media release, 4 August 2023, online at: https://www.trademinister.gov.au/minister/don-farrell/media-release/ resolution-barley-dispute-china

5. Andrew Tillett and Michael Smith, 'China has wins on Darwin Port, wind towers ahead of Albanese visit', *Australian Financial Review*, 20 October 2023, online at: https://www. afr.com/politics/federal/tariffs-on-chinese-wind-towers-to-be-lifted-to-help-seal-wine-deal-20231020-p5edrs

6. David Speers and Stephanie Borys, 'China agrees to review tariffs on Australian wine ahead of Anthony Albanese's visit to Beijing', ABC, 22 October 2023, online at: https://www.abc.net.au/news/2023-10-22/china-trade-tariffs-australian-wine-beijing/103006854

7. China Council for the Promotion of International Trade, 'China Chamber of International Commerce – Brief Introduction' 中国国际商会 – 简要介绍, online at: https://www.ccpit.org/dept/group/guojishanghui/. Ministry of Commerce, 'People's Republic of China Barley Industry Anti-dumping Investigation Application' 中华人民共和国大麦产业反倾销调查申请书, 9 October 2018, online at: http://images.mofcom.gov.cn/trb/201811/20181119081757833.pdf

8. Ministry of Commerce, 'Final ruling of the Ministry of Commerce of the People's Republic of China on the anti-dumping investigation of imported barley originating in Australia' 中华人民共和国商务部关于原产于澳大利亚的进口大麦反倾销调查的最终裁定, 19 November 2018, online at: http://images.mofcom.gov.cn/trb/202005/20200518192204750.pdf

9. Weihuan Zhou, 'China might well refuse to take our barley, and there would be little we could do', Conversation, 11 May 2020, online at: https://theconversation.com/china-might-well-refuse-to-take-our-barley-and-there-would-be-little-we-could-do-138267

10. World Trade Organization, 'Australia initiates WTO dispute complaint against Chinese barley duties', 21 December 2020, online at: https://www.wto.org/english/news_e/news20_e/ds598rfc_21dec20_e.htm

11. Ministry of Commerce, 'Application for review of the investigation regarding anti-dumping measures and countervailing measures on barley' 大麦反倾销措施和反补贴措施 – 复审调查申请书, 20 March 2023, online at: http://images.mofcom.gov.cn/trb/202304/20230414140740858.pdf

12. Penny Wong, 'Resolution of barley dispute with China', media release, 4 August 2023, online at: https://www.foreignminister.gov.au/minister/penny-wong/media-release/resolution-barley-dispute-china

13. World Trade Organization, 'WTO issues panel report regarding Chinese duties on Australian barley', 24 August 2023, online at: https://www.wto.org/english/news_e/news23_e/598r_e.htm

14. Michael Hogan and Naveen Thukral, 'China snaps up Australian barley after tariffs lifted – traders', Reuters, 30 August 2023, online at: https://www.reuters.com/article/china-australia-trade-barley-idAFL4N3AAAQ2/

15. Jonathan Kearsley, Eryk Bagshaw and Anthony Galloway, '"If you make China the enemy, China will be the enemy": Beijing's fresh threat to Australia', *Sydney Morning Herald*, 18 November 2020, online at: https://www.smh.com.au/world/asia/if-you-make-china-the-enemy-china-will-be-the-enemy-beijing-s-fresh-threat-to-australia-20201118-p56fqs.html

16. Andrew Tillett, 'Why Penny Wong says we can't "reset" with China', *Australian Financial Review*, 24 February 2023, online at: https://www.afr.com/politics/federal/penny-wong-on-the-thaw-with-china-and-bringing-all-of-yourself-to-the-job-20230112-p5cc1a

17. Benjamin Herscovitch, 'Caution and compromise in the Albanese government's China strategy', China Story, 21 August 2023, online at: https://www.thechinastory.org/caution-and-compromise-in-the-albanese-governments-china-strategy/

18. Penny Wong, 'Step forward to resolve barley dispute with China', media release, 11 April 2023, online at: https://www.foreignminister.gov.au/minister/penny-wong/media-release/step-forward-resolve-barley-dispute-china

19. Andrew Tillett and Michael Smith, 'China could back down on barley tariffs within days', *Australian Financial Review*, 4 August 2023, online at: https://www.afr.com/politics/federal/china-could-back-down-on-barley-tariffs-within-days-20230803-p5dtm6. Significant weaknesses in China's argument include using the price of Australian shipments to Egypt—a very minor export market—to determine the 'normal value' of Australian barley, and the claim that Australian barley imports damaged Chinese barley production, even though it had been in decline for decades (see Figure 1).

20. See World Trade Organization, DS589: 'China—Measures concerning the importation of canola seed from Canada', online at: https://www.wto.org/english/tratop_e/dispu_e/cases_e/ds589_e.htm

21. Matthew Knott, 'China's "blatant coercion" of Australia is a lesson for the world, says Antony Blinken', *Sydney Morning Herald*, 25 March 2021, online at: https://www.smh.com.au/world/north-america/china-s-blatant-coercion-of-australia-is-a-lesson-for-the-world-says-antony-blinken-20210325-p57duc.html

22. Michael Poznansky, 'Feigning compliance: Covert action and international law', *International Studies Quarterly*, vol. 63, no. 1 (2019): 72–84.

23. See for example Alexandra Hofer, 'The developed/developing divide on unilateral coercive measures: Legitimate enforcement or illegitimate intervention?', *Chinese Journal of International Law*, vol. 16, no. 2 (2017): 175–214.

24. Victor A. Ferguson, 'Economic lawfare: The logic and dynamics of using law to exercise economic power', *International Studies Review*, vol. 24, no. 3 (2022): 1–33. Regarding concerns of policy-makers that to be seen to be using sanctions might damage China's credibility and reputation, see for example Permanent Mission of the People's Republic of China to the United Nations, 'Joint Statement on Unilateral Coercive Measures at the Third Committee of the General Assembly at Its Seventy-Seven Session', 19 October 2022, online at: http://un.china-mission.gov.cn/eng/hyyfy/202210/t20221019_10786144.htm

25. Sarah Basford Canales, 'Australia and China suspend WTO wine tariff dispute before Anthony Albanese's trip to Beijing', *Guardian*, 22 October 2023, online at: https://www.theguardian.com/australia-news/2023/oct/22/australia-and-china-suspend-wto-wine-tariff-dispute-ahead-of-albanese-trip-to-beijing

26. Scott Waldron, Darren J. Lim and Victor Ferguson, 'Exploring the domestic foundations of Chinese economic sanctions: The case of Australia', *China Brief*, vol. 22, no. 18 (2022), online at: https://jamestown.org/program/exploring-the-domestic-foundations-of-chinese-economic-sanctions-the-case-of-australia/

27. Scott Waldron, 'China's tariffs on Australian barley: Coercion, protectionism or both?', *Diplomat*, 19 June 2020, online at: https://thediplomat.com/2020/06/chinas-tariffs-on-australian-barley-coercion-protectionism-or-both/

28. Jingyi Liu, Xiande Li and Junmao Sun, 'China–Australia trade relations and China's barley imports', *Agriculture*, vol. 13, no. 8 (2023): 1469.

29. Changxian Chang, 'With regard to malting barley, how to "treat" the perennial "choke point" problem?' 聚焦啤酒酒大麦，'卡脖子'顽疾如何'治疗'？, Sohu, 6 January 2022, online at: https://www.sohu.com/a/514763522_121124454

30. Scott Waldron, Colin Brown and John Longworth, 'Agricultural modernization and state capacity in China', *China Journal*, vol. 66 (2011): 119–42.

31. National Development and Reform Commission, 'Opinions on the implementation of comprehensively promoting the reform of decoupling industry associations, chambers of commerce and administrative agencies' 关于全面推开行业协会商会与行政机关脱钩改革的实施意见, 17 June 2019, online at: https://www.gov.cn/xinwen/2019-06/17/content_5400947.htm

32. Jonathan Unger, *Associations and the Chinese State: Contested Spaces*, Abingdon: Routledge, 2008.

33. Ni Hongxin, Yu Kongyan, Han Yijun, Ma Jianlei, Xu Ruizhao, Zhang Shu and Li Xue(Research Group, China Agricultural Trade Promotion Centre, Ministry of Agriculture), 'Phased characteristics and countermeasures of the country's trade in agricultural products' 我国农产品贸易阶段性特征与对策建议, *Agricultural Trade Research* 农业贸易研究, Issue 3 (2013), online at: http://www.agri.cn/V20/SC/myyj/201410/P020141215537843850939.pdf

34. One exception was on sorghum from the United States. See Ministry of Commerce, 'MOFCOM Announcement No. 13 of 2018 on countervailing investigation against imports of grain sorghum originating in the United States', 4 February 2018, online at: http://english.mofcom.gov.cn/article/policyrelease/buwei/201802/20180202710853.shtml

35. In 2022, the representative of the CCPIT was Secretary-General of the CCOIC. China Council for the Promotion of International Trade, 'Regular press conference August 2022' 中国贸促会举行2022年8月例行新闻发布会, 29 August 2022, online at: https://www.ccpit.org/a/20220829/20220829xeum.html

36. China Council for the Promotion of International Trade, 'Legal Affairs Department—key responsibilities' 法律事务部 – 主要职责, online at: https://www.ccpit.org/dept/internal/falvbu/

37. See China Alcoholic Drinks Association, 'List of organizations of the Beer Branch of China Alcoholic Drinks Association' 中国酒业协会啤酒分会组织机构名单, 20 July 2020, online at: https://www.cada.cc/Item/1125.aspx

38. Ministry of Commerce, 'Domestic and international dual circulation: China's choice in the era of globalization and reconstruction' 国内国际双循环：全球化重构时代的中国选择, 14 July 2020, online at: http://cacs.mofcom.gov.cn/article/flfwpt/jyjdy/cgal/202007/165119.html; Xinhua, 'To ensure food security, Xi Jinping thoroughly discussed these major issues' 确保粮食安全，习近平把这几大问题谈透了, Xinhuanet, 16 October 2020, online at: http://www.xinhuanet.com/politics/xxjxs/2020-10/16/c_1126617636.htm

39. Hu Chunhua, 'Accelerating the modernization of agriculture and rural areas' 加快农业农村现代化, *People's Daily*, 1 December 2020, online at: https://www.chinanews.com.cn/gn/2020/12-01/9351310.shtml

40. Jingyi Liu and Xiande Li, 'Impact of extreme weather disasters on China's barley industry under the background of trade friction-based on the partial equilibrium model', *Foods*, vol. 11, no. 11 (2022): 1570.

41. Ministry of Agriculture and Rural Affairs, 'Reply to Recommendation No. 6503 of the Fifth Session of the Thirteenth National People's Congress' 对十三届全国人大五次会议第6503号建议的答复, 29 July 2022, online at: http://www.moa.gov.cn/govpublic/XZQYJ/202208/t20220823_6407548.htm

42. See Wen Jing, 'In breaking the imported barley "choke point", Anheuser-Busch starts the domestic raw material war' 破解进口大麦'卡脖子' 百威率先打响国内原料大战, *21st Century Business Herald*, 27 October 2020, online at: https://m.21jingji.com/article/20201027/herald/1a71046e8bef5841342f7ccf56d60102.html. Wary of the distortions caused from previous interventions in the corn market from 2015, China has since refrained from large-scale, direct interventions in feed grains. See Scott Waldron, 'The exposure of Australian agriculture to risks from China: The cases of barley and beef', Asian Cattle and Beef Trade Working Papers No. 4 (2020), online at: https://www.researchgate.net/publication/342425277_The_exposure_of_Australian_agriculture_to_risks_from_China_the_cases_of_barley_and_beef

43. Ministry of Commerce, 'Application for review of the investigation regarding anti-dumping measures and countervailing measures on barley' 大麦反倾销措施和反补贴措施 – 复审调查申请书, 20 March 2023, online at: http://images.mofcom.gov.cn/trb/202304/20230414140740858.pdf

44. Ministry of Commerce, 'Ruling on the review on the necessity of continuing to levy anti-dumping and countervailing duties on imported barley originating from Australia' 中华人民共和国商务部关于对原产于澳大利亚的进口大麦 – 继续征收反倾销税和反补贴税必要性的复审裁定, 4 August 2023, online at: http://images.mofcom.gov.cn/trb/202308/20230804111101908.pdf

45. Ministry of Commerce, 'Ministry of Commerce Announcement No. 44 of 2018: Announcement on the termination of the investigation on anti-dumping and countervailing duties on imported sorghum originating from the United States' 商务部公告2018年第44号 关于终止对原产于美国的进口高粱反倾销反补贴调查的公告, 18 May 2018, online at: https://cacs.mofcom.gov.cn/cacscms/case/jkdc?caseId=53d8a6e261599d6e0161647d278a00b5

46. See Department of Foreign Affairs and Trade, 'Summary of Australia's involvement in disputes currently before the World Trade Organization', online at: https://www.dfat.gov.au/trade/organisations/wto/wto-disputes/summary-of-australias-involvement-in-disputes-currently-before-the-world-trade-organization

47. Scott Waldron and Zhang Jing, 'Chinese tariffs on Australian wine in 2020: The domestic drivers of international coercion', *Analysis and Policy Observatory*, 23 February 2021, online at: https://apo.org.au/node/311126

48. China Alcoholic Drinks Association, 'List of organizations of the Wine Branch of China Wine Industry Association'.

49. Chen Zhenxiang, 'Wang Qi: N factors that contribute to the sluggish development of China's wine industry' 王琦：中国葡萄酒行业发展不太景气的N个因素, China Wine News, 19 April 2018, online at: http://www.winechina.com/html/2018/04/201804294633.html

50. Trish Gleeson, Donkor Addai and Liangyue Cao, 'Australian wine in China impact of China's anti-dumping duties', ABARES Research Report 21.10, July 2021, online at: https://daff.ent.sirsidynix.net.au/client/en_AU/search/asset/1032321/0

51. 'Interview with Trade Minister Don Farrell MP', Asia Society, 28 August 2023, online at: https://asiasociety.org/australia/interview-trade-minister-don-farrell-mp

52. Australian Grape and Wine, 'China barely duties removed', 7 August 2023, online at: https://www.agw.org.au/china-barley-duties-removed/

53. Treasury Wine Estates, 'Treasury Wine Estates launches first China-sourced wine in prestigious Penfolds Collection', 20 July 2023, online at: https://www.tweglobal.com/media/news/twe-launches-first-china-sourced-wine-in-prestigious-penfolds-collection

54. Australian Grape and Wine, 'China barley duties removed', 7 August 2023, online at: https://www.agw.org.au/china-barley-duties-removed/

55. David Speers and Stephanie Borys, 'China agrees to review tariffs on Australian wine ahead of Anthony Albanese's visit to Beijing', ABC, 22 October 2023, online at: https://www.abc.net.au/news/2023-10-22/china-trade-tariffs-australian-wine-beijing/103006854

56. Darren Lim and Stephen Dziedzic, 'Ep. 119: When domestic policy is foreign policy (and the PM's travels)', Australia in the World, 30 October 2023, online at: https://australiaintheworld.podbean.com/e/ep-119-when-domestic-policy-is-foreign-policy-and-the-pm-s-travels/

57. Paul Karp, 'Australian government says "yeah, no" to deal with China to drop wine tariffs', *Guardian*, 24 September 2023, online at: https://www.theguardian.com/australia-news/2023/sep/24/australian-government-says-yeah-no-to-deal-with-china-to-drop-wine-tariffs

58. Ministry of Commerce, 'Spokesperson of the Ministry of Commerce answers reporters' questions on the China–Australia WTO dispute' 商务部新闻发言人就中澳世贸争端案答记者问, 22 October 2023, online at: http://www.mofcom.gov.cn/article/syxwfb/202310/20231003448049.shtml

59. Kirsty Needham, 'Australia says "not necessary" to cancel Chinese firm's lease on Darwin port', Reuters, 21 October 2023, online at: https://www.reuters.com/world/asia-pacific/australia-says-not-necessary-cancel-chinese-firms-lease-darwin-port-2023-10-20/

60. Daniel Hurst, 'Australia rules out cancelling Chinese company's lease over Port of Darwin', *Guardian*, 20 October 2023, online at: https://www.theguardian.com/world/2023/oct/20/australia-eyes-breakthrough-on-wine-as-it-moves-to-scrap-tariffs-on-chinese-wind-towers

61. Dali L. Yang, *Remaking the Chinese Leviathan Market Transition and the Politics of Governance in China*, Palo Alto, CA: Stanford University Press, 2004.

62. See for example Ministry of Foreign Affairs of Japan, 'G7 leaders' statement on economic resilience and economic security', 20 May 2023, online at: https://www.mofa.go.jp/fp/es/page1e_000684.html

63. Wilhelmine Preussen, 'EU takes China to WTO over Lithuania', *Politico*, 7 December 2022, online at: https://www.politico.eu/article/eu-seeks-2-wto-panels-for-chinas-discriminatory-trade-policies; 'Taipei to take PRC mango ban to WTO', *Taipei Times*, 22 August 2023, online at: https://www.taipeitimes.com/News/front/archives/2023/08/22/2003805095. 'Japan hopes to resolve China's seafood ban within WTO's scope', *Asahi Shimbun*, 5 October 2023, online at: https://www.asahi.com/ajw/articles/15021513

64. Andrew Mertha, '"Fragmented Authoritarianism 2.0": Political pluralization in the Chinese policy process', *China Quarterly*, no. 200 (2009): 995–1012.

65. Australian beef, for example, is imported by some 1,500 entities.

| CONTRIBUTORS

Debby Chan is a Lecturer in the Australian Centre on China in the World and Crawford School of Public Policy at The Australian National University. Her research interest include China's economic statecraft and public diplomacy.

Edward Sing Yue Chan is a Postdoctoral Fellow at the Australian Centre on China in the World, The Australian National University. His research focuses on China's foreign policy, East Asian security, sea power and maritime security. He is the author of *China's Maritime Security Strategy: The Evolution of a Growing Sea Power*.

Rogier Creemers is a Lecturer in Modern Chinese Studies. With a background in Sinology and International Relations, and a PhD in Law, his research focuses on Chinese domestic digital technology policy, as well as China's growing importance in global digital affairs.

Dorien Emmers is an Assistant Professor at the Chinese Studies Group and the Department of Economics, KU Leuven.

Victor A. Ferguson is a JSPS Postdoctoral Research Fellow at the University of Tokyo's Research Center for Advanced Science and Technology.

Ruben Gonzalez-Vicente is an Associate Professor in Political Economy at the University of Birmingham, specialising in South-South relations, particularly focusing on China's relations with Latin America and the Caribbean. Ruben serves as an editor for the Global China Pulse and the People's Map of Global China and chairs the Political Economy Research Group at the University of Birmingham.

Benjamin Herscovitch is Research Fellow at The Australian National University and author of Beijing to Canberra and Back, a newsletter chronicling Australia–China relations.

Ben Hillman is Director of the Australian Centre on China in the World, The Australian National University, Associate Professor at the Crawford School of Public Policy and editor of *The China Journal*.

Qian Huang is an Assistant Professor at the Centre for Media and Journalism Studies, University of Groningen. Her research interests and expertise include digital vigilantism, digital visibility, and digital cultures in China.

Willy Lam began studying and writing about China since his first visit to Beijing in 1972. He is a Senior China Fellow of the US think tank Jamestown Foundation. He teaches at the Chinese University of Hong Kong and Simon Fraser University, British Columbia.

Darren J. Lim is Senior Lecturer in the School of Politics and International Relations at The Australian National University.

Kevin Magee is a Policy Fellow at the Australian Centre on China in the World. He had a long career in the Department of Foreign Affairs and Trade during which he was the Australian Representative in Taipei, Ambassador to Saudi Arabia and Deputy Head of Mission in Moscow. His main research interests are China-Russia relations, cross Taiwan Strait relations and the Australia–China bilateral relationship.

Jean C. Oi is the William Haas Professor of Chinese Politics in the Department of Political Science and a Senior Fellow of the Freeman Spogli Institute for International Studies (FSI) at Stanford University. She directs the China Program at the Shorenstein Asia-Pacific Research Center and is the Lee Shau Kee Director of the Stanford Center at Peking University. She holds a Ph.D. in Political Science from the University of Michigan. Oi is the current President of the Association for Asian Studies.

Annie Luman Ren is a Postdoctoral Fellow at the Australian Centre on China in the World and a co-editor of The China Story. Her research focuses on the literary world of the Bannerman in eighteenth century China.

Scott Rozelle is Helen F. Farnsworth Senior Fellow and co-director of the Stanford Center on China's Economy and Institutions in the Freeman Spogli Institute for International

Studies and Stanford Institute for Economic Policy Research, Stanford University.

Graeme Smith is a Fellow in The Australian National University's Department of Pacific Affairs. His research explores Chinese investment, migration, military engagement, technology and aid in the Asia-Pacific. He also hosts the *Little Red Podcast* with Louisa Lim.

Brad Tucker is an Astrophysicist/Cosmologist at the Research School of Astronomy and Astrophysics, Mt. Stromlo Observatory and the National Centre for the Public Awareness of Science, at The Australian National University.

Scott Waldron is an Associate Professor at the School of Agriculture and Food Sustainability at the University of Queensland, where he leads the China Agricultural Economics Group.

Jiao Wang is a Research Fellow at the Melbourne Institute of Applied Economic and Social Research, the University of Melbourne. Wang's fields of research include monetary policy, open economy macroeconomics, macro-prudential policy, and the Chinese macroeconomy.

Kai Yang is a Research Assistant Professor at Lingnan University in Hong Kong. He employs qualitative and computational methods to study contentious politics and political trust, with a particular focus on veteran-state relations. His research articles have appeared in peer-reviewed journals such as *Comparative Politics*, *The China Quarterly*, *The China Journal*, and *Journal of Contemporary China*.

Peishan Yann is a graduate of the Masters in Translation and Interpretating Programme at the University of Melbourne. Previously she was educated in Singapore, Australia and China. She is interested in matters relating to cultures and languages.

Tan Zhao is Assistant Professor at the School of Public Administrative and Policy, Renmin University of China. His research focuses on rural governance in contemporary China.

PREVIOUS *CHINA STORY* *YEARBOOKS*

2022: *Chains*

Speaking to the Twentieth National Congress of the Communist Party of China, in October 2022, President Xi Jinping reiterated his commitment to the 'opening up' policy of his predecessors—a policy that has burnished the party's political legitimacy among its citizens by enabling four decades of economic development. Yet, for all the talk of openness, 2022 was a year of both literal and symbolic locks and chains—including, of course, the long, coercive, and often brutally enforced lockdowns of neighbourhoods and cities across China, most prominently Shanghai. Then there was a vlogger's accidental discovery of the 'woman in chains', sparking an anguished, nationwide conversation about human trafficking. That was part of a broader (if frequently censored) conversation about gendered violence and women's rights, in a year when women's representation at the highest levels of power, which was already minimal, decreased even further. There was trouble with supply chains and, with the Fourth Taiwan Strait Crisis, in August, island chains as well. Despite the tensions in the Asia-Pacific, the People's Republic of China expanded its diplomatic initiatives among Pacific island nations and celebrated fifty years of diplomatic links with both Japan and Australia. As the year drew to a close, a tragic fire in a locked-down apartment building in Ürümqi triggered a series of popular

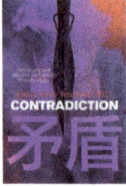

protests that brought an end to three years of 'zero COVID'. The *China Story Yearbook: Chains* provides informed perspectives on these and other important stories from 2022.

2021: *Contradiction*

In the second year of the COVID-19 pandemic, the many facets of crisis—the theme of last year's *China Story Yearbook*—fractured into pictures of contradiction throughout Chinese society and the Chinese sphere of influence.

Contradiction: the ancient Chinese word for the concept holds within it the image of an unstoppable spear meeting an impenetrable shield. It describes a wide range of phenomena that English might express with words like conflict, clash, paradox, incongruity, disagreement, rebuttal, opposition, and negation. This year's *Yearbook* presents stories of action and reaction, of motion and resistance.

The theme of contradiction plays out in different ways across the different realms of society, culture, environment, labour, politics, and international relations. Great powers do not necessarily succeed in dominating smaller ones. The seemingly irresistible forces of authoritarianism, patriarchy, and technological control come up against energised and surprisingly resilient means of resistance or cooptation. Efforts by various authorities to establish monolithic narrative control over the past and present meet a powerful insistence on telling the story from an opposite angle. The *China Story Yearbook 2021: Contradiction* offers an accessible take on this complex and contradictory moment in the history of China and of the world.

2020: *Crisis*

The *China Story Yearbook 2020: Crisis* surveys the multiple crises of the year of the Metal Rat, including the catastrophic mid-year floods that sparked fears about the stability of the Three Gorges Dam. It looks at how Chinese women fared through the pandemic, from the rise in domestic violence to portraits of female sacrifice on the medical front line to the trolling of a famous dancer for being childless. It also examines the downward-spiralling Sino-Australian relationship, the difficult 'co-morbidities' of China's relations with the United States, the end of 'One Country, Two Systems' in Hong Kong, the simmering border conflict with India, and the rise of pandemic-related anti-Chinese racism. The *Yearbook* also explores the responses to crisis of, among others, Daoists, Buddhists, and humourists—because when all else fails, there's always philosophy, prayer, and laughter.

2019: *China Dreams*

The year 2019 marked a number of significant anniversaries for the People's Republic of China (PRC), each representing different 'Chinese dreams'. There was the centennial of the May Fourth Movement—a dream of patriotism and cultural renewal. The PRC celebrated its seventieth anniversary—a dream of revolution and national strength. It was also thirty years since the student-led protest movement of 1989—dreams of democracy and free expression crushed by party-state dreams of unity and stability. Many of these 'dreams' recurred in new guises in 2019. Xi Jinping tightened his grip on power at home while calling for all citizens to 'defend China's honour abroad'. Escalating violence in Hong Kong, the ongoing suppression of Uyghurs in Xinjiang and deteriorating Sino-US relations dominated the headlines. Alongside stories about China's advances in artificial intelligence and genetically modified babies, and its ambitions in the Antarctic and outer space, these issues fuelled discussion about what Xi's own 'China Dream' of national rejuvenation means for Chinese citizens and the rest of the world.

2018: *Power*

In 2018, the People's Republic of China (PRC) was, by most measures, more powerful than at any other time in its history and had become one of the most powerful countries in the world. Its economy faced serious challenges, including from the ongoing 'trade war' with the United States, but still ranked as the world's second largest. Its Belt and Road Initiative, meanwhile, continued to carve paths of influence and economic integration across several continents. A deft combination of policy, investment, and entrepreneurship has also turned the PRC into a global 'techno-power'. It aims, with a good chance of success, at becoming a global science and technology leader by 2049—one hundred years from the founding of the PRC.

2017: *Prosperity*

A 'moderately prosperous society' with no Chinese individual left behind—that was the vision for China set out by CPC General Secretary Xi Jinping in a number of important speeches in 2017. 'Moderate' prosperity may seem like a modest goal for a country with more billionaires (609 at last count) than the United States. But the 'China Story' is a complex one. The *China Story Yearbook 2017: Prosperity* surveys the important events, pronouncements, and personalities that defined 2017. It also presents a range of perspectives, from the global to the individual, the official to the unofficial, from mainland China to Hong Kong and Taiwan. Together, the stories present a richly textured portrait of a nation that in just forty years has lifted itself from universal poverty to (unequally distributed) wealth, changing itself and the world in the process.

2016: *Control*

'More cosmopolitan, more lively, more global' is how the *China Daily* summed up the year 2016 in China. It was also a year of more control. The Communist Party of China laid down strict new rules of conduct for its members, continued to assert its dominance over everything from the Internet to the South China Sea and announced a new Five-Year Plan that Greenpeace called 'quite possibly the most important document in the world in setting the pace of acting on climate change'.

2015: *Pollution*

This *Yearbook* explores the broader ramifications of pollution in the People's Republic for culture, society law and social activism, as well as the Internet, language, thought, and approaches to history. It looks at how it affects economic and political developments, urban change, and China's regional and global posture. The Communist Party of China, led by 'Chairman of Everything' Xi Jinping, meanwhile, has subjected mainland society to increasingly repressive control in its new determination to rid the country of Western 'spiritual pollutants' while achieving cultural purification through 'propaganda and ideological work'.

2014: *Shared Destiny*

The People's Republic of China under the leadership of the Communist Party of China and Xi Jinping, has declared that it shares in the destiny of the countries of the Asia and Pacific region, as well as of nations that are part of an intertwined national self-interest. The *China Story Yearbook 2014* takes the theme of Shared Destiny 共同命运 and considers it in the context of China's current and future potential.

2013: *Civilising China*

As China becomes wealthier and more confident on the global stage, it also expects to be respected and accommodated as a major global force—and as a formidable civilisation. Through a survey and analysis of China's regional posture, urban change, social activism and law, mores, the Internet, history, and thought—in which the concept of 'civilising' plays a prominent role—*China Story Yearbook 2013* offers insights into the country today and its dreams for the future.

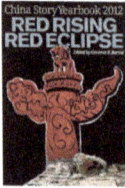

2012: *Red Rising, Red Eclipse*

The authors of *Red Rising, Red Eclipse* survey China's regional posture, urban change, social activism and law, human rights and economics, the Internet, history, and thought. This inaugural *China Story Yearbook* offers an informed perspective on recent developments in China and provides a context for understanding ongoing issues that will resonate far beyond the Dragon Year of 2012–2013.

www.ingramcontent.com/pod-product-compliance
Lightning Source LLC
Chambersburg PA
CBHW050808270326
41926CB00026B/4612